Craft Consciousness and Artistic Practice in Creative Writing

Research in Creative Writing

Series Editors
Janelle Adsit (Humboldt State University, USA)
Conchitina Cruz (University of the Philippines)
James Ryan (University of Wisconsin-Madison, USA)

Showcasing the most innovative research and field-defining scholarship surrounding Creative Writing Studies, Research in Creative Writing strives to discuss and demonstrate the best practices for creative writing pedagogy both inside and out of the academy. Scholarship published in the series wrestles with the core issues at the heart of the field including critical issues surrounding the practice of creative writing; multilingualism and diverse approaches to creative production; representation and the politics of aesthetics; intersectionality and addressing interlocking oppressions in and through creative writing; and the impact of teaching established lore. Responsive to emerging exigencies in the field and open to interdisciplinary and diverse contexts for creative writing, this series is designed to advance the field and push the boundaries of Creative Writing Studies. This series benefits from the guidance of and collaboration with the Creative Writing Studies Organization (https://creativewritingstudies.com/).

Editorial Board Members
Ching-In Chen (University of Washington Bothell, USA)
Farid Matuk (University of Arizona, USA)

Titles
The Place and the Writer, edited by Marshall Moore and Sam Meekings

Forthcoming Titles
A-Z of Creative Writing Methods, edited by Francesca Rendle Short, Julienne Van Loon, David Carlin, Peta Murray, Stayci Taylor and Deborah Wardle
Before and Beyond Craft, Micah McCrary
Digital Voices: Podcasting in the Creative Writing Classroom, edited by Saul Lemerond and Leigh Camacho Rourks

Related Titles
Beyond Craft, Steve Westbrook and James Ryan
Imaginative Teaching, edited by Amy Ash, Michael Dean Clark and Chris Drew

Craft Consciousness and Artistic Practice in Creative Writing

Ben Ristow

BLOOMSBURY ACADEMIC
LONDON • NEW YORK • OXFORD • NEW DELHI • SYDNEY

BLOOMSBURY ACADEMIC
Bloomsbury Publishing Plc
50 Bedford Square, London, WC1B 3DP, UK
1385 Broadway, New York, NY 10018, USA
29 Earlsfort Terrace, Dublin 2, Ireland

BLOOMSBURY, BLOOMSBURY ACADEMIC and the Diana logo are trademarks of Bloomsbury Publishing Plc

First published in Great Britain 2022
Paperback edition published 2023

Copyright © Ben Ristow, 2022

Ben Ristow has asserted his right under the Copyright, Designs and Patents Act, 1988, to be identified as Author of this work.

For legal purposes the Acknowledgments on pp. xi–xii constitute an extension of this copyright page.

Cover design: Eleanor Rose
Cover image: *This Way* by Nicholas H. Ruth, 2020, Monotype on Kozo. Photographed by Chris Cardwell.

All rights reserved. No part of this publication may be reproduced or transmitted in any form or by any means, electronic or mechanical, including photocopying, recording, or any information storage or retrieval system, without prior permission in writing from the publishers.

Bloomsbury Publishing Plc does not have any control over, or responsibility for, any third-party websites referred to or in this book. All internet addresses given in this book were correct at the time of going to press. The author and publisher regret any inconvenience caused if addresses have changed or sites have ceased to exist, but can accept no responsibility for any such changes.

A catalogue record for this book is available from the British Library.

Library of Congress Cataloging-in-Publication Data
Names: Ristow, Ben, author.
Title: Craft consciousness and artistic practice in creative writing / Ben Ristow.
Description: London ; New York : Bloomsbury Academic, 2022. | Series: Research in creative writing | Includes bibliographical references and index.
Identifiers: LCCN 2021041075 (print) | LCCN 2021041076 (ebook) | ISBN 9781350120686 (hardback) | ISBN 9781350120693 (ebook) | ISBN 9781350120709 (epub)
Subjects: LCSH: Creative writing. | Authorship.
Classification: LCC PN187 .R48 2022 (print) | LCC PN187 (ebook) | DDC 808–dc23
LC record available at https://lccn.loc.gov/2021041075
LC ebook record available at https://lccn.loc.gov/2021041076

ISBN: HB: 978-1-3501-2068-6
PB: 978-1-3502-9074-7
ePDF: 978-1-3501-2069-3
eBook: 978-1-3501-2070-9

Series: Research in Creative Writing

Typeset by Newgen KnowledgeWorks Pvt. Ltd., Chennai, India

To find out more about our authors and books visit www.bloomsbury.com and sign up for our newsletters.

For JJ

Bug

and June

Contents

Figure	ix
Series Preface	x
Acknowledgments	xi
Introduction	1
1 "*What Is the Good?*" The Seeds of Virtue in Craft Histories and Creative Writing	13
Stochastic *Technê* and the Virtues of Technique in the Classical Era	19
Virtuous Bourgeois and the (De)Radicalization of the Arts and Crafts Movement	25
Creative Writing Studies Histories and the (Im)mobilization of Craft	32
Bauhaus, Black Mountain, and Orchestrating the Liberation of Craft in Arts Education	41
2 Six Thought Experiments in Craft Consciousness	51
Thought Experiment #1	55
Thought Experiment #2	67
Thought Experiment #3	74
Thought Experiment #4	82
Thought Experiment #5	93
Thought Experiment #6	102
Conclusion: Pushing Creative Writing toward New Formations in Craft Consciousness	109
3 Radically (Un)Becoming: Qualitative Perspectives on Crafting an Artistic Practice	113
Introduction	113
MFA Programs in the Studio Arts and Process Scholarship in Art	116
Emerging Qualitative Research in Creative Writing Studies	123
Study Design and Methodological Rationale	127

	Findings: Thematic Correspondence across Craft Consciousness	130
I	Definitions of and Disputations with Craft	134
II	The Artist Triangulates—Metaphor, Material Source, and Form	139
III	Conceptual Processes, Spiritual Awakenings, and Institutional Influence	146
IV	Artists Out-of-Category and Metamorphoses within Craft Consciousness	150
	Discussion: Craft Consciousness and Artistic Ontologies, Ecosystems, Political Systemics	157
	Conclusion	160
4	Craft Consciousness Futures	163
	Pedagogical Principles in Craft Consciousness	168
I	Collective Knowledge and Community Building	168
II	The Nature of Workshop: Multiplicities and Contradictions in Space	174
	MFA Program Design + Hybrid and Emerging Forms	180
	Creative Writing Futures in Integrated Arts and Scientific Collaboration	186
	Conclusion	189

Appendix: Chart of Artist Interviewees	193
Notes	195
Index	211

Figure

1　Thought Experiment #4　　　84

Series Preface

Creative Writing Studies (CWS) is a field that exists at the interstices of creative writing, aesthetics, fine arts, composition, rhetoric, creativity studies, critical ethnic and queer studies, and literary studies and in countries around the world is regularly housed in departments and programs such as Liberal Arts, Cultural Studies, Creative Practice, Writing Studies, and Language. While there are few courses and programs that take the name "Creative Writing Studies" explicitly, the field is practiced whenever creative writing pedagogy, aesthetic theory for writers, craft criticism, and fictocriticism are studied deliberately.

Research in Creative Writing is a new series from Bloomsbury Academic designed to advance the academic field of CWS by publishing field-defining scholarly manuscripts. The series wrestles with the core issues of CWS: What is creative writing? What insights are currently emerging at the intersection of creative writing teaching and practice? What is the relation between the practices of creative writing and the practices of social justice? How does technology influence and inform creative writing practice? What kinds of creative writing happen inside the academy, and what sort of knowledge and ways of thinking do these practices produce? What kinds of creative writing happen outside the academy, and what meaning do these practices have for their participants?

Books in this series will explore all of these questions and more in an effort to build the research conversation that accompanies creative production.

Acknowledgments

This book was drawn from curiosities. Curiosities vanish without time, space, financial support, love, and the encouragement of other humans. And the best kind of humans gave to me and to this project in large and small ways. I was inspired by Erik Herman and Chris Bell who are true friends and true teachers of science and art. Before the book was ever a book, I was lucky enough to receive guidance and mentorship in my writing life from Chuck Rosenthal, Paul Harris, Gail Wronsky, Darrell Spencer, Sherrie Gradin, Elizabeth Evans, Jonathan Penner, Roxanne Mountford, Amy Kimme Hea, Ken McAllister, and, especially, Tom Miller, who saw the early incarnations of this project. In the proposal stage and in early drafting, I relied on Amy Green, David Reamer, Russell Payne, Quinn McFeeters, and Alex Carioty to turn raw material into something coherent and compelling to readers.

In order to enter the conversation in creative writing studies, I found Tim Mayers's work on craft criticism to be foundational; it allowed me to seek out craft studies and the work of Glenn Adamson, Jenni Sorkin, and T'ai Smith. From Wendy Bishop and Kate Haake's research, I saw modeled an approach to scholarship that was innovative in form and imaginative in style. Their research and the work of Janelle Adsit has fomented a sea change in the ways that creative writing is taught and the liberatory ends to which it serves. Matthew Salesses and Felicia Rose Chavez's recent books on craft and workshop will enact a further shift in how we talk about craft and how we run workshop. Among the group of creative writing studies scholars, I hold gratitude for Pat Bizzaro, Kate Haake, Graeme Harper, Stephanie Vanderslice, Trent Hergenrader, Susan Meyers, and Jon Udelson who have seen me along on my path.

The series editors for the Research in Creative Writing series for Bloomsbury, James Ryan, Conchitina Cruz, and Janelle Adsit, were tireless in their patience and perseverance, and I am indebted to their feedback and commentary on the manuscript. Along with Lucy Brown at Bloomsbury, who worked to keep the machine of my mind running and clacking along in cadence, I am grateful to the series editors for their labor in benefit to the project. Among the faculty at Hobart and William Smith Colleges, I am lucky enough to work with collaborators who double as friends, and in that spirit I want to thank Hannah Dickinson,

Maggie Werner, Geoff Babbitt, Alex Hanson, Cheryl Forbes, Kathryn Cowles, Leah Shafer, Lisa Patti, Melanie Hamilton, Sebastiano Lucci, Dot Vogt, and Alla Ivanichova for their guidance and support.

I found space to write because of the work of Susan Pliner and the staff at the Center for Teaching and Learning at Hobart and William Smith, including Sue Hess and Ingrid Keenan, who make space for writers to write. The retreats, and a generous research fellowship with the Fisher Center for the Study of Gender and Justice directed by Jodi Dean, allowed me time *and* space. Friends and family gave their homes to me to work, and I want to thank Glenn Lawson and Nima Dabestani, John Francis Walsh and Katrina Rudmin, Joseph Tonzola and Suzanne Scholten, and the A.D. White Library at Cornell University for housing me and my laptop.

For my family back home in Wisconsin, I want to thank my sister Amber and my brother Seth for being who they are, and for Zach, whose fight for life has been a model of perseverance for us all. For my dad, Bill, for showing me how to tell a story and how to do work of the hardest kind. My mother, Mary Kaye, brought me to the library, read to me, took me to the laundromat with my books, and somewhere in that spin cycle, I became literate and hungry to spread my imagination across a page.

For JJ, there are no words to express my true love for you and for your sacrifices in the making of this book. Your spirit is in here as it is in me, and it lives in our daughters, Alina and June, who are as bright and warm as the loving light you hold up for them each day.

Introduction

In the small square of life that constitutes my spare time, I volunteer on a school bus that is more spectacle than a means of transportation. The bus belongs to my friend Erik, and it's outfitted for something like psychedelic space travel. Aluminum foil is layered over the yellow bus paint, and stenciled on the sides are words in purple lettering: *Physics Bus*. Erik conceived of the bus as a way to engage children in physics phenomena through hands-on exhibits he has built from found objects and useless junk. We drive with a bullpen of volunteers to elementary schools, music and regional festivals, and local holiday parades throughout Central New York. When we park and the door accordions open, children pile on among the exhibits constructed of discarded hand mixers, microwaves, televisions, speakers, circuit boards, pencil sharpeners, and a hodgepodge of thrown-away contraptions that have been gutted, rewired, spliced, glued, soldered, or duct taped. From the mélange of junk, there emanates sparks, lasers, smoke, audio chirps, or bubbling, starchy goo. Outside, on the dark side of the bus, a group of kids, some as young as toddlers, will make giant soap bubbles or demonstrate what they have not yet learned to call the Bernoulli principle by running an electric leaf blower that suspends a beach ball magically above their parents' heads. Older adolescents snack on cheese curls frozen in liquid nitrogen or run electric jigsaws to repair a new hovercraft or launch soda bottle rockets into the shrieking crowd. To witness all this commotion is to see children sharpened by a tinker's concentration, a loving labor that appears antithetical to the passive absorption required of them in school. Erik's teaching on the Physics Bus stands at a distance from the environment of the laboratory. His philosophies work in the tradition of Frank Oppenheimer (younger brother of J. Robert Oppenheimer) by focusing children's energy on the experience of science, a sensibility based in curiosities more than prescriptive outcomes.

The Physics Bus conceives of science as an experiential art, an interactive space or swarming hive where craft and consciousness become kindred. Tinkering is a more subtle invitation into the scientific world, and it seems to displace the requirements of more formalized learning objectives. The Physics Bus shines a light on the domesticating tendencies of school, and it marks (through the repurposing of junk) the ways that throwaway culture and laptop distractions may corrupt our ideas of what constitutes living and learning. My volunteering on the bus with Erik and his co-teacher Chris has given me the opportunity to see kids returning to the old virtue of material exploration and making things by hand. Their building and repairing as young DIY scientists is a form of liberation and demonstrates an active engagement in science. The experience has circled me back to the animating principles of craft in my field of creative writing. As a writer myself, I have seen craft associated with a reduction rather than an enlargement of making principles. Craft has often been naturalized as technique, and Master of Fine Arts (MFA) programs in creative writing have systematized principles in writing under the auspices of literary formalism and a purely materialist focus on texts. Throughout this book, I argue for a more capacious definition for craft, and one that evolves through metaphor—as a lens, a sensibility, and an awareness.

The purpose of this book is to conceptualize craft through *consciousness* and to shift creative writing toward processism, a set of diverse philosophical, educational, and cultural traditions that views reality and the individual writer as in a *constant state of change*. Process philosophy represents a counterpoint to Western metaphysics and its fixation with substance and a material existence based in the fixed and observable features of reality.* Processism takes reality to be based in the *dynamicity* between stable entities and in the *processes* and *relationships* that form the basis of our world. Although processism is associated with formal philosophy and Alfred North Whitehead, its epistemic and cultural traditions are more diverse and expand beyond Western philosophies. For artists, processual traditions locate the action of art making in the *process* rather than the product, and by defining the artist as perpetually *becoming* rather

---

* A fuller account of process philosophy is taken up in Chapter 2 and is extended through diverse epistemic traditions from Buddhist philosopher Thich Nhat Hanh to the formal philosophy of Alfred North Whitehead. Common to the traditions of processism is the belief that reality is constituted by *processes in thought* rather than physical or material objects alone. Because reality is marked by instability and perpetual change, philosophies such as those in Thiên Buddhism focus on fluctuations and transformations rather than on substantive metaphysical ideas of reality that concentrate on materiality. I argue that processual traditions in art integrate creative writing (and the individual writer) into a more complex, diverse set of traditions and practices than those focused on materiality (text).

than being, processism centers craft on internal matrices rather than external criteria or eternal truths. The new term *craft consciousness* gives name to the internal awareness developed by creative writers as they explore the material and conceptual dimensions of the making process. Artistic practice becomes defined by the *habits in making* that integrate in the artist's consciousness as they consider how a medium's histories and cultural traditions inform their work. MFA programs in creative writing that adopt a prescriptive approach to craft through the lexicon of *technique* dictate a priori how and what the artist makes. I argue in the book that writers reduce the explorative, experiential, political, and spiritual dimensions of craft, and its embeddedness in an artist's culture, when they teach it as an objective, external criteria. For writers, this marginalization renders invisible conceptual processes and limits writing to an outcome, artifacts understood through the lens of literary genres rather than in the processes that expand a writer's understanding of the world.

Formalism in the hands of the New Critics dominated the post–Second World War era, and it has since been naturalized in creative writing in the form of what Janelle Adsit and other creative writing studies scholars refer to as dominant craft discourse.[1] Dominant craft in creative writing is defined tacitly through literary traditions and workshop pedagogies that are exclusive. Programs designed through legacies of domination are supplemented and reinforced by textbooks, curricula, reading series, writing retreats, book prizes and contests, and fellowships that exclude writers that do not identify with the race, gender, class, ability, and sexuality categories held up as exemplary. Western aesthetic traditions redouble dominant craft and determine *who* has access and who is fairly equipped to become a creative writer in an MFA program. This book complements those researching the exclusions in the field of creative writing, and it argues that craft is, and has been, the principal signifier that does the almost imperceptible work of circumscribing the processes and identities of writers.

Some MFA programs have tried to combat more perceptible inequities, such as the one at the University of Oregon, which developed a formal diversity action plan in order to become a more equitable, inclusive environment. There is consensus, nonetheless, that adding more faculty of color, diversifying reading lists, and initiating roundtables at the Association of Writers' and Writing Programs (AWP) Conference have been wholly inadequate.[2] In an essay for *Poets and Writers*, Sonya Larson points to a panel dialogue conducted at Warren Wilson College, "Shadow Boxing: A Faculty Panel on the Intersections of Culture and Craft." In the conversation, novelist David Haynes discusses craft as an artist of color: "But there's this imposed voice up here, outside of me, that I have no control over, that's doing this additional defining. How do I interact with it? Do I ignore it? Do I engage it?"[3] Haynes identifies the ineffable features doing the "additional defining" of him and his practice. For writers at the margins, or anyone that doesn't fit the categories of dominant literary tradition, there's a sense that "control" is "impose[d]" by external criteria and unnamed impediments. Matthew Salesses, in his book *Craft in the Real World: Rethinking Fiction Writing and Workshopping* (2020), identifies the exigence as he defines craft as an "expectation" foisted upon those not in a sociocultural position to view the idea as "just craft."[4] The neutrality of "pure craft" is an illusion in need of dissolution, and when it comes to craft, the intervention is far from straightforward; writers must contend with the ways the term has been mythologized *and* standardized in writing programs. Salesses holds a perspective that I share, namely, that the "rules are always cultural" and that craft has primarily been understood and disseminated in workshops through a white, cis-gender male perspectives on what is deemed *literary*. Any reappraisal of the literary, therefore, necessitates a redefinition of craft, and I draw this action through consciousness and into the multiplicity represented by understanding craft's allusions and applications outside of writing. Salesses articulates a sentiment in this vein, as he writes, "There are many crafts, and one way the teaching of craft fails, is to teach craft as if it is one."[5] The multiplicity of craft is central to a more expansive understanding of literature and art, and I will argue the task before creative writing requires artists to recenter on concepts of process and to build bridges between writing and other art forms. My hope in this book is to theorize and engage with a new artistic, philosophical, and historical orientation for the field of creative writing and to reassess how we teach writers to think as artists through constructing intersectional, coalitionary traditions.

To build a more inclusive, capacious understanding of craft, researchers must consider transdisciplinary methods for examining the histories, theories, and pedagogies of craft. Transdisciplinary methods are interactive and relational and are used in the sciences when concepts and problems require collaboration across fields of study. For example, and according to Harvard University's T.H. Chan School of Public Health, transdisciplinary research is defined as "efforts conducted by investigators from different disciplines working jointly to create new conceptual, theoretical, methodological, and translational innovations that integrate and move beyond discipline-specific approaches."[6] Transdisciplinary perspectives and methodologies have the benefit of aligning writers with the processes undertaken by other artists. Creative writers share a common belief in process with fine, performing, and studio artists, and despite their shared psychosocial and cultural position in the world, writers are often compartmentalized and estranged from other artists in higher education. Collectively, the labor of writers, whether visible or not, inflects upon the network of living practitioners that negotiate making processes. These processes apply to materials as much to lived experience, and artists find their way through a continual self-reinvention, a progression that includes moving beyond the boundaries of one discipline or medium. Given the circumstances of transformation that are natural to the living artist, how does craft remain adaptable to an individual and collective consciousness that is ever growing and ever developing in the artist's mind?

Through navigating formal or material conditions, artists develop an awareness, and this internal sensibility is what I term *craft consciousness*. Craft consciousness represents a departure from an outcome-based model of production in higher education, and it presumes that writers should not be trained as specialists in a genre. Rather than taxonomizing techniques in a single genre, craft consciousness recognizes how material and conceptual explorations parallel the ways that artists transform their identities in a perpetual process of *becoming*.[7] In my argument, becoming a writer is not about conferring an MFA degree or publishing a book: it involves continuous practice and the integration of know-how from a range of art forms and composing practices.[8] To understand how artists interact in the world, this book analyzes twenty-five artist interviews, and the qualitative research complements narratives, theoretical discussions, and histories from craft studies scholarship. A broader cultural analysis of craft draws writing studies scholars out of textbooks and traditions and toward interdisciplinary *and* transdisciplinary methods for intervening in dominant craft discourse. Historically, craft has been evoked to intervene in industrial, educational, and cultural movements. Because of its malleability as a signifier, it can easily be subsumed as an empty marketing symbol in late capitalism, but no matter the purpose it serves, craft legitimizes and authenticates most any cause for which it is summoned.

As anyone knows walking through the grocery store, craft has reascended into popular consciousness in the last decade as a signifier of the *authentic*. It has been interpreted as a marker of consumer goods often produced through smaller scales of production, and the term unifies buyers in the abstract virtue of resisting globalization through shopping local. It marks the genuine, or if you make something as a DIYer, it can refer to the techniques of how-to in crocheting or woodcarving. Consumers are positioned at a remove from the maker and from knowing the real difference between *craft* hummus and regular hummus, but they can be sold the illusion they are getting the *real* thing. But what is real about craft? In this model, it serves as a linguistic modifier we hope will foment our resistance to exploitative global manufacturing and bring us closer to what we consume. Buying local does offer a modicum of resistance to exploitive global production methods; however, capitalist evocations obscure our view of the true revolutionary potential of the term. Craft can function as a signifier of radical social change and what rhetorical theorist Sonja Foss would call a *feminist rhetorical principle of disruption*.[9] DIY punks and other misfits, according to political scientist Kevin Dunn, form a line of resistance to capitalism, industrialization, globalization, and the march of an robot overlords toward automation.[10] Theorizing craft consciousness in creative writing means generating energy in this tradition, in delivering more kerosene for cosmic propulsion. If writers wish to reclaim craft from co-optation or its function as an oppressive doctrine, we have to invite collaborators and conspirators of a common and uncommon feather, those of artistic *and* scientific mind.

Preeminent craft studies scholar Glenn Adamson writes that craft originated in the opposition between the handmade and machine-made objects during the industrial revolution in Britain and America.[11] The philosophical and political interventions of William Morris in the nineteenth-century Arts and Crafts Movement fused craft to cultural resistance movements. It has also responded to collective anxieties during the processes of industrialization, nuclearization, climate change, and global pandemics. During the AIDS epidemic, a group of strangers in San Francisco began the AIDS Memorial Quilt, which became a traveling monument to loss and arguably the most important work of public art in the twentieth century.[12] And as we have seen in the surge of mask-making during the Covid-19 pandemic, we respond to crises through collective actions even when governmental agencies and presidential leadership fail to respond. Definitions of craft that narrow to technique or capitalist signifiers don't capture the collective force of art practiced by women and others dispossessed of power. Under the banner of craft arts (textiles, pottery, ceramics), women artists have been categorically dismissed and subordinated to the fine arts (painting, sculpture, architecture), which is often dominated by male artists. Recuperating craft means challenging patriarchal legacies that are situated in traditionally gendered, racialized, and classed interpretations of who is an artist and whose art is valued in the world.

Craft consciousness brings into relief the ways that creative writing workshops and programs tacitly marginalize writers and naturalize the dissemination of dominant craft based on race, gender, class, ability, sexuality, or other cultural exclusions. Craft studies scholars T'ai Smith and Jenni Sorkin are working to recuperate and reassess women artists. Their labor reclaiming the processes, embodied practice, and collective action of craft affords creative writing studies scholars a new vantage from which to imagine an inclusive, liberatory mission for creative writing. To accomplish this objective means synthesizing creative writing studies and craft studies. Although Glenn Adamson waved "Goodbye [to] Craft" in his essay for *Nation Building: Craft and Contemporary American Culture*, his research over the last decade has expanded my understanding and made this fusion of scholarly traditions possible. I hope my training in writing and rhetoric extends the research of Adamson and craft studies scholars T'ai Smith, Sandra Alfondy, Jenni Sorkin, Sandra Corse, Howard Risatti, Richard Sennett, and Kim Grant and popular authors of craft Matthew Crawford and Alexander Langlands.[13]

Among creative writing studies scholars, Tim Mayers's research in craft criticism illuminates the ways that writers share pedagogical and intellectual space as practitioners of the word.[14] Mayers's research complements Matthew Salesses's critical intervention into craft and his assertion that the term is *always* situated in cultural values. In addition to benefiting from Salesses and Mayers's work, this book extends writing on craft by Felcia Rose Chavez, David Mura, Kate Haake, Kelly Pender, Bryon Hawk, and the growing list of creative writing studies books interested in disrupting the inequities of the status quo, including Janelle Adsit's *Toward an Inclusive Creative Writing*, *Critical Creative Writing Studies*, and with Renée Byrd *Toward Intersectional Identities: Keywords for Creative Writers*; Felicia Rose Chavez's *Anti-Racist Workshop: How to Decolonize the Creative Writing Classroom*; Sherry Quan Lee's *How Dare We! Write: A Multicultural Creative Writing Discourse*; Kate Haake's *What Our Speech Disrupts: Creative Writing and Feminism*; Anna Leahy's *Power and Identity in the Creative Writing Classroom: The Authority Project*; and Steve Westbrook and James Ryan's book *Beyond Craft: An Anti-Handbook for Creative Writers*.[15] These books serve as a commons from which to move the field of creative writing toward inclusive, intersectional collaborations with artists and scholars from beyond writing. Through the journey of this book, craft becomes the navigational star and ontological foundation for creative writing in MFA programs. In defining craft as a nexus across intersecting formations in consciousness, I hope to extend understandings of process from the textual toward the lived experiences, local and traditional cultures, and the socialization process needed to write and keep writing.

Any reclamation or revision to craft must contend with classical histories that push craft (*technê*) to the margins and define it in the Platonic tradition as the antithesis of knowledge (*epistêmê*). Chapter 1 analyzes the binary between techne and episteme and provides perspective on why practitioner knowledge has been theoretically and historically diminished. In *Nicomachean Ethics*, Aristotle argues that happiness comes through a *virtuous practice*. Virtue is not a by-product of happiness, according to Aristotle; instead, practice reflects the virtue of human activity, what is referred to as a stochastic art. Despite the redemptive qualities of *technê* (craft, skill, art) in the treatises *Nicomachean Ethics*, *On Rhetoric*, and *Poetics*, I argue that Aristotle codified craft in lockstep with Plato, and both philosophers limit craft to a technical or physical skill. Chapter 1 also works to link these classical Greek treatises to contemporary craft studies research in order to analyze the ways that craft eventually became inscribed with radical, political values in the Arts and Crafts Movement of the late nineteenth and early twentieth century.[16] Philosophies from the Arts and Crafts Movement and William Morris explain how craft operated in the cultural milieu. Originally born in resistance to modern industrialization, the idea came to function symbolically as liberation for the upper-class bourgeois who claimed it as their signifier.

Chapter 1 synthesizes historical studies of craft with histories of creative writing by D. G. Myers, Mark McGurl, and Eric Bennett. Historians of creative writing characterize craft through the Platonic, formalist legacies of genre and technique, and by and large, they see the term as a by-product of mass market textbooks, celebrity author culture, and the process of institutionalization of creative writing in higher education, what McGurl calls the "Program Era."[17] The codification of craft reflects the process of institutionalization to be sure; however, I argue that writers should view their historical and institutional orientation through studio arts histories such as Howard Singerman's *Art Subjects: Making Artists in the American University* (1999) and arts education models based on the Bauhaus and Black Mountain College.[18] Chapter 1 aligns creative writing with experiential educational and process-based pedagogies associated with MFA arts training. Strict oppositions between knowledge (episteme) and craft (techne) reduce practitioner knowledge to disembodied technique. Craft consciousness attempts to intervene in the objectification of craft through external criteria, and it traces histories of creative writing in order to suggest that the field recuperate its future through looking to arts education training outside of writing.

Chapter 2 transitions from the historical toward the theoretical as it structures and defines craft consciousness through six *thought experiments*. Exploring intersections between writing studies, craft theory, consciousness studies, feminist craft studies, cultural studies, spiritual philosophy, and Marxist thought, the chapter describes how institutionalization as an academic field pushed writing studies toward definitions of craft based in verifiable standards and away from exploratory processes. Scholars Tim Mayers and Kelly Pender discuss how craft was/is reduced through the exigencies of professionalization in rhetoric and composition studies. Mayers and Pender resist reductions of the term by identifying the potential in interdisciplinary and process-based understandings of techne or craft. In addition to analyzing examples from writing studies, the chapter examines legacies in aesthetic theory from Immanuel Kant, Martin Heidegger, and Howard Risatti. Dominant aesthetic theories define craft as *functional* (Kant) and present the artist as a specialized, stable being (Heidegger). My argument pivots the term toward the interactional and political, and it sees the artist on unstable ground, as a being always still transforming and perpetually becoming.

Transitioning from the domain of aesthetics, the third thought experiment delves into consciousness studies and the philosophies of Gloria Anzaldúa, Thich Nhat Hanh, Susan Blackmore, Ned Block, and Thomas Nagel. From understandings of material, phenomenal, mind, store, and access consciousness, craft consciousness takes shape in the spiritual and cultural life of the artist. For women and artists from nondominant traditions, craft consciousness can form a resistance to disembodied or objective instructions for making. Among scholars Gloria Anzaldúa, T'ai Smith, and Jenni Sorkin, craft integrates identity and embodied forms as it negotiates against patriarchal society and the oppressive forces of colonialism, racism, and capitalism.[19] Craft is subversive, disruptive, and revolutionary, and like creativity, it must resist commodification and institutional propensities to domesticate its power. The chapter closes by challenging the valorization of the individual artist and argues for collectivity and collaboration from across disciplines. Craft consciousness is hand-shaped more than it is defined through the six thought experiments, and it operates through interactions and processes based on internal principles rather than external standards.

Following from the six thought experiments of Chapter 2, the third chapter analyzes qualitative data from interviews with twenty-five US and international artists. The analysis reflects how artists evolve through the processes, collaborations, and explorations they experience. The findings challenge the prevailing wisdom in current MFA program design, which bases training on genre specialization. Living artists leave behind or evolve through and past technical training in a single medium. Through conversations with artists, it is clear that identity forms and reforms through explorative processes, and in the findings, it is revealed that artists try to push past the impediments of craft when they circumscribe their material and formal explorations. Artists remain less fixed inside disciplinary boundaries because they don't stay put in one medium, genre, or material. Chapter 3 highlights how artists seek the edge of what they know and explore material and conceptual processes rather than through institutional parameters designed in predetermined forms.[20] The artists I interviewed spoke to the challenges of making art that is validated by institutions and other audiences for their work. One consequence of this finding is that educational, industrial, or academic pressures may silence artists from communities outside of the literary canon, and these pressures, observed in creative writing, work in conjunction with dominant craft discourse to silence writers in MFA programs. Drawing experiments with craft consciousness into praxis means reassessing how an internalized notion of craft integrates into how we teach and design MFA programs.

The final chapter incorporates discussions of the interactive potential of craft consciousness with urban theorist Keller Easterling's concept of *medium design*. Drawing from processist wisdom in the field of design theory, Easterling presents a way of thinking about creative writing that centers on interactions, potentials, and the collaboration within art and science. Using the coalescing momentum of medium design and craft consciousness, I apply craft consciousness to the thinking work of teaching workshop and designing MFA programs. Planning for these tectonic shifts requires imagining new paradigms like those discussed by Felicia Rose Chavez's *anti-racist workshop* and Matthew Salesses's alternative workshops. Chavez, Salesses, and Adsit provide a blueprint for an inclusive, liberating creative writing pedagogy in workshop, and in complementing their frameworks, I experiment with other pedagogical improvisations that shift the authority of the workshop from the Socratic to the anti-racist, neosophistic, improvisatory, and collaborative workshop. Working artists evolve perpetually, and I argue that MFA programs should be sites of interaction, collaboration, and experimentation; they should be workshops for cognitive expansion and acculturation into thinking as an artist rather than the assimilation into dominant craft, aesthetic, and literary tradition. To accomplish this liberatory task, the last section of the chapter encourages writers to consider the ways that they might seek collaborations with artists and scientists. Seeking out collaborations with scientists as well as other non-writing artists will redefine the processes, philosophies, and pedagogies that are carried in the minds of writers.

We're lucky. Craft makes use of junk deemed unsuitable for use. Leftovers. Rubbish. Whatever we call it on the Physics Bus, artifacts have real meaning when they are reused and born anew. Craft also bears our burden as it encircles us. For example, when my grandfather became ill with leukemia, my mother Mary Kaye gathered together fabric scraps from all the quilts she had made previously for baptisms, weddings, and newborns in our family. The quilt kept her father Glenn warm during chemotherapy, and swaddled in it, she hoped it might bring him the same comfort of his children and grandchildren. Like the AIDS Quilt, craft lives immemorial; it serves, too, as a model approach for the writing of this book. The style and structural choices remain unconventional and there is a deliberate meander through personal narratives, craft criticism, historical surveys, qualitative research, and speculations on the future of creative writing. If you travel on this bus, readers must be willing to get a bit lost or frustrated by writing that builds by squares as with quilts or by accretion as with space particles. I'd never utter this on the Physics Bus, but in astrophysics, *accretion* is associated with the amassing of particles in an astronomical object by gravitationally attracting more matter.[21] Astronomical objects like planets, suns, galaxies, or even black holes are built through the spinning accumulation of particles found above us in the night sky. My hope is that all the whirling about in prose will be worthwhile and that theorizing a definition of craft consciousness works to draw writers, artists, and scientists to communal action.

1

"*What Is the Good?*" The Seeds of Virtue in Craft Histories and Creative Writing

I see Ruth Asawa and her fingers separating root tendrils from black earth. Remember, she experienced internment as a girl during the Second World War in California, her family was torn apart, and yet she, remarkably, never claimed any hostility for the injustice later in life. I have been thinking of her kneeling before a garden, her father sent to internment in New Mexico, her sister unable to return from Japan. How she must have felt the absence, and how she planted seeds like my family does to remember who we are when we are together. Asawa would become an artist at Black Mountain College despite violent oppressions and displacements of a magnitude that are hard to imagine enduring. She said later in an interview, now in the Smithsonian archives: "Powdered dirt, for example. Or brick. That does not appeal to me. Just I learn from my parents. If I plant a tomato seed I will get a tomato plant out of it. Then I will get tomatoes from that. I like that."[1] In the interview, Asawa speaks of planting as process, one from which the outcome, though sometimes uncertain, creates hybridities and surprises. New definitions permeate gardens. Material is unmade or is remade by the artist processing the world, she says: "Or what if I got a cucumber and a mixture, a hybrid. I like that too because I get something new." For Asawa, gardening was a form of material exploration and one that was not invested in the politics of categories; it was process focused, utilitarian, interactive, and based on an outcome loosened from the living earth. Unfettered by demands for the recognizable. Later in the interview, she turns from gardening to artistic process:

> It doesn't bother me. Whether it's a craft or whether it's art. That is a definition that people put on things. And what I like is the material is irrelevant. It's just that happens to be material that I use. And I think that is important. That you take an ordinary material like wire and you make it, you give it a new definition.

Craft evolves from interactions between an artist and their material, and in this way, new definitions of craft come through planting seeds.

I save my grandfather's Polish heirloom tomatoes year after year on a swatch of paper towel, and I germinate the seeds in April before planting them in June. The tomatoes look like Edward Weston's pepper photos and grow huge before folding into themselves like deflating globes. With the heat they grow to a red, sweet swollenness and an acidic balance that requires nothing or, sometimes, the extravagance of salt and pepper. I pinch the slices between my thumb and forefinger and then drop them onto my teeth. Their flavor seems to fill every cavity of my head. It's a simplicity my grandfather cherished and shared with everyone, his family, his neighbors, and strangers who entered his chatting distance between June and August. The seeds are an origin for me, for all tomatoes, and though I plant Sunny Golds and black Brandywines, these tomatoes reflect a virtuous practice, a tradition in family, and a history bound to processes lost to gardening methods. Seeds remind me of the spiritual danger Aldo Leopold identifies when we live at remove from farming, namely that we think tomatoes come from the grocer.[2] We must see, too, alternative propagation methods in roots that don't grow from seeds but from rhizomes and tubers that worm under soil.

In the Sonoran Desert of Tucson where I spent a decade, I didn't grow tomatoes. At first glance the native plants seemed to be cultivated on Mars. Plants required little water save the torrential monsoons of July and August. In the informal garden filled with combat squadrons of hummingbirds, the agave and cacti could be rearranged like living room furniture. Roots were insignificant and the plants could imagine roots from nowhere and from lying on their backs. Some were torn from the mother plant by a hungry javelina and cacti would grow down through the hard pan of caliche soil. Blue-green century plants, king of the agaves, led their children away and small "pups" were perpetually springing horizontally from the mother plant. Each spring and summer, a gardener could share pups or a purple Santa Rita or beavertail cactus pad with a friend. Tucked into ground they grew wherever, in a shallowness that was horizontal and not vertical. For the *Agave americana*, the pups sent horizontally lead eventually to a single crescendo when it would send a stalk out to the height of a house. The stalk flowered and sent seeds down before the agave desiccated, and dying, left its sprouting "pups" and seeds to propagate the next generation of agaves. I have been thinking about roots, as in histories, and how they define who we are and what we teach in creative writing.

After almost a century since the Iowa Writers' Workshop's founding (1936), and more than five decades since the formation of the Association of Writers & Writing Programs (1967), it seems strangely belated to suggest that the roots of creative writing are not the sole artifact of Iowa City and the heritage of literary studies and the iconic workshop there. Histories of creative writing by D. G. Myers, Eric Bennett, Stephen Wilbers, and Mark McGurl situate Iowa as the seed; however, these historians also reflect a more variegated landscape where regionalist literature, New Criticism, Progressivism, Cold War politics, New Humanism, artists' colonies and collectives provided seed material for the "Program Era" and the proliferation of creative writing programs to more than three hundred today. Locating creative writing in the University of Iowa suggests that histories depend on fidelity in the genomic material and the perfect replication of my grandfather's tomatoes. Tomatoes sometimes cross-pollinate and change almost imperceptibly between generations and plantings. Cross-pollination happens invisibly and sometimes without the gardener's knowledge, and it is likely that my grandfather's heirlooms have been slightly modified with each planting, and the garden at my mother and father's house doesn't have the same heirloom tomatoes despite coming from the same original seeds. Certainly, writers of contemporary literature depend upon those traditions in writing workshops that were ritualized in Iowa, but this historical positioning tends to obfuscate a historical legacy in art that is more natural to writers, a rhizomic or nodal propagation in other arts. Creative writers actively migrate, appropriate, and experiment as artists who conceptualize and labor to make things.[3] Critiques or studios in the arts parallel the writing workshop and function as the mechanism for *delivery*; the *substance* of creative writing is understood to be craft, an idea that has hardened and narrowed to become synonymous with a select genre and its conventions within formalist ideologies and materialist philosophy.

Appeals for reform to creative writing pedagogy have often been moot, and it's no wonder as the field is held precariously between the bulwarks of the interpretative (literature), the pedagogical (composition and rhetoric studies), and the theoretical (critical theory) in English Studies. Creative writing has been subordinated by the traditional dominance of faculty lines in literature or been taken to task—and oftentimes appropriately and legitimately so—by a growing number of rhetoric and composition scholars for the oppressive conditions in which marginalized writers experience workshop and MFA programs. Competition among individual students is often *valued* and program mechanisms such as student rankings, fellowships, and coveted networking or mentorship opportunities are reserved for those in privileged positions already. Educating creative writers has become less a matter of artistic development and more a matter of developing students' ability to train in one genre. Fidelity to genre conventions and literary studies' interpretative model has drawn writers away from teaching traditions that value artistic practice and process philosophies. Creative writing studies scholars have engaged the field in critical questions of how and why artists teach, but they (myself included) have often been too eager to bring composition theory and its unique obsessions with assessment, accountability, and transferable skills to creative writing practitioners. The field of creative writing studies has expanded considerably and globally since the field was established in the 1990s by Wendy Bishop and others who began to theorize about how one might teach creative writing.[4] My argument demonstrates an affinity to early creative writing studies scholars and pushes the field toward arts scholarship and craft studies, a field developed in the past decade through the work of Glenn Adamson, Sandra Alfondy, Jenni Sorkin, T'ai Smith, and Sandra Corse, among others. Both fields share a common intellectual and artistic space, and it is my argument that it is at *the intersection of craft* where creative writing's virtue as a field is defined. As practicing artists, creative writers find themselves in a challenging position to articulate their history outside of literary studies and their teaching outside of composition studies. It is my intention to operate under the assumption that literary studies and composition studies are integral and have contributed to the study of creative writing but that the field is primarily, not exclusively, a field of artistic engagement and practice. Arguments for reforms to workshop teaching that do not account for the ways that writers of literature are artists are in danger of missing the point entirely. The arts are not free from prejudice, of course, and it is my argument that looking at craft arts and craft studies positions us to reconsider how we write histories, how we teach, and how we position the field to be a more inclusive and equitable site for educating artists as thinkers. We define the mission of creative writing through rewriting our understanding of craft as Tim Mayers and Matthew Salesses have suggested, and we must develop coalitions outside of English that define "the good" in art practice.[5]

Practitioner knowledge is squishy stuff; it's live bacteria or a biome, and not inert matter like data on retention or annual departmental reports. Artistic engagement is defined through a virtuous practice and a pursuit explored during the execution of a project. Craft philosophies in creative writing have been stripped of their verve and the ability to animate the process of creation, and in this dangerous will to domesticate under the banners of the interpretative or pedagogical, scholars must remember that we are teaching an approach built from experience. Without accounting for this wildness and recognizing its value to our student artists, scholars become ideologically bound to reproducing in creative writing what is meant for another field and what is not meant for practitioners or creative writers. Italo Calvino speaks about the quality of "multiplicity" in *Six Memos for the Next Millennium*. Among the traits of the storyteller, and through the traits of quickness, lightness, visibilty, exactitude, he outlines, Calvino sees multiplicity as a "mental encyclopedia" and the "network of possibilities" that emerge from the self as they encounter the world: "Who are we, who is each one of us, if not a combinatoria of experiences, information, books we have read, an inventory of objects, a series of styles, and everything can be constantly shuffled and reordered in every way conceivable."[6] The knowledge of the practitioner comes from artistic engagement in the world and beyond literary studies and the textual traditions of the literary canon. What Calvino suggests can revive creative writing, namely a dedicated engagement with practitioners and processes outside of writing.

To engage in inquires focused on process philosophies and practitioner knowledge, creative writing studies scholars must interrogate deeply held beliefs about the virtue of the field outside of literature and composition and through (non)traditional terminology such as lore. In the tenth anniversary edition of *Can Creative Writing Be Taught?*, editors Stephanie Vanderslice and Rebecca Manery assemble creative studies scholars who question the value of "lore" in creative writing.[7] Lore is associated with what Stephen North called "practitioner knowledge," a knowledge that is adaptable to teaching and sites of production but that does not hold up to the academic rigor of scholarship. Lore is storytelling built on histories of a practitioner's engagement with the processes of making. In *Terms of Work for Composition: A Materialist Critique* (2011), Bruce Horner points to the ways that lore is sapped of vigor by the tendency of North to isolate it from the reified knowledge valued in academic disciplines.[8] As a consequence, we have a tendency to view lore as a form of practitioner knowledge that is different from academic knowledge; lore is oppositional or antagonistic to academic discourse. If we argue that lore is knowledge situated from the perspective of the practitioner, we set it up as inevitably subordinate to those forms of discourse that are more easily academized. Practitioner knowledge in the form of lore or (the slightly more digestible term) craft has been academized through the process of institutionalization in MFA programs. Craft more than lore has been reenacted and ritualized as a discourse over and over through the writing workshop. The term has academic and commercial visibility in ways that are central to understanding what creative writing is and what it does; and as a result, it has come to authors' lips as a way to describe their processes, their rationale for teaching, and, most importantly, as the substantive content of creative writing. It articulates more than workshop does "the good" of creative writing's mission, and I argue it lies at the center of rearticulating the virtue of the field. It is my objective in this chapter to analyze its pedagogical and artistic merit through engaging the broader histories of craft.

Calls for a coalition between creative writing and the arts have been relatively muted in the scholarly context of creative writing studies.[9] The exigence of this book emerges from the absence of scholarship linking the arts to creative writing, and as a consequence, I use DIY methodologies to synthesize craft studies and creative writing studies. Making becomes equitable and inclusive if it's built on processist, feminist, and marginal aesthetic principles of craft that consider it as a mode of consciousness rather than as a technical proficiency. Craft consciousness articulates making as a way of thinking that remains unfixed in a static *being* and rearticulates education as a perpetual state of *becoming*.[10] Artists don't fix themselves in one field and remain the same person forever; they evolve, get stuck, expand in their thinking, and as a result, they change genres, mediums, processes, and identities throughout their lives. Artists are migratory and remain unpersuaded by static processes or the techniques that oftentimes stand in for what we call craft. Students in creative writing can prepare for these migratory patterns and learn to think about their practices outside of the genre that defines their identity in the MFA program. Through displacing technical, formal, and generic associations with craft, an alternative, less visible definition surfaces. Any new definition must materialize from outside the handbooks or textbooks and celebrity culture that have become expansive and hypervisible in creative writing. Craft represents a revolutionary alternative to commoditization, and it is defined by craft studies scholars as a force of revolutionary potential.

This chapter examines the craft legacies in *technê* from the classical period (Aristotle and Plato) and accounts for craft in creative writing studies scholarship and histories. The analysis surfaces the ways craft has been corrupted by institutionalization and marginalized through associations to the technical, the teachable, and the sentimental or nostalgic. Craft revivals like those first experienced in the nineteenth century Arts and Crafts Movement are foundational to our understanding of craft as creative writing scholars. The revivification of craft happens in the wake of seismic shifts in the cultural milieu (mass industrialization or the turn toward the World Wide Web) and as artists and citizens reexamine the basic virtues of life. Craft authenticated creative writing's right to be in the early twentieth-century American university, and though this legacy has been driven toward the chomping mouth of industries and institutions of higher education that hold tightly to the moniker of the authentic, we must not forget that craft is revolutionary. To enact a shift away from the purely technical, nostalgic, or profiteering connotations of craft, I argue that we must return to experiential educational models like those first created at the Bauhaus and Black Mountain College. These historic educational sites serve as models for *becoming* where young artists such as Ruth Asawa and Anni Albers found virtue in developing a practice. From static renderings in technique—*thinking of craft as a noun*—this chapter migrates on a pathway toward understanding craft as a practitioner's sense—*thinking of craft as a verb and an attendant sensibility*—that frames craft consciousness as the state of *becoming* rather than *being*. Becoming an artist requires an engagement with process philosophies that perpetuate, that complicate, and that multiply in the mind of the artist as they experience the virtue of making over time. The mission of creative writing, its teleological end, is not solely beholden to literature; it is premised on the need to prepare writers for the thinking they will do as working artists after the MFA.

Stochastic *Technê* and the Virtues of Technique in the Classical Era

Aristotle argues in *Nicomachean Ethics* that human happiness (*eudaimonia*) pivots on the following question: *What is the good?*[11] In asking the question, Aristotle posits that happiness is not so much an outcome, but in fact, it's a virtuous practice. As activated through *doing*, happiness should be the desired end (*telos*) of human existence. His argument presents virtue as a productive concern rather than as an outcome of reason; for Aristotle, virtue is a craft that benefits the soul. Knowledge in Aristotle's formulation must account for actions through the lens of virtue and the being that acts justly through action. Humans cultivate knowledge that is productive and contained in the producer not only in the artifact. He writes, "Every craft is concerned with coming to be; and the exercise of the craft is the study of how something of being and not being comes to be, something whose origin is in the producer and not in the product."[12] By locating the origin of virtue in the someone rather than in the something, Aristotle also demonstrates the dialogic relationship between the something made and the being who makes. Virtue is neither a by-product nor an end point, and Aristotelian logic frames craft as an ongoing process happening within the artist. From Aristotle's perspective, the link between who we are and what we make is inseparable and craftspeople do the work of embodying virtue in the practice of their given art form. Aristotle's question has a way of turning practitioners inward toward *process* and away from the virtues currently animating creative writing as a "good" in service to literary studies or to tangible professional outcomes, such as enrollment in esteemed MFA programs, publications and awards, and celebrity author status.

The mission of creative writing has been confused in the turn from process to outcomes, from virtuous practice to a focus on publications, technical refinement, and the marshaling of students under the banner of genre. Professionalization shapes the field's mission away from Aristotle's virtuous practice and toward a raw and dangerous specialization. In this bind, and to better represent a more collective and inclusive cause, we must reshape craft to reconfigure the educational mission of creative writing. Histories of art education in the early twentieth century provide meaningful precedent, and I argue that the Bauhaus, Black Mountain College, and MFA programs in studio arts and music shaped the ideological, pedagogical, and aesthetic foundations of creative writing in the decades *before* the establishment of the Iowa Writers' Workshop in 1936.[13] Dominant craft discourse in the form of textbooks and craft criticism (artists on artistic process) along with workshop protocol and program design circumscribe alternative models, and this discourse continues to augment the restrictive formalism and language of technique and natural talent. By surveying eras of craft revival from the classical period to the present, I demonstrate that histories of craft in the radical, collective, and disruptive are subsumed by those that diminish craft and its virtue in artistic labor processes. The virtue of creative writing in the twenty-first century cannot be separated from histories of arts collectives, makers' guilds, or craftspeople who have worked and taught together. Aristotle's question serves as a provocation for historians, scholars, and artists to reevaluate the core values reflected in their treatment of craft in the classroom and in their own practice. How is virtue reflected in process and in the mentorship of artists? Questions of "the how" and "the good" have oftentimes gone unasked in creative writing, and I hope asking invites a reexamination of our ontological and epistemological orientation to craft in creative writing studies. Contemporary rhetorics of craft and the discourse that girdles the term are built on forerunners in the classical schism between *epistêmê* and *technê*, cultural resistance movements formed against industrialization in the nineteenth century, and those definitions that separate talent from craft and its association with mere technique or material knowledge. Through surveying relevant histories and scholarship in writing and craft studies, I argue that the limitations of craft are not insoluble and that its restoration is possible in light of Aristotle's question and through listening to artists discuss their process philosophies.

The historical origins of craft are bound to its classical antecedents in *technê* (art, skill, craft) and the stochastic arts as discussed by Aristotle, Plato, and Longinus. A number of books, especially Jeffrey Walker's *The Genuine Teachers of This Art: Rhetorical Education in Antiquity* (2011), have been devoted to *technê* and its counterpart in *epistêmê* (knowledge).[14] The schism constructed between techne and episteme in Plato's dialogues is critical to scholarly understandings of techne and our understanding of contemporary craft. In Plato's dialogues, *Charmides, Ion, Sophist,* and *Theaetetus,* there are contradictions in the evaluation of techne, and for contemporary readers it may seem odd that woodworking, medicine, horsemanship, and rhapsodic poetry were all associated with techne.[15] For Plato, techne was not pure knowledge, and therefore, it merited less attention and a measure of suspicion. Techne was defined in Platonic thought by the *ergon* (the function) of an activity. Farming's goal is to produce food, medicine to produce health, building to produce shelter, weaving to produce a garment, and so on. The Platonic schema for techne in the dialogues separates activity from function (*ergon*). Reflective knowledge does not produce the wisdom of pure knowledge and the idealized forms associated with theoretical knowledge. For example, when Socrates pushes the celebrated rhapsode Ion to explain the endeavor of poetry, Ion produces an insufficient, blithering response, and Socrates ascribes the activities of the rhapsodic poet to performance or, worse, imitation.[16] Techne produces an inferior knowledge in the Platonic cosmology and it threatens to undermine purer forms of knowledge. Platonic legacies of techne follow craft and lead to its contemporary associations with technique. The function of craft produces more than reflection, it produces knowledge of experience and activates a productive reconfiguration in the artist's thinking; this is the knowledge that artists use to interpret past actions and to formulate future actions in-process for the new artifact.

The function of craft parallels the Platonic indictment of rhetoric, and Plato casts techne as a useful pursuit only when it demonstrates its function *and* can give an account of what the activity produces. The practitioner who does not bridge practice to pursuit through reflection is a fool or is manipulating the audience. The function of craft that distinguishes Plato's position on techne is counterbalanced by Aristotle's conception of techne as a form of productive knowledge, an art. Aristotle's treatises *On Rhetoric* and *Poetics* are the most compelling arguments for establishing the crafts of drama (classical tragedy) and rhetoric (the art of persuasion) as stochastic arts. Stochastic arts deal with knowledge that is *conditional* or *contingent*, an art form that aims but does not always rest on material outcomes. Aristotle's approach to *stochastic technê* in *Prior Analytics* reflects a more dynamic understanding of the aims of craft and a framework that displaces mastery with a form of techne that is aspirational and governed by chance.[17] For stochastic techne, the function of an art accounts for what may or may not happen, a negotiation of contingencies in a pursuit. The virtue of medicine does not mean that the doctor will always achieve health for the patient. Virtue is not a question of mastery or a perfect account of the measures taken. Craft remains open, attentive, and conjectural to what's not known beforehand. Platonic techne contrasts with Aristotelian techne; the former carries associations with technical mastery and the latter strives for a form of soul-building, a virtuous practice that need not arrive at mastery.

In his book *Shop Class as Soulcraft: An Inquiry into the Value of Work* (2009), Matthew Crawford points to the ways that Aristotle draws out the nuance of techne by suggesting that *stochastic arts* are reparative or aspirational and do not require mastery of an object. We don't master; we tinker, we mend, we engage in practices of reconstruction and demolition that are "variable, complex, and not of our making, and therefore not fully knowable; they require a certain disposition toward the thing you are trying to fix. This disposition is at once cognitive and moral."[18] The difference between mastery and "fixing things" feels as large as the chasm between the philosopher and the motorcycle mechanic, according to Crawford; however, the author maintains that craft in the tradition of the stochastic arts is "attentive" rather than "assertive." Like Aristotle, Crawford suggests that craft may take its purpose from an attentive pursuit rather than an absolute mastery. In the Platonic tradition, we see craft as prosaic or the technical penance of the amateur learning art for the first time. The craftsperson who approaches mastery is permitted to express true insights on practice. In this configuration, one based on traditional teacher–student hierarchies and exemplified in arts education and creative writing alike, the master craftsperson is the authority instructing the uninitiated. Separating those "who know" from those "who do not" establishes a social order that is based on individual talent and an apprentice–master bond. Inequities, then, are cemented in the technical lexicon that follows arts fields and elevates the master over the apprentice artist.

Defined and opposed to knowledge in the Platonic sense, the function of craft should be measurable, standardized, and dictated by those who know to those who do not. If we follow this model for construction, we end up operating on what woodworker David Pye calls a "workmanship of certainty," a practice that is analogous to Henry Ford's assembly line.[19] Specialists know their roles and perform them well and have a limited sense of the outcome. Ascribing craft to the condition of inductive reasoning and uniformity requires an aversion to deviation and a fidelity to replicable processes, specialist labor, and capital accumulation. Production in this craft tradition is less a virtue of practice and more a pursuit of an achievable standard. Standards may be codified by handbooks of technique and come to define a particular craft in light of the *ergon* (function) and the *telos* (ends) it serves. Aristotle's association of techne with a virtuous practice is contradicted by his taxonomies of technique in *Poetics*. Aristotle's treatises offer a case in point for the central paradox dogging craft, and just as the philosopher defines craft as a virtuous practice, he also creates taxonomies in *Poetics* that entrench the term with the guidelines that delimit craft. The function of *Poetics* seems to liberate technique from its Platonic relegation while simultaneously reprogramming craft with criteria governed by objective truths. *Poetics* represents the quintessential craft handbook, and it is best understood through its elisions, those spots in the text where Aristotle appears to acknowledge that artistic practice has gaps.

Aristotle's *Poetics* and Longinus' *On the Sublime* serve as some of the earliest examples of the ways that oratory and poetics were systematized through literature and ascribed a taxonomic function. For Aristotle, the dramatist is concerned with developing plot, music, and staging elements that lead the audience members to *catharsis*. This ineffable feeling, a tragic pleasure, forms the purpose of the dramatist and their purpose as a creator. Aristotle's treatise liberates poetics and dramatic tragedy from the indictments of techne by Plato; however, it also tends to narrow perceptions of what tragedy may be and how writers construct a play. Codifying principles of making in a field simultaneously narrows outcomes and moves practitioners away from exploratory principles. In reading *Poetics*, Aristotle embodies the fastidious taxonomizer who cannot fully account for the poet's labor. His ambivalence marks tragedy as a stochastic art even in spite of the philosopher's potent desire to systematize craft. He writes,

> The poet's job is not to report what has happened but what is likely to happen: that is, what is capable of happening according to the rule of probability or necessity

> ... The reason is that what is possible is persuasive; so what has not happened we are not yet ready to believe is possible: for it would not have happened if it were impossible ... The poet ought not to cling at all costs to the traditional plot, around which our tragedies are constructed.[20]

Aristotle seems to cede that contingencies govern the principles of construction, and it is fair to see his contribution in *Poetics* as redeeming *and* reducing craft simultaneously, a paradox that does not fit in his penchant as a philosopher and rhetorician to classify even the ineffable.

Longinus' *On the Sublime* (from around 100 CE) frames the craft of writing and oratory using the lens of the sublime rather than catharsis. Sublimity (*hypsos*) elevates the writer and reader to an ethereal plane through the use of figurative words, imagery, and style. The state of the sublime is reciprocal and affects the reader and writer alike. Longinus says that the sublime may be achieved through imitation of the masters (Homer, Sappho, Plato) or through inborn talents. He writes, "Most important of all, we must remember that the very fact that there are some elements of expression which are in the hands of nature alone, can be learnt from no other source than art."[21] Much like Aristotle's stochastic arts, Longinus' treatment of the sublime synthesizes attainable sources (devices, strategies, diction, exemplars) and internal sources (inspiration, aspiration, passion). This combination of source elements summons the power of the sublime through the ineffable and mysterious, a dangerous suggestion in the Platonic cosmology. The cosmologies of classical techne estrange craft from knowledge in the Platonic tradition; however, craft's codification in Aristotle's *Poetics* and Longinus' *On the Sublime* also fuses art making with virtue making. The virtue of making in the stochastic arts tradition acknowledges that mastery is not the only outcome. Virtue is exemplified in the maker who acknowledges the past and the master craftsperson, and in contrast to Platonic thought on techne, Aristotle and Longinus see practitioner knowledge as partly conjectural and predicated on outcomes of a process. Virtuous practice and "soul building" demonstrate "the good" for the maker and the audience, and as a consequence craft (in its etymological predecessor in *technê*) is set on two divergent paths. One path leads toward the codification of craft in terms of mastery, individual genius, or natural talent, and in this reduction of processes, it approximates certainty and a definable outcome. Technical proficiencies can be measured, can be taught, can be wielded by those who profess to know to those who do not; this path holds dominance in our contemporary definition of craft. The alternative path initiated in the classical period positions craft as a process whereby virtue is not measured by the outcome; instead, the journey of the artist in their practice reflects a moral imperative, an imperative that suggests that the student artist is at the center of our educational purposes, not the content. We rarely speak of the moral dimensions of craft because this conception of the term is foreign and harder to monitor or accumulate or govern in our educational institutions. It challenges us to think in terms of the processes and the virtue as expressed in collective artistic practice. It yields craft as a verb rather than a noun; making rather than the made, or, gardening rather than the harvest. The moral imperatives and "the good" expressed in the processes of art making are what constitute the fluctuating identity of the artist, and nineteenth-century industrialization brought this fact into relief.

Virtuous Bourgeois and the (De)Radicalization of the Arts and Crafts Movement

As discussed in the introduction, the radicalization of craft is rooted in its resistance to industrialization. The nineteenth-century Arts and Crafts movement in England (and later in the United States) drew directly from traditions in stochastic techne and further naturalized craft as a philosophy that countered dominant modes of production. With the massive proliferation of industrialization in England by the mid-nineteenth century, William Morris, influenced in large part by the writings of John Ruskin, argued for a return to methods of small-scale production that had preceded machinery and factories.[22] Industrialization, according to scholar Glenn Adamson, became the antithesis against which craft came to be defined in the modern sense. Adamson writes in "Goodbye Craft" in *Nation Building: Craft and Contemporary Culture* that "the most powerful, and paradoxical, idea about craft that has come down to us from the nineteenth century is that craft was invented as an absence. It came into being as a figure of cancellation, an 'X' marking a spot that had never existed in the first place."[23] There might not be a way to ascribe the handwork of artisans (potters, blacksmiths, weavers) to something called "craft" without the hands-off mechanized production represented in industrialization.[24] Before craft there was only the labor that sustained people in livelihoods and traditions that passed from older to younger generations. From this perspective modern craft was born in England, and where the handbooks of techne codified the elements of rhetoric and oratory, the Arts and Crafts Movement further systematized the moral imperatives of practices and philosophies working against dominant modes of production. The philosophies of the Arts and Crafts as they migrated to the States through the writings of William Morris characterized craft as a utopic vision for making, and thus it ushered in a definition of craft that has followed us into contemporary forms of small-scale production made by artisans outside the purview of the factory. The Arts and Crafts Movement was more than a commentary on the social and economic dimensions of production; it formed a quasi-religious ideology that sought to radically intervene in modernity. The movement also came to define *who* had access to identifying themselves as a craftsperson. In *No Place for Grace: Anti-Modernism and the Transformation of American Culture 1880–1920* (1981), T. J. Jackson Lears describes the Arts and Crafts Movement as a fiercely "anti-modernist" sentiment that sought to recapture an authentic life through a return to the land and the embrace of artisanal practices.[25] In the wake of Victorian "overcivilization," Lears writes about American society as lost. He describes the social milieu in a fashion that echoes the sentiments of a digital age: "For many, individual identities began to seem fragmented, diffuse, perhaps even unreal. A weightless culture of material comfort and spiritual blandness was breeding weightless persons who longed for intense experiences to give some definition, some distinct outline and substance to vaporous lives."[26] Through the desire for intense experiences and an identity authenticated through practice, the Arts and Craft Movement came to embody a bourgeois resistance to Victorian ornamentation and the rising tide of industrialization and labor alienation.

The upheaval in modern life presented people with a way to redefine civilization through the virtue of thinking as a craftsperson. The disciples of John Ruskin and William Morris in England became American craft evangelists, and Elbert Hubbard of Roycroft and furniture maker Gustav Stickley, among others, integrated transcendental philosophies of making into a referendum on the modern world. Lost were the ways of the medieval artisans (according to Ruskin and Morris) who had toiled and refined their skilled trades with the noble attentiveness of people who knew their work and for whom work defined their happiness. The irony, as pointed out by T. J. Lears, is that the artisans who formed the labor force of the preindustrial medieval guilds were not fairly treated and often abused and indentured to their master's wishes. The ideologies of craft and the figure of the artisan came to be defined by an anxious bourgeois nostalgia for work that was at once *authentic* and *genuine*. Arts and Crafts philosophies in the tradition of Morris came to be appropriated by those who were privileged to choose to produce or consume artifacts in the American craft tradition. The idealism of craft became less signified by a revolutionary impulse and more by nostalgia for material quality by a group of Americans who yearned for a real existence. Highlighted in this historical lineage of Arts and Crafts are the ways craft became framed as a pursuit or a social apparatus among the elite who were more freely positioned to evoke, imitate, and perform traditional craft practices for their inherent cultural virtue.

The class exclusions suggested in Lears's critique of Arts and Craft are echoed in contemporary critiques of creative writing as an elitist pursuit that provides some (not all) with the time to pursue writing. These critiques are repeated by historical precedents wherein manual laborers are left behind and individuals with leisure time are free to evoke craft and its liberating virtue. For example, in his book, *Cræft: An Inquiry into the Origins and True Meaning of the Traditional Crafts* (2018), Alexander Langlands blends a historical and archeological analysis of traditional crafts such as hay making, beekeeping, weaving, and wool gathering, and other farming practices with the suggestion that "*lost* knowledge of traditional crafts, as we know them, are about so much more than just making. We don't have cræft in our lives any more."[27] An archeologist, historian, and television host for a BBC *Historic Farms* series, Langlands bemoans industrialization in the tradition of Ruskin and Morris: "As I became more and more engrossed in the traditional ways—and not just historical methods of farming but ways of making and living in the past—it occurred to me that the modern world was depriving us of many of these skills."[28] Langlands's critique of modern society implies that revitalization of the traditional crafts may lead to a new way of living. In a world that has been dominated by industrialization since the late nineteenth century, Langlands's critique uses a preservationist tone to suggest that enacting antiquated farming practices may stave off further encroachment by throwaway culture, the erosion of physical skills, and the rapid digitization and automation of our world. As the craftsman, farmer, and archeologist, Langlands sees the preservation of vanishing farming practices as a method for archiving past values in the present. As with Ruskin and his characterization of the medieval craftsmen, the question emerges: Whose values or cultures are performed through a method for making? Who is rendered liberated in the process of traditional or ritual modes of old labor methods?

The preservationist gesture of Langlands may seem removed from the radical treatises of William Morris; nonetheless, each evokes a reinvigoration of moral values in handwork and the well-made thing. If work is no longer an authenticating experience for a capitalistic society, we are left to look for production methods that recover a sense of self within culture. Craft ideologies in the tradition of Morris, Hubbard, and Langlands reflect the nostalgic, but more than that they demonstrate craft's ability to authenticate labor for those who may be in danger of losing their purpose. *What does my labor produce?* It is a transcendental question or a question from Marx that emphasizes the laborer rather than the artifact. Craft traditions produce a *self* where there might otherwise be disembodied labor. Although labor in the spirit of craft traditions has a tendency to be aggrandized and mythologized, the arguments outlined by Langlands and Morris also characterize craft as a productive form of resistance. In our contemporary expansion of local producers like artisan butchers and cheese makers, craft breweries and cideries, potters and stain glass makers, and farm-to-table restaurants, what is often lost is the way that support for smaller businesses forms a resistance to the interminable march toward globalization in late capitalism. Is craft by its nature anti-capitalistic by the forms of labor it supports? Richard Sennett and Matthew Crawford analyze the ways that conceptions of craft subvert dominant modes of production and labor that separate the worker from work that is meaningful for the soul. In *Shop Class as Soulcraft*, Crawford tries "to avoid the mysticism that gets attached to 'craftsmanship' and the term craft."[29] He employs the term "trades" to describe the work of those who fix other people's things rather than toil in a workshop with an object based on the standards of their craft field. Crawford sees the erosion of individual agency in office work and other forms of disembodied intellectual labor as contributing to a decline in human happiness. Choosing labor in the trades or crafts allows for the reestablishment of "meaningful work" and "self-reliance."[30]

> Both ideals are tied to a struggle for individual agency, which I find to be at the center of modern life. When we view our lives through the lens of struggle, it brings certain experiences into sharper focus. Both as workers and as consumers, we feel we move in channels that have been projected from afar by vast impersonal forces.[31]

The consumer and worker are given a dizzying array of choices in capitalism and expanding global markets; these choices perpetually privilege the new and newer. Crawford presents vocational education and the trades as reparative soul work and as an intervention into production narratives of capitalism, narratives that fixate on brands rather than William Morris's well-made thing. By aligning the tradesperson and consumer in a parallel struggle for agency, Crawford points to the ways that the crafts and trades undermine disembodied labor and the profound disconnection to production.

In his argument, Crawford draws on the work of Richard Sennett, a craft studies scholar at Yale who connects making to the cultures of capitalism. In *The Culture of the New Capitalism* (2006) and *The Craftsmen* (2008), Richard Sennett employs a philosophy of American pragmatism to analyze craft's role in contemporary culture. His argument stems in part from Hannah Arendt's *Human Condition* (1958) and posits a philosophical distinction between *Animal laborans* and *Homo faber*. *Animal laborans*, as defined by Arendt, takes man's labor "to be an end in itself," whereas *Homo faber* encompasses "men and women doing another kind of work, making a life in common."[32] Sennett clarifies Arendt's distinction by discussing the ways that labor defines humanity. He writes, "In one way we make things; in this condition we are amoral, absorbed in a task. We also harbor another, higher way of life in which we stop producing and start discussing and judging together. Whereas *Animal laborans* is fixated in the question of 'How?' *Homo faber* asks 'Why?'"[33] In Sennett's argument, an emphasis on *Homo faber* repositions craft as a mediating force that balances "the how" with "the good." When labor is done blindly for its own end, it has the consequence of undermining humanity in the name of scientific and technological progress, ideals shown to us in the travails of nuclear and climate destruction.

Like Crawford, Sennett believes craft reflects a complex mechanism for negotiating materials through the processes of making. Balancing how and why allows the craftsperson or tradesperson to negotiate ethical principles during the making, and Sennett and Crawford see the ideology of craft activating individual agency and reinvigorating humanist, pragmatist, and processist philosophies. These philosophies resist tendencies in culture to embrace technological and capitalistic progress, and they advocate for labor that enriches and enlivens the worker in a common or collective endeavor. Crawford and Sennett adopt less of the inherent nostalgia or preservationist's tone, and their scholarship along with Glenn Adamson's work opens up the possibility that artistic practice may be more than the singular refinement of one's material or a purely manufactured outcome. One's craft may be more akin to a virtuous practice that is embodied in a craftsperson's *way of thinking*.

In *Thinking through Craft* (2018), Glenn Adamson continues an important shift in craft studies by arguing that craft is not a *category* in art but a *subject* of study.[34] As stated earlier in this chapter, Adamson argues that craft as a subject of study did not exist before industrialization. Before factory production, most objects were made by hand or with rudimentary tools. In the context of the fine arts, craft has been ascribed an inferior value and swept toward categorical distinctions (pottery, woodworking, weaving) or ascribed a functional rather than an intellectual value. In *Thinking through Craft*, Adamson focuses on the five dimensions of craft that make it foundational to art: the qualities of the supplementary, the sensual, the skilled, the pastoral, and the amateur. Adamson works through these overlapping frameworks in order to demonstrate how craft elicits definitions based on the context and purpose of its application. Through the lens of the functional and provincial, craft arts are situated categorically beneath the fine and performing arts in the dominant discourse of the arts; as a consequence, and ironically, craft has the unique ability to include the moral or spiritual dimensions of process in ways that are excluded from fine arts.

One legacy of the past decade in craft studies scholarship has been the liberation of craft arts from the categorical margins, and Adamson, Sennett, and Crawford have moved philosophies of techne back toward the spiritual, virtuous idealism of the classical period. Classical legacies of techne from Aristotle and Plato, however, characterize it as outside knowledge or a philosophical tradition, whereas Adamson, Sennett, and Crawford see craft as an ontological and ideological practice and intervention. Sennett suggests simply that "making is thinking" and not the object to be categorized by the philosopher.[35] Sennett frames his argument in *The Craftsmen* by discussing what he calls "material consciousness," a principle he describes as "the craftsmen's proper conscious domain; all his or her efforts to do good quality work depend on curiosity about the material at hand."[36] Materiality is understood in-process and cannot be abstracted or disassociated from embodied processes of the laborer. Material consciousness does not occupy the domain of certainty but of *curiosities* in the artist and of *contingencies* of material exploration. What Margaret Atwood has said of gardening holds true; art is more than a spiritual gesture performed for social reward. She writes,

> But in truth the point of this gardening is not vitaminization or self-sufficiency or the production of food, though these count for something. Gardening is not a rational act. What matters is the immersion of hands in the earth, that ancient ceremony of which the Pope kissing the tarmac a pallid vestigial remnant. In the spring, at the end of the day, you should smell like dirt.[37]

In the "pallid vestigial remnant," I can see the grocery store tomato, not red exactly, not sweet or acidic either, more of a representation grown to serve an aesthetic purpose at the grocer. The vestigial remnants of craft operate similarly when evoked by the privileged and the disembodied as they conceptualize art as objects to be sold rather than as processes combining earth and hand. Garden tomatoes, even mediocre ones, are still the antithesis of the "workmanship of certainty" and the principles of commercial agriculture; they do not standardize for purposes of the shelf; they approximate, they do not perfect; they project across a mind in labor. David Pye's oppositional idea to certainty is the "workmenship of *risk*," and it captures material consciousness in the artist. Artists have a penchant to disrupt processes even of their own making and to see curiosities in forms and conjecture as a method of thinking.

Our thinking is craft. More than the battery of techniques codified in textbooks or the teaching spaces of workshop, studio, or art critiques, craft consciousness, as we see in Chapter 2, maintains that mastery is illusory. Farmers like artists are generalists more than specialists. In *The Gift of Good Land: Further Essays Cultural and Agricultural* (2018), Wendell Berry suggest as much: "We have neglected the truth that a good farmer is a craftsmen of the highest order, a kind of artist."[38] The kind of artist we imagine teaching should not imagine craft as a static framework to master. It is not an industry standard. It is a mule-harnessed troika between material and consciousness and body. To return to craft is not really to return in any spiritual sense to a woebegone era; it is crucial, instead, to first dispense with definitions of craft that operate on the purely historical, technical, functional, hegemonic exclusions that are based in sectioning off artistic practice and identity from those who do not have the time or training. Exclusions can nullify the liberating gesture and reduce creativity to an individual pursuit in one form or medium. Oppression in arts training begins with this gesture toward formal exclusions. As we consider the education of artists, we must invite and facilitate the play of formal and generic interplay. In jazz, and spoken word performance, we can see artists pushing form past its limits. According to Kamau Daáood and the Army of Healers in their song "Liberator Spirit (for John Coltrane)," Daáood repeats in his refrain, "John Coltrane is a freedom fighter that liberated the spirit from the shackles of form."[39] The liberating gesture in craft as a *disruption of form* allows us to think about other artists' role in disruption; Daáood suggests that Coltrane's intervention flies in the face of dominant jazz forms and their oppressive tendencies. For artists to mentor students, it is critical to see craft as supportive of a way of thinking that recognizes material constraints and acknowledges that the good of practice should be initiated through individual agency *and* a collective of artists. With the agency to negotiate processes in a project (no matter its medium), students can invite the unintended and view *process* as the center of their educational training.

In the next section of this chapter, I examine how craft has been analyzed and historicized in creative writing studies and how terms were formulated, integrated, and sometimes eschewed in arts schools prior to the establishment of the Writers' Workshop at Iowa in the late 1930s. To undertake a reconfiguration of the term, my argument pivots from creative writing studies to art education philosophies in the groundbreaking schools of the Bauhaus in Germany (est. 1919) and Black Mountain College (est. 1933). These educational sites along with MFA programs in the United States in music, theatre, and studio arts figured critically in the conceptualization and delivery of craft ideologies and the marginalization of the term. Women artists were (and are) often associated with craftswomenship and mediums involving traditional handwork or functional artifacts. Liberating craft from the margins and situating it at the center fundamentally shifts arts training from the individual male genius to a more collective, inclusive, and intersectional group of artists. Legacies in craft are often associated with the codified, technical, formal, or otherwise dismissed, and these classic legacies are buttressed by nostalgic bourgeois gestures to the past that ignore the real beings who make art. Reconfiguring craft as a mode of thinking through practice allows marginalized artists to smash through conceptions of their labor as inferior or simply technical, and it is my argument that process philosophies (not artifacts) recenter us on those artists we tend to ignore, marginalize, or make invisible. New intellectual bridges are built between art forms when we see process as vital to training young artists. *Technique*, more than process, defines craft in current historical studies of creative writing, and the next section examines the ways that literary studies scholars eschew the term's association with process. In histories of creative writing, Platonic and Aristotelian legacies are visible, and craft becomes associated with the teachable and technical in ways that diminish the power and agency of the creative writer.

Creative Writing Studies Histories and the (Im)mobilization of Craft

Histories of creative writing have been written primarily by literary studies scholars. Much like the interventions into workshop teaching made upon creative writers by well-intentioned compositionists, histories of the field have reflected a latent tendency to characterize creative writing as a product of the institutionalization and systematization of literary production in the late twentieth century. The historical approaches of D. G. Myers, Eric Bennett, and

Mark McGurl have aligned conception of craft that correlate the term with dominant discourse and its association with technique. This characterization sees craft as a product of textbooks written by prominent writers, common pedagogical practices, and the residual philosophies of programs that proliferate like an "elephant machine" (Myers) and that offer students an "experiential commodity" (McGurl).[40] Seen in this light, craft is rather uncomplicated, and it is seen implicitly and reductively as a mechanism for legitimizing writing in the university and as a discourse of artistic professionalism from which dogmas like "show don't tell" were enfranchised. Craft is teachable. Teaching creative writing means teaching the *only* thing measurable in art: craft. In this section, I survey historical studies of creative writing in order to diagnose the omission and/or technification of craft and to initiate a movement toward examining histories in the arts and away from literary studies. Through these foundational histories, studies essential to our field to this point, scholars have marginalized craft *and* creative writing through recodifying craft as technique and ascribing the teleological value of creative writing's past, present, and future to literary studies. Notably, writers Tim Mayers, Paul Dawson, and Matthew Salesses extend understandings of craft from these histories. They have developed critical terminology in "craft criticism," "sociological poetics," and "real-world craft" that invite writers to embrace social and artistic multiplicity beyond dominant literary traditions and through coalitions of arts practitioners and teachers.

On the surface, the establishment of the University of Iowa's creative writing program in 1936 appears to be a radical, breakthrough historical moment, a "sudden adoption of creative work" for course credit as D. G. Myers has written, and as a site through which a who's who of writers (Wallace Stegner, Flannery O'Connor, Kurt Vonnegut) have circulated through.[41] In *The Iowa Workshop: Origins, Emergence, and Growth* (1980), Stephen Wilbers places the origin of creative writing in the cornfields of Iowa with the formation of the first MFA creative writing program in America.[42] The objective of creative writing, according to Wilbers, began as a way to support grassroots and regional efforts toward literary production from outsiders to the university. The first true architect of the Iowa Writers' Workshop was Norman Foerster, and according to the Association of Writers & Writing Programs' former Director D. W. Fenza, creative writing "sought to repair the divorce in the study of literature, the divorce between aesthetics and scholarship, between practice and theory, and between art and criticism. Foerster did not intend for his school to become 'a vocational school for authors and critics,' but he did implement classes in creative writing and a new emphasis on literature as an art."[43] As an art form, creative writing at Iowa came to symbolize a shift in literary production from the main hub in New York City to the environs of Iowa. Wilbers's history is dominated by nostalgia for Iowa's pioneering educators: Norman Foerster and, later, program architect Paul Engle. Omitted in Wilbers's history of creative writing are the ways that educational models for arts training were already afoot in both international arts schools and MFA programs. In *Art Subjects: Making Artists in the American University* (1999), Howard Singerman outlines the history of the MFA through the lens of studio arts and music.

> The first MFAs were awarded in the mid-1920s at the University of Washington and Oregon; Yale and Syracuse, the oldest campus based art schools place their first MFAs in the late 1920s ... At the beginning of the 1940s there were 60 graduate studio candidates enrolled at eleven institutions; in 1950–51 there were 320 candidates at thirty-two institutions.[44]

Singerman's history situates creative writing in a context where the arts degrees and the MFA were no longer anomalous or even new; for example, and according to department websites, Yale University conferred its first MFA in playwriting in 1931 and the undergraduate program in creative writing was established at Columbia University as early as 1911.[45] Even at the University of Iowa, the Department of Speech and Dramatic Arts (est. 1929) and its tenacious department chair, Edward Charles Mabie, had secured rights to stage productions outside of New York City and approached the Rockefeller Foundation for grant funding to construct a new theatre that opened on the banks of the Iowa River in 1936.[46] It seems likely that the first creative writers at Iowa, including Foerster, saw the success of the dramatic arts, music, and studio arts on campus and across the nation as models of educational missions to emulate. Singerman's history illuminates people and MFA programs we are likely to elide in glorifying the Writers' Workshop. For example, the first MFA in studio art was conferred at the University of Washington to the painter Mabel Lisle Ducasse in 1924 and the College Art Association was formed in 1911 long before the Association of Writers & Writing Programs. Singerman traces histories of artists on campus, and in this history, writers appear to be integrated later and after waves of artists and arts schools were already established.

In the first major historical scholarship on creative writing, *The Elephants Teach: Creative Writing since 1880* (1996), D. G. Myers looks for the foundations of creative writing at Iowa in the context of the progressive educational movement advocated by John Dewey, Hugh Mearns, and other national educational scholars who emphasized creativity.[47] Deweyian philosophies certainly influenced Norman

Foerster and provided focus for workshop; however, robust artistic learning communities were well-established and already being modeled at institutions such as the Bauhaus (operated in Germany from 1919 to 1933) and Black Mountain College, which was established in 1933. Perhaps even more than "creativity," the educational ideology mantra of the interwar era was "experiential" and later adapted from arts institutions into the ideologies of formalism and New Criticism. Additionally, popular interest in the short story form in the first golden age of literary magazines in the interwar period came to influence writing programs' conceptions of craft. Writing programs, in the later histories of creative writing presented by Mark McGurl, would begin to influence literary production and aesthetic principles in postwar literature. The earlier influences in publishing solidified craft in the lexicon of technical formalism and the taxonomic gestures of Aristotle's *Poetics*. In *Creative Writing and the New Humanities* (2004), Paul Dawson discusses the proliferation of handbooks in creative writing at the beginning of the twentieth century.[48] Aided by the proliferation of short stories in literary journals, handbooks like *Short Story Writing* by Charles Barrett (1898), *A Study of Prose Fiction* by Bliss Perry (1902), and *The Short Story: A Technical and Literary Study* by Ethan Allen Cross (1914) were absorbed into teaching creative writing courses in the university. These handbooks served more than the early students of creative writing classrooms; they permitted apprentice writers to develop techniques for writing, and more importantly, they cultivated an appreciation for literature among readers. The former provided a rationale for teaching the short story in the context of universities and the latter bolstered literary studies as interpretative *and* practitioner knowledge. Handbooks form the pedagogical and teleological framework from which creative writing became professionalized and understood in the university. Paul Dawson analyzes Brander Matthews's 1905 essay "An Apology for Technic," and he argues that Matthews's essay separated character and talent in the technique of the short story form.[49] Technique served as the foundational rationale for teaching creative writing in the twentieth century and allowed for a technical and formalist notion of craft to serve as the footing for the Writers' Workshop.

Eric Bennett frames the mission of creative writing as inclusive of New Humanist and democratic principles, and in his book *Workshops of Empire: Stegner, Engle, and American Creative Writing during the Cold War* (2015) he expands D. G. Myers's research and claims that the New Humanism advocated by Irving Babbitt became the foundational ethical principle of creative writing under Norman Foerster, and, later, Paul Engle.[50] Echoing the sentiments of former AWP Director D. W. Fenza, Bennett presents the Iowa

Writers' Workshop as an ideological endeavor bent on resisting and disrupting dominant tropes in the post–Second World War age—the ineffectual Romantic figure and the machinery of a communist revolution. Bennett marks Iowa as a factory of ideological fervor where the workshop and craft came to symbolize a force for democratic good. This history is echoed in D. W. Fenza's suggestion that creative writing is born of a fundamental democratic principle, a radical egalitarianism. For Bennett, the progressive educational movement is only one backdrop for understanding the good of creative writing, and he focuses on the pedagogical dimensions of the "whole person," a "productive self knowledge" that "could do the work of humanistic synthesis … integrat[ing] what the university otherwise split apart: facts of material reality, faculties of mind, traditions of literature, and the experiences of lives as lived."[51] The important shift initiated by Bennett's archival research allows creative writing studies scholars to conceive of the ways that a mission of self-knowledge and humanistic education in writing helps spread global democracy. Bennett's analysis draws progressivism and New Humanism into conversation while suggesting that the ideological forces of creative writing were used as political propaganda. In Bennett and Myers's creative writing histories, there is a scarcity of discussions of craft; it is discussed, as with Mark McGurl, through the concept of formalism and technique.

Eric Bennett credits Mark McGurl's *The Program Era: Postwar Fiction and the Rise of Creative Writing* (2009) with establishing creative writing studies scholarship.[52] McGurl's extensive study of programs in the postwar era is an examination of creative writing through a "system theory" approach, one that organizes the field through the lens of literary studies. As with Myers, Bennett, and Wilbers, McGurl argues that the mission of creative writing centers on its underpinnings as the practitioner subdiscipline of literary studies. In McGurl's argument, New Criticism mobilizes creative writing and gives it purpose following the Second World War, and McGurl devotes considerable energy to characterizing the field's proliferation through the lens of a "systemic creativity."[53] Although he says that the "Program Era" does not constitute a decline in quality but a "fall into institutionality," McGurl affixes aesthetic categories to the literature of the period: High Modernism, Technomodernism, Lower-Middle Class Modernism, and High Cultural Pluralism.[54] By defining craft as "technique" and "show don't tell," McGurl presents craft as oppositional to creativity and self-expression. "For the champion of self-expression, 'craft' is likely to be seen as a cipher for conventionality and timidity, while for his opposite number, paeans to 'creativity' invite the production of half-baked fantasy."[55] McGurl's presentation creates a familiar binary that locates craft in the gritty persistence and professionalism of New Criticism and iconic popular authors like Ernest Hemingway or Ray Carver. McGurl suggests that experience forms the synthesis between craft and self-expression, and he works to elevate the superficial dimensions of creative writing to argue that it constitutes a "experiential commodity" that valorizes the individual through the identity of authorship.[56] Such a perspective certainly echoes the suggestion of T. J. Jackson Lears in critiquing the bourgeois indulgences of the Arts and Crafts movement, and McGurl identifies the features of the Program Era in a way that takes the good of creative writing to be a sort of "self-tourism" and a process of authentication in MFA programs. McGurl meticulously identifies features of aesthetic strains without aligning himself fully with the detractors of creative writing; however, he continues to see craft as a limiting force and focuses on prominent biographies of creative writers. Speaking about writers as teachers, he argues: "What the literary artist is presenting to students in the classroom is a charismatic model of *creative being*."[57] One way to read this sentence is to see the enormous chasm between craft and "creative being." Another way to read the sentence is to see that charisma is a stand-in for creativity. Creative beings don't *give* creativity away in their teaching, they model it, they show don't tell. Creativity and craft become monikers for what cannot be taught—only modeled or imitated—and both terms are ascribable to systemic and programmatic forces more than to the individual creative writer. Beings are created who are creative, but creative beings cannot be made. McGurl applies his system theory and aesthetic lens to contemporary literature of the postwar period, what he calls the Program Era, and his history functions as a lens for literary scholars to understand contemporary literature more than to illuminate how writers practice.

In *Creative Writing and the New Humanities* (2004), Paul Dawson makes an intervention into the historical characterization of craft and creative writing by literary studies scholars. He suggests that the field evolved "as a series of local pedagogical responses to the international crisis in English Studies which accompanied the rise of theory. As a result the emergence of Creative Writing in Australia is emblematic of its emergence around the world as the disciplinary and imperial coherence of English Studies fractured."[58] Dawson challenges Wilbers and Myers's conclusions that skills-based training in literary craft became absorbed by universities and colleges through progressive and regionalist motives, and in contrast, Dawson observes in creative writing's development a much more intentional, grassroots resistance to the theoretical shift of the 1980s and 1990s. Although Dawson's observations are centered on Australian writing programs, the analysis he provides is disruptive to the neutral language typically ascribed to craft. "The author is not a craftsman who employs an ideologically neutral and formalistically pure language to express a unified personal vision or to master the objective world. Instead, writers represent in the literary work a range of extra-literary languages which organise social relations."[59] Dawson creates an opening in craft that allows for a critical, constructive element, what he refers to as a "sociological poetics." Advocating for an expansion that parallels Tim Mayers's craft criticism and Matthew Salesses's cultural situated definition of craft, Dawson writes,

> A sociological poetics would thus require a recognition that aesthetic or craft-based decisions of a writer are always the result (consciously or otherwise) of ideological or political choice: the choice to employ social languages and ideologies they embody in certain ways, and hence the choice to position a literary work in relation to these languages, as an active intervention in the ideological work they perform.[60]

Dawson argues that artists should be cognizant of the ways their art operates in the world. The New Humanist approach advocated by Dawson holds craft to a moral good in a way that echoes the political charge of Bennett's strong archival research. Tim Mayers, Paul Dawson, and Matthew Salesses's research expands craft through framing works in the genre of craft criticism and through the sociocultural poetics of craft.

In his book *Craft in the Real World* (2021), Matthew Salesses draws Dawson's sociological poetics into direct conversation with dominant craft discourse. Through defining centering on cultural traditions and the identities of artists, Salesses breaks the spell of *neutrality* and argues that Western traditions in art tend to obfuscate or nullify the diverse traditions in literature. Focusing on examples from Asian literary traditions and their practical application to fiction writing workshops, Salesses renders a lineage in craft that differentiates itself from craft traditions based on Western aesthetics and dominant literary traditions. Salesses models an approach to reading literature and teaching craft in workshop that inflects upon the aesthetic and rhetorical dimensions of the term. Our values are never *apart* from craft—they *are* craft—and the degree to which MFA programs endorse approaches to realism in the vein of Hemingway or Carver, in Salesses's example, they enfranchise a narrow conception of what constitutes art and literature.[61] In this arrangement, Asian literary traditions become *exceptions* outside of expectations and rhetorically inadequate for a white readership.[62] Salesses positions his argument through a rhetorical awareness; craft cannot be ahistorical, acultural, or deracialized because it has arrived through the lens of a white, Western readership. It is taught in fiction workshops through a dominant aesthetic lens that is transfixed on traditions based in exclusions and exceptions. Understood in this manner, and institutionalized through workshops, professors of creative writing must take an active role in illuminating the ways that readers apply their own normative biases upon a workshop submission. Salesses asks the creative writing student and professor to question their own readership: "Which audience are we?"[63] For Salesses and Dawson, traditions in craft are political, culturally embedded, and, most importantly, not beyond the purview of a creative writing education. Craft is integrative of the set of values negotiated between reader and writer, and given this fact, craft must analyze the cultural traditions from which art and literature originate and live.

Tim Mayers's book *(Re)Writing Craft: Composition, Creative Writing and the Future of English Studies* (2005) extends craft's potential as a collaborative nexus among practitioners.[64] Mayers argues for a productive alliance between compositionists and creative writers in English Studies, and he bases his argument on the position that composition and creative writing are interested in *production* while literary studies is primarily involved in the *interpretation* of texts. By connecting both fields to a practitioner's ethos, Mayers addresses the ways that craft forms a bridge between disciplines and provides an opportunity for a reciprocal intellectual and pedagogical exchange; he writes,

> By expanding the concept of craft beyond its prevailing sense as mere technique, craft criticism harbors the promise of bringing sociopolitical understandings of literacy into the discourse of creative writing, where such concerns have often been absent. This expanded concept of craft also harbors the promise of returning aesthetic concerns to the discourse of composition studies, where they have sometimes been eclipsed. In other words, a "rewritten" notion of craft might provide common ground.[65]

In Mayers's argument, the opportunity for coalition exists in craft criticism, a genre inclusive of practitioners and pedagogues who are interested in examining their processes of producing writing and the sociopolitical consequences of making. The alliance suggests that composition and creative writing have a mutual interest in narratives of production and that craft criticism underlies the tenets of each field and offers the possibility of rethinking English Studies. In this coalition, literary studies figures as the institutional behemoth against which composition and creative writing have thus far defined themselves. Mayers's radical suggestion in identifying craft criticism is that practitioners rather than critical theorists and interpreters of literature may determine the future of English Studies. Mayers points to the ways that craft has formed the rationale for teaching creative writing in higher education, but more than this, he identifies it as a mode of collaboration and future liberation for both fields.

When discussing the substance of what creative writers teach, Mayers identifies the ways that poets and fiction writers have relied on an "institutional conventional wisdom" that keeps the inborn and "mysterious" dimensions of creative process outside the parlance of formal instruction.[66] The examples in Mayers's text are numerous and provide the backdrop for his argument: craft remains the cornerstone from which pedagogical philosophies of creativity have been grounded. Detractors of creative writing, and there are many, argue that creative writing cannot be taught or point to the ways that teaching practices are ruining contemporary literature. For the moment, I want to avoid the quagmire of this debate and point to the ways that Mayers bridges creative writing to fields beyond English Studies. In discussing the teachability of creative writing, Mayers notes that the poet Mary Oliver has gestured to the ways that painters, sculptors, and other artists question whether art can be taught and, if so, what elements can be *learned*. The language of academic discourse in standards, assessment, or outcomes doesn't often pair well with writers or artists in the imaginative tradition. Questions surrounding the viability of teaching art are not germane only to creative writing. The litany of books asking this question includes: *Why Art Can't Be Taught* by James Elkins; *Teaching Painting: How Can Painting Be Taught in Art Schools?* by Ian Hartshorne and Donal Moloney; and *Can Creative Writing Really Be Taught?* by Stephanie Vanderslice and Rebecca Manery.[67] The question of whether art or creative writing can be taught has the rhetorical effect of suggesting, albeit implicitly, that there may *never* be a way or that there may be a *new way* contained in the book. Depending on who asks the question, creative writing and the arts are portrayed as outsiders in the university, and the question does the work of creating narrative tension by suggesting that creative writing may be exiled.

The expulsion of creative writing (or art) from the academy is unlikely and could not happen without also excising craft from academic discourse. Craft is perfectly nebulous, and it systemizes teachable elements even while conjuring up unteachable principles that are mystical or natural. In the tradition of creative writing handbooks, a prominent artifact in undergraduate workshops, there is the potential to make writing mechanical, and it is at our own peril that we expand craft to those spheres of making that give credence and value to the more nonlinear, spiritual, or mysterious dimensions of practice. If we include craft in these fuzzy conceptual realms, we risk further mystifying the circumstances from which apprentice writers and artists become excluded because they do not represent the ideal artist. One way forward is to banish craft as a teaching rationale. The other solution fits with Mayers and Salesses's research and would involve radically intervening in what we imagine craft to be. A protracted and potentially disruptive definition could work to further expand craft criticism to include essays, interviews, collaborations, intermedia or transmedia projects, and the host of artifacts that have been and are being produced by artists in creative writing and beyond. Given craft's prominence in creative writing's history, pedagogy, and ideological framework, it would seem that its role as a "threshold concept," according to Janelle Adsit, precludes its banishment, and so it may be better to see it as an artistic heuristic that has the potential to impact pedagogical values and support new virtues for the field.[68] Histories of creative writing characterize craft in ways that serve to sever it from imagination and the ontological forces guiding the living practitioner, and it is critical to see how craft's recurrent codification works in conjunction with forces that conceal the experiences, processes, and explorations of the artist.

Bauhaus, Black Mountain, and Orchestrating the Liberation of Craft in Arts Education

Craft evokes nostalgia for the preindustrial or predigital past, or it becomes a reduction of principles relating to strict formalism or fidelity to the techniques of a medium. Craft philosophies tend to narrow when integrated into instructional textbooks or taxonomies of art or when wielded by the master craftsperson in their teaching. These actions of codification and institutionalization are not felt evenly by artists, and it is my argument in the final section of this chapter that definitions of craft are far from innocuous; they are the epistemological, ideological, and pedagogical foundation from which the virtue of a creative writing education is understood and integrated into MFA programs. In the final section of this chapter, I synthesize critiques of creative writing with a brief historical examination of experiential educational sites such as Black Mountain College and the Bauhaus. Through examining these two early-twentieth-century art institutions, I will demonstrate how experiential educational philosophies form the bridge for craft's migration into higher education in the United States. In that migration, a movement obfuscated by references to the University of Iowa as creative writing's birthplace, scholars and practicing artists are granted a more variegated and complex understanding of craft's ideological base in arts training and gain perspective on how craft has been feminized and reduced to an oppressive heuristic for arts training. Anni Albers and Ruth Asawa, artists discussed in this and later chapters, offer case studies in how to navigate around dominant craft discourse, and I theorize a new definition in craft consciousness that liberates marginalized artists through an emphasis on process philosophies and intersectional aesthetic traditions. Coalitions can be built around process philosophies and embracing intersectional aesthetic traditions promises to redefine and reorganize craft consciousness and allow for new histories and teaching to take root in creative writing.

Our insistence on static definitions of craft creates exclusions and privileges some groups of makers. In *Social Medium: Artists Writing 2000–2015* (2016), Bill Beckley speaks to this tendency and presents art in terms of our political sphere: "If there is any division in our American culture right now it is between those of us who are *text oriented*, making decisions gleaned by acknowledging the ever-changing circumstances of our lives, and those of us who are *grammar oriented*, going by rules already formulated in our mind and in our culture."[69] Our current grammar orientation for craft pins the term rather than letting it occupy a text-oriented definition, a definition that pushes past text-as-text and considers texts as flexible, immaterial, and about "decision making" in "the ever changing circumstances of our lives." Like Tim Mayers, Beckley's sentiments extend disciplinary boundaries and create an internalized, process-based approach for artists and artistic training. A grammar orientation for craft operates in a manner similar to Standard English, and it creates a mechanism for controlling artistic practice and those identities enfranchised through the artistic process.

In her book *Toward an Inclusive Creative Writing: Threshold Concepts to Guide the Literary Writing Curriculum* (2017), Janelle Adsit refers to the ways that craft acts as a governing heuristic and implicitly dictates the "ideologies of taste," while Adrienne Perry suggests that craft limits "anyone outside of the dominant cultural and economic position."[70] If craft functions as a dominant heuristic, it is in danger of curtailing artists through mediating their productive action and aesthetic choices, and worse, it limits who may call themselves artists. This last point about identity may seem superficial, but it is primary to the questions of inclusivity surrounding creative writing. In his 2014 essay "MFA vs. POC" for the *New Yorker*, Junot Díaz wrote, "Simply put: I was a person of color in workshop whose theory of reality did not include my fundamental experiences as a person of color—that did not in other words include *me*." Exclusions in workshop and programs are made through pedagogical, aesthetic, and social conditions, sometimes invisible to white, male, abled, hetero, classed writers. Craft plays to the monopolizing whiteness and classedness in workshop and among the program cohorts. Díaz speaks to how MFA programs separate writers of color from aesthetics *and* mentoring and peer support *and* a sense of self in the world as an artist. These divisions leave the artist without aesthetic, pedagogical, or creative social spaces to operate; they exclude them from the MFA and often push them out of graduate programs. The Voices of Our Nation Arts Foundation (VONA), an organization committed to the support of writers of color, cited that "in 1999, less than 0.2% of writers of color were represented in writing workshops across the country." Organizations like VONA operate in conjunction with *de-canon: A Visibility Project*, a database of craft criticism from writers of color. VONA provides workshops in the community and *de-canon* offers resources to actively question the aesthetic and pedagogical traditions inherited from MFA programs. In the overview to the *de-canon* project, the organizers point to the aesthetic domination and the ways that dominant craft discourse invalidates some in MFA programs:

> At the heart of the MFA vs POC discussion is the contention that any discussion of craft does not take place in a vacuum—that race is part of the one's lived experience and how we see ourselves and are seen does impact how and what we write. Much of what is taught, for example, about craft in writing workshop presumes the primacy of a Western European aesthetic tradition, ignoring 1) that tradition's historical debts to other cultures and traditions; 2) the multiple aesthetic traditions in literature and the arts elsewhere in the world which were concurrent or preceded the European tradition; 3) the complexity and fluidity of cultural exchange happening presently—that we live in a global society where our literature and art should more accurately reflect the reality of our communities, not look back nostalgically to whitewashed world that never was.[71]

According to Díaz and Salesses, dominant craft discourse is mobilized through workshop and through program structures that tend toward obfuscating traditions, languages, and identities of those who do not come from the Western aesthetic tradition. In the histories surveyed in this chapter, craft forms the pivot from which these dominant traditions are dispersed and made rigid through reenactments of traditional workshop and the literary canon. As creative writers, the de-canonization of a dominant aesthetic tradition can be achieved through a dedicated reconfiguration of craft from more intersectional aesthetic traditions. In Chapters 2 and 4, I explore ways in which craft consciousness and an intersectional aesthetic approaches to craft can enfranchise creative writers currently marginalized in MFA programs.

Traditions in craft are built upon the contradiction expressed by Aristotle in his rendering of techne as technique and as virtuous practice. From the dominant traditions signified through codification and institutionalization, there is a less discernible tradition that is built upon the radical cultural upheavals and revolution expressed in the Arts and Crafts Movement. Craft represents the radical intervention and collective opposition to industrialization, digitization, and the march of capitalism. The revolution of craft is a resistance to those methods that dehumanize the maker and create the conditions of artistic oppression. Ideologies of dominant craft discourse create the methods and categories of art (especially in craft arts) that relegate women and other marginalized artists to something less than art. Despite its contradictions and marginalization as a term in art, craft was adopted in creative writing at the University of Iowa and elsewhere *because* it authenticated writers' practices and represented a radical intervention into interpretative frameworks in literary studies. Practitioners in creative writing sought to intervene, ritualize workshops and programs, and make their practice as artists visible to higher education institutions devoted to contemporary literature. Creative writing may have lost it's revolutionary charge in its rush into English Studies. Historians of creative writing, like Myers, Bennett, and McGurl, are painstaking in their examination of the sociocultural factors (Progressivism and New Humanism) that allowed creative writing to be adopted in the American university system; however, they have neglected factors defining craft in creative writing and its legacy in the revolutionary experiential education schools at the Bauhaus and Black Mountain College. The birthplace of creative writing is not the University of Iowa, and I argue it was presaged by the sociocultural factors defining craft from the classical period to the Arts and Crafts movement and by those workshops, arts programs, and pedagogical foundations established at the Bauhaus (Germany) and Black Mountain (North Carolina). Recovering these histories along with sociocultural and pedagogical traditions from arts schools and MFAs, we are afforded an alternative and an opportunity to redefine craft as a *mode of becoming*, a fluid way of thinking through practice that is collective and liberatory and will redefine the virtue of creative writing. Turning toward those histories of the Bauhaus and Black Mountain requires us to embrace the radical interventions that redefine craft and artistic practice. We are no longer beholden to craft as craft or educational models that are implicitly built to enfranchise those who fit within dominant traditions in art.

Neither the Bauhaus nor Black Mountain represents perfect idylls for arts education and they were never free of prejudice or political or social challenges for artists, especially women. Both schools *did* fundamentally change the ways artists were trained in the past century, and they represent the definitive sites for understanding craft's institutionalization and marginalization. The Bauhaus School in Weimar, Germany, formed as a radical educational experiment in 1919. By following the impulses of the earlier Arts and Craft Movement and rejecting ornamentation in the high Victorian style, Walter Gropius and the arts educators of the Bauhaus sought a more apolitical path forward, in which experimentation might lead to a fluid relationship between form and function, and between art and industry. At the Bauhaus, Gropius conceived of a school on track "to create a new guild of craftsmen, without the class distinctions which raise an arrogant barrier between craftsman and artist."[72] Although the Bauhaus' influence on art, architecture, and industry cannot be understated, the pedagogical dimensions and their causes merit discussion in relation to craft and creative writing. Bauhaus educational philosophy drew craft into a project of redefinition that framed the mission of the Bauhaus over the subsequent decade. In *Bauhaus Weaving Theory: From Feminine Craft to Mode of Design* (2014), T'ai Smith points to the ways that Gropius projected "the image of a medieval *Bauhütte* (guild) in which a 'working community' of artists and craftsmen could produce together in harmony."[73] The community principle saw crafts (primarily pottery and weaving) as bridges between art and industry; however, as Smith points out, craft's allusion to community soon had to expand into "an alliance of artisanship with fine arts, an approach more in keeping with German expressionism's spiritual-utopian ideals. *Craft*, in other words, was redefined as a product of workers to the service of idealized communities rather than say, industrialists."[74] The synthesis of craft and fine art, Smith argues, slowly eroded through curricular development and the teaching philosophies of the male-dominated Bauhaus. Fine art and craftsmanship had value, whereas arts-and-crafts were associated with female artists working textiles and ceramics such as Anni Albers, Marianne Brandt, Gunta Stözl, Gertrud Arndt, Benita Koch-Otte, Otti Berger, Ilse Fehling, Alma Siedhoff-Buscher, Margarete Heymann, and Lou Scheper-Berkenkamp.

The feminization of craft at the Bauhaus created a division between *being* (identity) an artist and the *practice* (doing) of crafts such as pottery and weaving;

the doing (it was presumed) involved less of the thinking or conceptual work of high art. In this configuration, craft served on the surface as a rationale for articulating art and industry and highlighting the working community, and paradoxically, it subordinated craft to fine arts such as sculpture, painting, and architecture and the esteemed male artists working in these mediums and design like Josef Albers, Wassily Kandinsky, Láslzló Moholy-Nagy, Paul Klee, Johannes Itten, and Walter Gropius. German expressionism elevated painting and other fine arts above craft, and this framework determined that hierarchies in art could be maintained only when the undoing or theoretical work of fine art was authenticated by craftsmanship and craft. This legitimizing principle was folded into a working community of artists that would become a legacy that followed educators Anni and Josef Albers as they emigrated to the United States after the Bauhaus closed under pressure from the Nazis in 1933.

Anni and Josef Albers resettled at Black Mountain College in North Carolina and brought with them Bauhaus educational philosophies that cross-pollinated with Deweyian educational philosophies and the eccentricities of Black Mountain founder John Andrew Rice. Although the connection between the Bauhaus and Black Mountain College and the creation of the Iowa Writers' Workshop by Norman Foerster is neither literal nor definitive, it is inarguable that the two arts schools played the primary role in defining craft in the twentieth century. Black Mountain and the Bauhaus are the foundation of a revisionist history from which we may reinscribe philosophies of craft through an alternative heuristic, one activated in a community of artists. Josef and Anni Albers arrived from the Bauhaus and were foundational in the creation of Black Mountain as an experiential liberal arts model. Through its life span as an educational community from 1933 to 1957, Black Mountain College's influence on Modern art is difficult to quantify. Helen Molesworth's book and exhibition *Leap before You Look: Black Mountain College 1933–1957* (2015) has done considerable work to recover the artistic work and pedagogies that permeated the school throughout its existence.[75] The illustrious list of students and art professors reads like a who's who of the twentieth century's avant-garde: John Cage, Merce Cunningham, Buckminster Fuller, Karen Karnes, M. C. Richards, William de Kooning, Anni and Josef Albers, Charles Olson, and students Robert Rauschenberg, Cy Twombly, and Ruth Asawa. In collaboration with their students, Black Mountain faculty presented the possibility that making could be grounded in community and actions-in-process that brought artists together for collaborative productions.

Anecdotes from Black Mountain read like pedagogical lore. For example, during summer school in 1952, Merce Cunningham describes the first "happening": "John Cage organized a theater event, the first of its kind. David Tudor played piano, M.C. Richards and Charles Olson read poetry, Robert Rauschenberg's white paintings were on the ceiling, Rauschenberg himself played records, and Cage talked. I danced."[76] These happenings and workshops provided the rationale for teaching art in a university and they took Deweyian experiential educational philosophies toward the avant-garde and experimental. Dewey's regular visits to Black Mountain College underscored the importance of the new experiential educational model afoot and amid the artistic collectives, retreats, and communes that began to thrive nationally by mid-century from MacDowell to Carmel.[77] Although John Dewey figures prominently in current histories of creative writing, Black Mountain and the Bauhaus defined craft in the humanities and in the cultural milieu of early twentieth-century arts training.

To this point creative writing histories have not engendered craft with its virtue in consciousness or artistic practice and it has come to represent a static, if not tired, signifier. The promotional materials developed by the Bauhaus saw craft as a malleable signifier for authentication, a legacy born of Arts and Crafts philosophies and echoed later in creative writing MFA programs. Beyond acting as a signifier of authentication, a thread I discuss in detail in relation to writing studies in Chapter 2, craft has come to be characterized as prescriptive, reductive, or, worse, mechanically driven to suppress those artists who are gendered, raced, classed, or differently abled. When mobilized in fidelity to a chosen technique or aesthetic, craft excludes and privileges. Janelle Adsit and Matthew Salesses echo these sentiments and point to the ways that creative writing instructors might utilize threshold concepts like craft in order to make teaching creative writing more equitable. Adsit points to the ways that "craft pedagogy mobilizes a set of aesthetic standards that are framed as heuristics for composing and revising literary texts."[78] By framing craft as a heuristic (Adsit) or as a rhetorical awareness (Salesses), craft becomes a thinking-through-practice that provides new ways to imagine our teaching. In fact, it allows for more than a redefinition of teaching practices, it fundamentally changes the mission of the field and its role in higher education and arts training.

From Aristotle and Plato to the Arts and Crafts Movement, techne and craft tend to drift toward a set of standards or formalist principles. I argue that formalist philosophies or standardizing impulses do more than reduce the available means of making in creative writing—they also determine *who* is considered a writer. To resist deeply held ideologies of technique, creative writers must turn toward the radical collective action represented in craft histories and the virtuous practice embodied in the artists who navigate a set of philosophies, histories, materials, and aesthetic traditions in their thinking. MFA programs in creative writing (and the arts more broadly) have created something incredible in scale: an expansive system of graduate and undergraduate programs and an international network of practitioners laboring to conceptualize and construct art. Programs in creative writing can reflect more than a "systemic creativity," narrowly defined by a set of aesthetic or formal criteria, and it is necessary to resignify craft anew and provide the rationale for teaching process philosophies that are exploratory, inclusive, and reflective of a virtuous practice. The virtue of creative writing is too easily subsumed in literary or composition studies, and it is my argument that the thinking practice that artists employ in their work *is* craft. To this end, I use Chapter 2 as the space to articulate what craft consciousness signifies and how it might be activated in relation to artistic practice and through an intersectional aesthetic tradition. As outlined in this chapter, craft must continue to resist codification, institutionalization, and signification of the term that limits making principles for artists and narrowly define it as technique in one medium. Postmodern theories of genre have obliterated and determined that terminology is never as static as we presume.[79] There is virtue in reconceptualizing craft and the good expressed in creative writing. The impetus for reforming craft must come from *the good* and *the who*. Who can participate in creative writing MFA programs is determined by the boundaries of craft, and feminist principles in craft studies and creative writing studies intervene in static notions of "being," a legacy of Heideggerian philosophy. In place of static notions of dominant craft discourse a rigid sense of being, we must explore the idea of "becoming," a legacy of the eccentric philosophies of Alfred North Whitehead. *Becoming* presumes that variability and change are the essence of existence, and it shifts artists' thinking away from formalist and technical fixations on rendering foundational principles in a medium. The shift from *being* to *becoming* opens up craft pedagogies to modes of thinking that are more inclusive and intermedium and reflective of *what it is like to be an artist*. Artistic identities and practices are ever-evolving, nonlinear, and based in conditional negotiations young and experienced artists alike must navigate through their working projects. Operating through a principle of craft consciousness means understanding the good in-process through thinking that is open to the conjectural. I will define creative writing's mission through craft consciousness and argue for utilizing this heuristic in support of artists' thinking processes. For students, this means that the process of their labor is more important than the outcome. Becoming an artist is not being fluent only in a set of techniques; it is learning how processes are traversed through individual projects and over the course of a lifetime as a working artist. We have lost the virtue in creative writing because we have lost craft to the aphoristic dogma that controls aesthetic principles and cordons off artistic practice from writers outside of dominant traditions. Processism in the form of craft consciousness returns creative writing to its radical roots and to philosophies built upon a collective of artists seeking a liberatory educational model.

A processist approach will draw gardening (more than the gardener) to the center of creative writing education. To achieve a more collective and dynamic approach to artistic thinking, we must wrestle away the concept of craft from its association with technique and the marginalization of artists by dominant craft discourse. Legacies in craft hold more nuance and integrate through cultures and lives in ways that honor the experiences of a diverse of set of writers. We have to work with artifacts that are not textbook adjacent and embrace nontraditional, non-canonical reflections on artistic practice from a more inclusive set of creative writers. The next chapter draws from black earth the roots of practice and those who are invisible inside current MFA programs. Gardening requires sight, but more than vision, the tactile, the corporeal, the familial experience, the oral histories, and the facts of existence form the good of art for the maker. Ruth Asawa learned how to garden from her family, worked on the farm at Black Mountain College as a student of art, and traveled to Toluca, Mexico, to learn the weaving with metal that allowed her to explore material and spatial dimensions. For her, it seemed the land and materials were one. She wrote, "Sculpture is like farming, if you just keep at it you can get a lot done."[80] Asawa never settled in sculpture, just as she never settled in landscape art; she weaved, she moved earth, she sculpted, and in these practices, she accessed a mode of thinking we are in danger of losing when we locate art in technique. Her art was a progression and evolution in thought, and like the garden, it's life from year-to-year is complicated by the circumstances of existence and the necessities of the heart that drive vision.

To prescribe a technique, a material, a form, or a genre is to limit who may call themselves an artist. It is a strange thing—the imposition of the material against the will of the artist is a necessary constraint—and yet, when educators, mentors, textbooks, and institutions dominate the thinking of the artist, we are left with reductions and begin to privilege exclusionary traditions in literature and aesthetics. The next chapter turns toward the critical-creative term that animates this book, craft consciousness, and in the six *thought experiments* sketched in the next chapter, the term is taken as a mode of consciousness and as a process-based philosophy that I hope will change the landscape for how we educate creative writers in future MFA programs.

2

Six Thought Experiments in Craft Consciousness

As suggested at the outset of this book, craft forms the foundation of creative writing and it can, if redefined, change the artistic and educational values of the field. This second chapter defines craft through *consciousness* and by way of six thought experiments. Thought experiments serve as a methodology of discovery for scientists, and like the line studies used by artists, they can serve as a preliminary sketch of a concept or design. This methodology generates multiple definitions of craft consciousness rather than one, and in this multiplicity it offers perspectives on craft through an exploration across fields in writing studies, consciousness studies, Marxist criticism, craft studies, and marginalized aesthetics. To synthesize this range of perspectives on craft, I situate processism as a theoretical framework for understanding the new term: craft consciousness. Process philosophies (and a reality signified by *change* or *perpetual becoming*) are integrated with what Sonja Foss calls feminist *strategies of disruption*, and the chapter generates *multiple perspectives, juxtaposes incongruities, cultivates ambiguities*, and *reframes* craft as consciousness in order to disrupt hegemonic craft definitions reliant on substantive rather than process metaphysics.[1]

Current craft discourse is dictated by substantiative metaphysics, a cosmology that sees the *text*—and often textual *interpretation* based in literary formalism—as the preferred method for learning how to produce one's own literary texts. Grounded in substantive metaphysics and its materialist considerations, writers are in danger of becoming attached to formalist literary analysis and neglecting what is required to develop an artistic practice. Formalist legacies in craft become exclusionary *because* they divorce the artist from processes that are culturally and spiritually embedded and *because* they obscure a more primary need: an evolving, iterative artistic consciousness. The ability to develop as an artistic thinker may be seen as outside the purview of a creative writing education, but I argue that this practitioner thinking must fall inside our goals as educators and in the structure of new and existing MFA/PhD programs. What is required is a radical shift in metaphysical and educational principles, from materialism to processism, a shift that will encourage developing writers to consider the changing nature of the textual and the instabilities of form and genre. Process philosophy equips writers to challenge dominant literary and aesthetic traditions, and it better captures the reality of artistic life, *a perpetual state of becoming*. Artists are always becoming artists, never arriving fully, never leaving entirely. In this condition they develop a practice across thresholds or formations of consciousness as they negotiate material and conceptual terrains. Knowledge of literature is critical to the development of creative writers, but put into practice, a fidelity to material philosophies alone creates an overdetermined system that may prohibit marginalized writers from becoming artists.

It is my argument that dominant craft discourse outlines craft a priori through workshops as an undergraduate to more specialized workshops, craft seminars, literature classes in a genre as a graduate student. What is lost? Or missed? In this steady march through degree programs, specialization and professionalization in a genre are built upon certain predominances. Traditions can be inheritances of the best sort, but for the field of creative writing, the literary canon, workshop procedures, and the traditional design of graduate programs have come to dominate over process. The simple truth is that creative writers, like all artists, are defined by internal processes, and they have the uncanny ability to metamorphosize, switching genres or mediums, testing new material, and adopting a cosmology marked by a practitioner's exploration.

Processism more than materialism underpins the reality of what it is to be an artist, and the turn toward process enacts a powerful shift that changes how we conceive of the reality of a creative writer's life. Outlined by Alfred North Whitehead during his Gifford Lectures at the University of Edinburgh in 1927–8, processism presents a cosmology that sees *change as perpetual* and the *dynamics of life* as central to reality. Artistic practice is formed in the dynamic *interplay* between concept and material, what Whitehead would refer to as "occasions of experience" and through modifications precipitated in-process and between ideas, people, or things. Process philosophy is most often associated with Whitehead's book *Process and Reality* (1929). Though Whitehead is not discussed in D. G. Myers's extensive history of creative writing *The Elephants Teach* (1993), I argue that processism held an influence on par with Hugh Mearns and John Dewey's educational philosophies as MFA programs in the arts were being formed in the early twentieth century. Whitehead's process philosophies were fundamental to experiential education and during the formation of Black Mountain College and in the artist colonies discussed by D. G. Myers, such as Carmel, MacDowell along with Penland, Haystack, and other craft schools.[2] These collaborative sites for experiential education shifted artists away from substance metaphysics to the *experiences* and *processes* upon which art and artist are created. In this shift in thinking, the object or artifact is considered less important than the social interactions that form the foundation of experience. To put it simply: art is more experience than object. Process philosophy closely aligns with John Dewey's early-twentieth-century philosophies and his experiential educational models that suggest "the world is an assembly of physical, organic, social, and cognitive processes that interact at and across levels of dynamic organization."[3] Nonetheless, process philosophy extends beyond Deweyian educational principles as it resists the notion that being and object are static entities, and it argues that *processes, dynamicity,* and *becoming* form the substance of our reality. In the tradition formalized by Whitehead, and preceded by classical philosophers such as Heraclitus, process philosophy offers an alternative way of conceptualizing reality outside the purely materialist impulse and need for hard substance as the basis for reality, consciousness, or aesthetics. The process philosophies of Whitehead set out to resist substantive metaphysics in the Western tradition and complements research by consciousness studies scholars who believe the hard problem of consciousness is not to be resolved through a purely materialist understanding of reality and cognition.

Processism captures what creative writers do. The artist is not simply a pupil to be trained, and the philosophical tradition suggests that the artist is "a basic entity that is individuated in terms of what it 'does.'"[4] Therefore, and based in process philosophy, the artist is by definition "what they do," and the interviews analyzed in Chapter 3 indicate overwhelmingly that artists adapt more than they specialize. Artists are characterized by the fluctuations required to explore new conceptual spaces. Craft discourse as it has been institutionalized in creative writing at present has defined craft as static, purely material, and, even more uncreatively, as a *verifiable standard*. Craft is reduced to the functional, material, and categorical in institutional contexts, and these signifiers limit writers' ability to deviate from dominant literary traditions. Process philosophies, as outlined by Whitehead, carve out a more capacious, inclusive space in craft consciousness where a diverse group of writers can navigate beyond the substance of the text and explore new concepts and process philosophies.

To develop craft consciousness beyond the text ought to be the objective of a creative writing education, and it better serves the MFA/PhD student to inhabit craft as an internal awareness that it is to be cultivate over a lifetime.

With this in mind, writers who teach or administer MFA/PhD programs have the responsibility to draw away from dominant craft discourse and toward the redefinition of craft through consciousness. To this end, the thought experiments in this chapter are organized with the objective of disrupting old definitions of craft and initiating new definitions of craft consciousness. No one definition will solidify in this chapter, and to some readers' chagrin and others delight, multiple perspectives will be constructed to complement new and existing hypotheses and theories of craft. Taken as a whole they demonstrate how fragmentation, co-optation, and the subordination of marginalized artists have been historically entrenched and institutionally reinforced *through* craft. These thought experiments synthesize potential definitions and scrutinize the conditions that have constrained craft to dominant aesthetics, institutional parameters, and unexamined educational principles. The experiments will not be comprehensive and they invite future scholars and artists to labor toward new craft consciousness definitions through a collectivity that seeks renewing, liberating arts practices. My hope is to use the thought experiments as more than imaginative leaps or hypothetical calisthenics, and I want to sketch a conceptual map in craft consciousness that benefits future artists and scholars in creative writing and reframes what we mean by "craft."

Craft Consciousness …

Experiment #1

… *identifies* the marginalization of craft in higher education and in disciplines that circumscribe the term to an assessable standard or verifiable technique.

Experiment #2

… *recuperates* cultural traditions and intersectional process philosophies that include indigenous, disability, queer, feminist, and non-Western aesthetics.

Experiment #3

… *frames* consciousness as thresholds or formations that displace theoretical and philosophical traditions that define craft as oppositional to art (or knowledge).

> *Experiment #4*
>
> ... *traverses* material, phenomenal, store, mind, and access consciousnesses and reflects a dynamic, inclusive understanding of "what it means to be an artist."
>
> *Experiment #5*
>
> ... *shares* a lineage with the labor of women and those who have had to renegotiate their cultural identity in the face of colonialist, gendered, racialized violence.
>
> *Experiment #6*
>
> ... *resists* being subsumed or commoditized through a collective of practitioners that fights against the forces of capitalism, industrialization, and digitization.
>
> (Chart 1)

Thought Experiment #1: Craft Consciousness ...

... identifies the marginalization of craft in higher education and in disciplines that circumscribe the term through assessable standards or verifiable techniques.

Experiment 1 examines what happens to craft as it crosses thresholds into the academy, and it uses scholarship into craft (*technê*) by writing studies scholars Tim Mayers, Kelly Pender, and Byron Hawk to examine how the term is standardized as it migrates into higher education. Scholarship on craft from composition and rhetoric studies, often referred to more broadly as writing studies, provides a valuable case in point because it demonstrates how the standardization of craft comes at a cost. What is lost in the migration into the academy modifies the ways scholars, artists, and teachers deploy the term, and as it becomes associated with techniques and standards, craft becomes detached from the processes used by individual writers. Pender, Hawk, and Mayers resist the denaturing of craft, and through drawing the term back to process philosophies, invention practices, and composing traditions shared in common, they provide a foundation for including writers and artists whose processes don't easily fit the mold. It is my argument that the standardization of craft reinforces the impulses initiated by literary formalism and the materialist inclination to detach artist from art object. Both formalism and standardization have the consequence of affecting creative writers on the macro-level (institution/profession) and at the micro-level (program/workshop) and as developing writers are forced to measure their work against criteria that by design and implementation exclude marginalized writers and the aesthetic and cultural traditions they value. My objective in this experiment is to look closer at the tendencies in literary studies and writing studies to standardize and detach craft from the artist, and to disrupt these inclinations, I examine the ways that artists Joy Harjo, Sandra Cisneros, Gloria Anzaldúa, Esther Díaz Martin, Dawoud Bey, Susan Sontag, and Victor Vitanza conceptualize craft as a process in consciousness.

Before moving toward the stories of individual artists and writing studies research, it is vital to discuss legacies in materialism and formalism and how literary production detaches the artist from their text. Philosophies in materialism suggest, "everything that exists is material."[5] Materialist philosophies are based in substantive metaphysics and focus the writer on the textual artifact; formalism provides an analytical framework in materialism that separates literary writing from practitioner knowledge, process philosophies, and consciousness. In the mid-twentieth century, the New Critics theorized formalism in literature by suggesting that it was a deviation from ordinary discourse. The *poetic* became associated with the mantra "make it new" or "making strange," and the establishment of interpretative frameworks in English Studies owes much to the New Critics and their dual roles as writer-critics.[6] Terry Eagleton describes how Formalism sought to differentiate the poetic from ordinary language: "The Formalists, then, saw literary language as a set of deviations from a norm, a kind of linguistic violence: literature is a 'special' kind of language, in contrast to the 'ordinary' language we commonly use."[7] Throughout the end of the past century, the *deviation* that formalism once represented in discourse had become systematized. As Susan Sontag suggests, deviations in art give way to institutionalization, and in the case of formalist definitions of craft, the *artifact* has come to supersede the *artist*.[8] In "Problematizing Formalism: A Double-Cross of Genre Boundaries," Mary Ann Cain also speaks to this point: "formalism asserts that the text stands on its own as a complete entity, apart from the writer who produced it."[9] This detachment of artist from object has had the consequence of framing creative writing as a battery of literary devices to be understood and then applied in practice. Formalism has been systematized in creative writing through dominant craft discourse and *detachment* has become foundational to the workshop procedures governing submission discussions. In this environment, workshop peers can be encouraged to strike the affect of objectivity, and a cohort enters into an inequitable arrangement where formalist principles and social pressures breed competition and oppressive conditions that can be hostile.

Anecdotes about famous writers have a tendency to be aggrandized and become the pithy, punchy stuff of MFA lore. The Iowa Writers' Workshop is legendary in this regard, and David O. Dowling's book *A Delicate Aggression: Savagery and Survival in the Iowa's Writers' Workshop* (2019) works to examine the experience of individual writers in the Workshop. In fifteen biographies of famous writers who have passed through, Dowling chronicles the depths of sexism and racism facing Workshop participants. Dowling details that the masculine ethos and celebrity writer status dominate the Workshop, and the book chronicles the mire of intolerance, violence, and sexism that were endemic and characteristic of the program under the directorship of Paul Engle and Frank Conroy. Dowling captures the raucousness of the competitive fray in the Workshop, and he shows how Joy Harjo and Sandra Cisneros resisted oppressive conditions and supported each other through their experience as students. In addition to enduring the "intellectual theatres of combat" that were the writing workshops, Joy Harjo was not granted funding through program and had to cobble together the means to support two small children. Dowling writes, "Cisneros and Harjo mainly clung to each other for emotional support while also mutually enriching each other's creative and professional growth at this stage in their career ... their alternative collaborative approach to writing into externalized, horizontal planes of sociocultural context, rather than the narrow psychological introspection of confessional male poetry."[10] Harjo and Cisneros's collaboration and support of each other, according to Dowling, was antithetical to the dominant ideological and aesthetic bent of the Workshop, which was decidedly individualistic and predicated on the mythos of the white male author. In her memoir *A House of My Own: Stories from My Life* (2015), Cisneros describes the challenges in overcoming traditions in dominant craft discourse at Iowa:

> I asked myself what I could write about that my classmates couldn't. I didn't know what I wanted exactly, but I did have enough sense to know what I didn't. I didn't want to sound like my classmates; I didn't want to keep imitating the writers I'd been reading. Their voices were right for them but not for me.[11]

Like Cisneros, Joy Harjo reflects on her time at the Workshop as the context in which she overcame the tendency to write like her peers in class. In an interview with the University of Iowa, Harjo said, "And of course that fell flat ... And then I just decided 'Well, I am going to be who I am.' I came to learn to deal with poetry on my own terms, and maybe that's what writing programs ultimately do."[12] Perhaps that's what MFA creative writing programs *should* do: allow the writer to *deal with literature/craft/identity on their own terms*. Harjo and Cisneros's testimonies and Dowling's history of the Iowa Writers' Workshop point to the ways that marginalized writers inherit social and aesthetic conditions that are potentially oppressive in past and current MFA programs. To understand craft's role in these conditions, writers must demonstrate a resistance to sexism, racism, homophobia, ableism, and other forms of discrimination while also examining how dominant craft discourse and the impulse toward professionalization may obscure approaches to process by artists not already enfranchised by MFA programs. Our work as scholars and artists must challenge micro-level oppression *and* examine the ways that craft has been codified through the process of institutionalization. Reductions of craft to technique or transferrable skills leaches the term of its essence and obscures more vital invention practices.

In *Techne: From Neoclassicism to Postmodernism—Understanding Writing as a Useful, Teachable Art* (2011), Kelly Pender presents the two dominant definitions of techne (craft) in the field of composition and rhetoric: the *New Classicist* and the *New Romanticist* approaches. Pender traces these definitions back from the classical period to contemporary composition studies scholarship, and she identifies the danger in the New Classicist tradition and techne's association with the verifiable. Used as an instrument for assessment in evaluating student writing and invention practices in higher education, New Classicist conceptions of techne ascribe value through conceiving of craft as an instrument for standardization and the verifiable dimensions of language. Conceiving of techne as the preordained and the procedural locks the term in the bind of industrial efficiency, which is a common symptom in institutional contexts where writing becomes a vehicle for cultural reproduction. Janice Lauer and Kelly Pender echo the industrial standard evoked here: "New Classicists emphasize heuristic procedures, a generic conception of the composing process through rhetorical knowledge can be carried from one situation to the other, and rational control of some processes that can be taught."[13] Capturing composition scholars' fixation on transferable skills, New Classicists draw techne toward what Lauer and Pender see as a prescriptive, closed system approach to composing and invention. As with composition studies, creative writing approaches techne in a similar manner when dominant craft discourse prescribes the characteristics of a genre and the invention practices associated with these literary genres. The ideological underpinnings of industrialization and institutionalization—with their drift toward uniformity, efficiency, and standards—integrate rather seamlessly into the

New Classicist approach. Pender suggests that the standardization of invention practices within the lexicon of techne changed the trajectory of composition in the 1980s; it provided composition and rhetoric studies a mechanism to legitimize itself in English Studies. This Pyrrhic victory, as Pender argues, has obfuscated the expressive, exploratory dimensions of the writing process.

> Acknowledging that there are a number of explanations for this trend, I argue that it is attributable, at least in part, to the oppositions that have been created between the term "writing" which, in various ways, has come to refer to a kind of "opening up" activity—that is, an inherently valuable, sometimes unteachable activity—and seemingly mundane, "closing down" activities that often fall under the rubric of "composition" and "scribing."[14]

Pender analyzes the role dominant craft discourse plays and argues that invention practices are narrowed as a field begins to migrate toward professionalization. Legitimacy is built upon standards. Writing standards in craft dictate the protocol of process and product. And if invention practices are dictated by these standards, the writer is encouraged to seek the verifiable rather than explorative invention practices that are uncertain, tenuous, politically disruptive, or grounded in the cultures and communities that sustain them. To extend Pender's argument, it's essential to recognize the *legitimating* gesture of standardization as implicitly *delegitimizing* making practices from outside of academy and from the cultural traditions where artists are engaged with the histories, traditions, and languages that make them who they are.

In the collection *Voices from the Ancestors: Xicanx and Latinx Spiritual Expressions and Healing Practices* (2019) edited by Lara Medina and Martha A. Gonzales, the authors express the abiding and replenishing sensibility connecting artist to community and culture. Martha A. Gonzales speaks to the role of the artist in the face of violence and oppression: "The poets of the Moviemento period wielded poetry as means to speak truth to the community, to invoke knowledges and lifeways that survived the genocide and ethnocide of colonialism."[15] Classical definitions of truth are framed by Plato as eternal and externalized from the thinker. Gonzales's evocation resists truth in the Platonic, New Classicist sense by defying the alienation and corruption of the artist under the banner of colonizing *standards*. Read in light of Gonzales's description—the poet "invok[es] knowledges and lifeways"—artists draw life from the lifelessness of professionalization and standardization. Craft dehumanizes when it requires the artist to detach from processes and lived practices that are culturally embedded or which enrich the mutually reciprocal relationship between artist and community or culture. Prescriptive craft in the New Classicist tradition is fundamental to building a dominant craft discourse, and it serves colonialism and capitalism more than it serves the artist. Definitions of techne/craft that erase culturally embedded making practices in the name of prescriptive standards create the illusion of verifiable, rational criteria.

New Classicist definitions mark techne as an instrument for increasing certainty (and decreasing uncertainty) in invention, a rational heuristic that gives a well-defined outcome: "When understood as a rational ability to effect a useful result, techne is deemed instrumental because the value of that result lies in its use ... When techne is understood as a way to produce resources, however, production never ends, which is to say that every product has the potential to become a means in future rounds of production."[16] Rather than characterizing techne as an outcome, Pender points to the circular, intuitive nature of techne and its legacy in spiritual renewal (an idea identified by theories in Anzaldúa and Gonzales as well). As a New Classicist notion of techne closes writers off from exploration, Pender invites the alternative often elided by dominant craft and those pseudo-industrial practices that seek to verify standards.

Characterizing craft as a simple instrument leads toward accumulation *not* exploration, and for Pender, Byron Hawk's concept of "post-techne" provides a way of thinking about techne in terms of post-process theory. He presents post-techne as an "understanding of techne from an instrumental means of production to a non-instrumental mode of bringing-forth."[17] To "bring forth" rather than to "verify" or serve as an "instrument" shifts craft (and techne), according to Hawk and Pender, away from a technical or instrumental definition toward one with an aleatory function. In *Counter-History of Composition: Toward Methodologies of Complexity* (2007), Byron Hawk outlines *post-technê* as a philosophy that acts as a forerunner to the concept of craft consciousness sketched in this chapter. Hawk realigns techne with a broader redefinition that elides its reduction to the instrumental and the functional, and he draws the term back to a vitalist origin in Aristotelian thought. He writes,

> [Techne] is both a rational, conscious capacity to produce and an intuitive, unconscious ability to make. All of the contextual elements that affect a technique, pedagogy, or method can never be fully accounted for. The bodily knowledges and contextual constraints also produce art along with conscious knowledges that move techne away from an instrumental conception of the technical toward a more complex model.[18]

Hawk orchestrates a pivot through post-techne that allows creative writers to conceive of their processes of making as akin to an ecosystem that broadens rather than constricts invention. To draw this conception of techne into conversation with craft consciousness, Chapter 3 discusses how writers and artists understand their process as ecosystemic, intersectional, and inclusive of ways of making from beyond their chosen field. Processes intersect and are organized by methodologies that do not succumb to easy labels or follow strict disciplinary or material categories. Hawk resists "the reduction of techne to 'technical rhetoric'" just as he refuses the conflation of techne with romanticism, expressivism, and process philosophies.[19] Like Pender, Hawk concentrates on the reductions of techne in composition studies, and he identifies Victor Vitanza, James Berlin, Richard Young, and Paul Kameen as scholars who provided alternative philosophies of techne in the 1980s. Hawk returns to a vitalist thread in craft, and he echoes previous generations of compositionist who sought—at the dawn of the field—to preserve an expanding notion of invention that would not be domesticated into a standard, New Classicist definition. Hawk undertakes the reinvigoration of techne using research methodologies and counter-histories that center on humanist philosophies that hold renewed value in the digital world. Organized against the standardized, institutionalized framework of techne that has come to dominate the field of composition, Hawk casts techne as historically oppositional to codification, perpetually inventive, and essentially governed by an "internal heuristic." The argument for post-techne pivots the field of composition toward methodological renewal predicated on "open methods" that have not been dulled in order to position techne/craft into standards for institutional assessment.

Ascribing aleatoric function to craft allows for a modicum of uncertainty. This uncertainty is dynamic and invaluable for the practitioner. It leads the writer toward the unassumed and the unverified, all impulses that resist the transferable, skills-based assessments desired by institutions and academic fields. Pender emphasizes that anxieties about whether or not writing is teachable led to the instrumentation, standardization, and professionalization of craft in writing studies; these worries have led toward capitalist and colonialist impulses where production and accumulation of resources (tuition, publications, authorial merits) supersede the consciousness required for developing artists, an awareness of craft's imaginative potential.

Dominant craft discourse extracts from canonical literature the methods of production; this impulse aligns creative writing with a closed, static system of craft where value is ascribed to the past and a workshop submission is evaluated based on canonical literature. Who becomes a creative writer is a matter of explicit *and* implicit institutional biases; it also becomes embedded in more surreptitious and inconspicuous ways, namely through the available methods of production. A pluralistic, multicultural literary canon does work to reflect a broader conception of literary production, but it cannot do the work alone and it does not fundamentally change the available methods of production and the writer's access to diverse invention practices. In considering the ways that craft consciousness might expand the making practices in the field, it is important to consider the material inequities that saddle the field, including hiring practices, editorial positions in literary journals, the rank of student writers in cohorts, artist fellowships, and book and writing contests. Fuller cultural representation at the level of the student cohort or course reading list doesn't mean more faculty of color will be hired, and it doesn't change the access given to some writers to agents, journals, contests, and funding that changes who *becomes* a creative writer. When craft consciousness changes the path of writers in invention it must simultaneously be echoed by a resistance to a host of operating procedures endemic to creative writing as a field: from the material (tuition waivers, fellowships, faculty leaves) to the social and pedagogical (diverse visiting writers, reading series, inclusive workshop practices) and onto the university and field (AWP recommendations for hiring traditionally marginalized artists, conference funding, health insurance). When craft consciousness builds from a focus on invention and process philosophies to the macro-level of creative writing field, it promotes inclusive making practices that affect artist and field alike. Compositionists Kelly Pender and Byron Hawk have worked against the reduction of techne, and their writing studies scholarship supplements a broader shift in definition that disrupts inequities of small and large scales in creative writing.

Complementing the work of Hawk and Pender, creative writing studies scholar Tim Mayers draws artists and writers to less visible sites of practitioner knowledge. In his book *(Re)Writing Craft: Composition, Creative Writing, and the Future of English Studies* (2005), Tim Mayers coins the term *craft criticism* to illuminate an interdisciplinary genre shared by scholars, creative writers, and artists alike. In chapters 2 and 3 of his book, Mayers outlines the four basic species of craft criticism, including: (1) Process, (2) Genre, (3) Authorship, and (4) Institutionality.[20] Mayers describes craft criticism as a genre of practitioner knowledge, a productive shoptalk among artist and scholars that brings forward questions central to academics and artists. His inquiry brings him to a common touchpoint with Pender and Hawk—Martin Heidegger. For Mayers,

Heideggerian theory influences the ways we conceive writers' ontological processes. By definition, ontology is the examination of the nature of being and becoming—existence itself—and Heideggerian theories, according to Mayers, influence poets and their task as artists. For Heidegger, poets are compared with modern technology and modern science because both serve to "reveal being" from concealment. Mayers writes, "Heidegger believes truth should be more properly understood in the sense of the Greek word *aletheia*, or, as he translates it, 'unconcealment.' ... In the sense of Greek word *poiesis*, things may be brought out of concealment to stand 'as they are,' or in their own Being."[21] In his analysis of Heidegger, Mayers compares craft to a "tool" or technology that extends the creative writers' ontological processes and their function as revealers of the world. This conceptual shift "eradicates the problematic and artificial distinction between craft and talent (and it may, in fact, eliminate the category of talent altogether or at least make it secondary rather than primary to craft)."[22] In redefining craft, Mayers offers the possibility of asking more basic questions of creative writing: What is the nature of the writer and how does their work reveal existence and being?

To understand the poet is to understand how they think. According to Mayers, it's helpful to understand the "poet as craftsperson," and if we push Mayers's analysis further it is logical to argue that "language is not a medium for the poet; the poet is a medium for language."[23] Mayers stops short of saying that "poetry is thinking"; however, his characterization of Heidegger leads us to see the poet as a craftsperson who reveals the world to the reader through a process metaphysics. The poet reveals, according to Heidegger, that "language is the house of Being," and Mayers destabilizes substantive metaphysics by defining the poet as the medium.[24] Rather than seeing the artist (poet) and the object (poem) as lying outside of being, Mayers draws craft criticism (and Heidegger) into line with process philosophy. The poet is perpetually "becoming" and they remain as irresolute and as fluctuating as text itself. Mayers's reading of Heidegger invites scholars and artists to see craft as ontological—at once process-driven and material—and he reveals how the poet evolves within their material, and even as a medium themselves. Unsettling craft in this manner allows for artists to rearticulate what they do and how they do it, and craft criticism, like craft consciousness, identifies the ontological space of the artistic process. Like Mayers, Pender and Hawk rewrite the historical, ideological, pedagogical, and ontological dimensions of techne/craft. For composition and creative writing studies, their research has a practical function by building interdisciplinary coalitions (Mayers), establishing new research methods (Hawk), and reexamining histories of the field (Pender). For the theoretical purposes of defining craft consciousness, their scholarship situates craft in consciousness and in the ontological process of art making.

Craft consciousness disassembles purely materialist and formalist approaches to arts training, and in the case of the writer, it can offer a method that is more inclusive, collaborative, exploratory, and inspired by artists like Anzaldúa, Gonzales, Cisneros, and Harjo who seek to establish individual *and* collective agency in their practice. In place of standardization and the verifiable measures required of institutions, craft consciousness embodies the iterative processes and internal awareness that artists traverse through and between mediums. Creative writing can build a new institutional framework through an inclusive model of craft consciousness that includes the ancestral, the spiritual, and the transformative. The erasure of cultural identity continues when we don't actively resist colonialist, capitalist, and industrial educational models. If marginalized artists are to be trained as artists in institutions of higher education, there must be an *atechnê* as Victor Vitanza suggests, a space for recognizing the organic nature of being and becoming. The artist claims freedoms to be visible and to become someone different. As the late poet-musician Gil Scott-Heron writes, "I didn't become someone different I did not want to be."[25] Heron's allusion suggests that we are non-static beings andthat we are becoming someone different throughout our lives. To accommodate artists "shedding plates like a snake," MFA programs must be reorganized around philosophies dictated by the artistic process, and their stages of awakening and (re)creation must form the foundation of training, not its incidental by-product.[26] Artists have created adaptive, collective strategies to work against dominant craft discourse and hostile programmatic social and aesthetic conditions; nonetheless, Harjo and Cisneros's experience at the Writers' Workshop shows the need for a wholesale resistance to domination. Rather than being dictated to the artist as institutional criteria, craft must be reimagined and reprogrammed through consciousness.

In her 1967 essay "The Aesthetic of Silence," Susan Sontag discusses the role of consciousness in defying and expanding the goals of art for a new generation of artists. She writes, "Whatever goal is set for art eventually proves restrictive, matched against the widest goals of consciousness. Art, itself a form of mystification, endures a succession of crises of demystification; older artistic goals are assailed and, ostensibly, replaced; outworn maps of consciousness are redrawn."[27] I argue that we have reached the eventuality described in Sontag's landmark essay; restrictive conditions have worn the artist threadbare. Art is not technique, "art is consciousness," and retracing craft requires writers to expand the term into the realm of consciousness and to displace the ideologies of formalism.[28] The consciousness shift Susan Sontag describes in her essay aligns with the transformative potential in art making Gloria Anzaldúa refers to in the book, *this bridge we call home: radical visions for transformation* (1981), as "*el camino de conocimiento.*"[29] *Conocimiento*, in Anzaldúa's theory of personal, political transformation in art, requires the artist to shake loose consciousness from the oppressive forces binding them to the capitalistic, colonialist project. Solidarity begins with shedding dogma in literature or art and beginning as "an inner exploration of the meaning and purpose of life ... a form or spiritual inquiry ... reached via creative acts—writing, art making, dancing, healing, meditation, and spiritual activism."[30] Through an inner exploration premised on the integration of spiritual inquiry and imaginative pursuits, Anzaldúa conceptualizes craft as a blending of spiritual, cultural, political, and arts expression.

In *Light in the Dark/Luz en la Oscuro: Rewriting Identity, Spirituality, Reality* (2015), Anzaldúa further theorizes the ontological dimensions of the artistic journey. In the chapter "Now Let Us Shift ... *Conocimiento* ... Inner Work, Public Acts," Anzaldúa formulates an "onto-epistemology" based on an intersectional relationship between the inner spiritual work and outer public work as an artist.[31] She describes the process as: "an intensely personal, fully embodied process that gathers information from context, *conocimiento* also incorporates emotion, spiritual-activist, and ontological dimensions."[32] Her theory of *conocimiento* integrates inner explorations with the outer work of artistic–cultural–political interventions in culture. Anzaldúa's critical term *el conocimiento* relates closely Paulo Freire's concept of *critical consciousness* and György Lukács's term *class consciousness*; in these terms, craft consciousness identifies the psychosocial position artists find themselves in as they work to resist oppressive sociopolitical conditions. Lukács and Friere's theories serve different political and cultural objectives, nonetheless, the political and pedagogical import of craft consciousness parallels the evocations of Anzaldúa, Freire, and Lukács as they seek liberation from political, educational, and cultural domination. For creative writers, dominant craft discourse imposes impediments to practice and the formation of an artistic practice and identity. To resist institutional and cultural impediments requires scholars and artists to diagnose and then disassemble the oppressive conditions through a collective, intersectional, and transdisciplinary approach to the process and procedures for training artists.

As Anzaldúa and Sontag argue, the first step is to rupture dominant discourse and the second step is to seek transformation through "spiritual inquiry" and an "inner exploration" of consciousness. I argue here (and in later thought experiments) that craft criticism by marginalized artists makes visible what we can't see in dominant craft, namely the process philosophies and narratives of those who face and resist institutional oppression. For example, in the essay collection *Voices from the Ancestors: Xicanx and Latinx Spiritual Expressions and Healing Practices* (2019), Esther Díaz Martín describes how learning embroidery from her mother allowed her to develop *mi forma de bordar* or a process for art making that served to shield her from institutional violence and microaggressions. Martín's narrative integrates concepts of art as a form of recovery:

> Bordar is meditation that allows me to disconnect from the anxiety of *"el trabajo que no se ve"*—the work of teaching and writing—and to connect to the tangible work of the hands, vision, and creativity ... By weaving this practice with the work of my academic profession, I honor the technologies passed down by my mothers and grandmothers and I find in their knowledge guidance that is not grounded in violence and competition but in creative love and humility.[33]

Martín's description of her process reveals the culturally embedded methods and the identity negotiations necessary to survive in an academic or artistic field. Embroidery in the form of *bordar* provides an interior meditative space for accentuating home cultures, and it activates process and practice as a form of resistance against institutional violence. Marginalized artists remain less visible, and the interiority of their subjects is obfuscated by dominant aesthetics and literary traditions. In another medium, contemporary photographer Dawoud Bey seeks to capture interiority in his subjects, an interiority not often permitted in representations of Black communities.

Bey describes his process in an interview for *BOMB Magazine*: "I want to convey a sense of the subjects' interiorities, particularly for people—such as black people and young people—whom the larger society does not always consider to have rich and complex inner lives."[34] For Bey, his representation of Black identity resists the oppression facing Black cultures in urban spaces. In order to reclaim marginalized subjectivities, craft must do more than shed oppressive representation of BIPOC lives; craft consciousness must reflect the process philosophies, personal and cultural values, and subjectivities of a diverse set of artists beyond those parameters dictated by formalism or the forces propelling artists toward professionalization and specialization.

Thought Experiment #2: Craft Consciousness ...

... recuperates cultural traditions and intersectional process philosophies that include indigenous, disability, queer, feminist, and non-Western aesthetics.

If we do not accept dominant literary traditions and craft discourse at face value, artists at the margins are less vulnerable to erasure (or invisibility) and artists may build through a collective. Through a collaborative, intersectional ethos, creative writers can pivot the field toward more diverse aesthetic traditions. In this second thought experiment, I discuss how craft consciousness integrates marginalized aesthetic traditions and builds a decidedly different educational model through indigenous, queer, disability, and feminist aesthetics. Janelle Adsit, in her discussion of marginalized aesthetics in *Toward an Inclusive Creative Writing*, suggests that critical creative writing studies may unify aesthetic traditions and allow writers to adopt and teach more inclusive approaches to process.[35] From this second experiment, I hope to draw the discussion away from formulations of craft based in institutional standards (Experiment 1) and toward considerations of how marginalized aesthetic traditions offer alternative conceptualizations of process and consciousness. The experiment, therefore, relies more on craft criticism by marginalized artists, and their practitioner wisdom presents lived experience as central to the definition of craft consciousness.

In her essay for the collection *How Dare We! Write: A Multicultural Creative Writing Discourse* (2019) "Notes in Journey from a Writing of the Mix," Anya Achtenberg suggests that the "placelessness" experienced by marginalized writers is a consequence of workshop dogma and dominant craft discourse, both of which emphasize linearity and cohesive approaches to story construction. Achtenberg argues that polyvocal narratives and *instabilities* of literary form better reflect the lived experience of some artists. She writes, "Fragmented, diasporic experience often births a fragmented story structure with multiple narrative voices. Part of our work is finding narrative forms to hold the fullness of our story and reveal the interconnectedness of its shards."[36] The search for form that Achtenburg describes locates itself in the challenge of representing diasporic experience in its "fullness" and "interconnectedness." This challenge of artistic representation—whether representing characters' experience or the experience of the author—is doubly challenging for the diasporic writer who must attempt to fit lived experience within the boundaries of literary genres or formal criteria. As institutional forces move toward the standardization, the "writer out of category," as Achtenburg describes, must take imaginative action by leaping between genres. She writes, "Writers out of category and placeless can be embodied for an instant as boundary jumpers, border crossers, shapeshifters, in flight and magical appearance; we can disappear into the whirring of atoms that move together in form that is permeable; the membrane of self, permeable."[37] Achtenberg's description offers insights into the relationship between identity and form, and the shapeshifting she describes is necessary because it better captures her lived experience. In "Some Thoughts on Diaspora and Hybridity," conceptual artist and photographer Lorraine O'Grady echoes Achtenburg's characterization of the diasporic experience, and she extends the critique to the compartmentalizing tendencies of academic disciplines, saying,

> For me, art is part of a project of finding equilibrium, of becoming whole … We do not look at or produce art with aesthetic and philosophy over here, and politics and economics over there. In fact, as these false barriers fall, we find ourselves in a space where more and more the entrenched academic disciplines appear inadequate to deal with the experience of racially and imperially marginalized people.[38]

Later in this chapter, I will equate artists' lived experience with phenomenal consciousness or the ability to render experience into an artistic form. For the moment, Achtenburg and O'Grady's descriptions offer a way to understand how craft consciousness may allow writers to shapeshift and boundary leap as they explore their own process. As an internalized process rather than an external criteria, craft consciousness provides artists a platform to explore, sample, remix, and challenge the categories, forms, genres, and boundaries that may limit the imagination. Dominant craft cannot capture what it means to live in the spaces where one's cultural traditions have been erased or made unwhole through racial, colonial, capitalist domination.

Craft criticism, the cross-disciplinary genre identified by Tim Mayers, can liberate and reinvigorate the process philosophies expressed by writers out of category. Oral histories, craft manifestos, artists' statements, and interviews expand the process philosophies of developing writers, philosophies that liberate them from the material limits of text. For example, the avant-garde collection of craft criticism edited by Jennifer Liese, *Social Medium: Artists' Writing 2000–15* (2016), offers a reinterpretation of the textual boundaries understood by artists as they navigate the warp and weft of consciousness.[39] Immersed in these networks of craft criticism, developing writers are given models for process-based inquiry where they can expand the range, complexity, and diversity of approaches to text and to process as developing artists. *Artists-out-of-category,* to use Achtenburg's deft coinage, develop through traditions not currently modeled in MFA programs designed for genre specialization, and I argue that creative writers are networked with practitioners of materials beyond the word. To integrate these networks and model the process philosophies of artists, craft consciousness requires explorations of process from beyond the text. At the intersection between marginalized aesthetic traditions, new possibilities emerge in process and as artists seek a resistance to domination or standardization in a chosen medium.

In *Queer Threads: Crafting Identity and Community* (2017), a collection of LGBTQ+ craft artist interviews, Nathan Vincent describes the ways that the exploration of a medium parallels his reexamination and reconfiguration of masculinity and norms of sexuality.

> I don't know that I would have thought to go there had I not been gay. I think there was some freedom to explore mediums that were not "masculine" because I wasn't living within the rules or boundaries anyway. One thing the feminist movement did was open up the definition of femininity to include things that we think of as masculine. With a lot of my work, I'm trying to expand the definition of masculinity, giving masculinity some tenderness and vulnerability.[40]

Vincent intervenes in dominant norms of gender and sexuality through his practice, and his strategies to disrupt gender boundaries aligns with O'Grady and Achtenburg's insistence on disruptions to the limitations prescribed through form, genre, or field. In the book *Queer Threads*, artists discuss how explorations of process are, at their heart, inextricable from examinations of identity and technique. Curator and designer Pierre Fouché articulates this phenomenon by referencing chance, saying, "I often feel my works and my process are quite random; I engage with subjects and techniques like a butterfly—whatever pulls with more urgency, whatever technique seems more interesting to engage with at the moment. In retrospect, the common threads and the narrative reveal themselves."[41] Moving from technique to technique or subject to subject as a "butterfly" suggests that Fouché operates on a process that is enriching because its stability comes from fluidity and placelessness. The process Fouché describes has value to all developing creative writers; however, it is striking how Achtenburg, O'Grady, and Vincent suggest that the need to disrupt boundaries or fields comes as a need (not a want) for diasporic and gay artists. Because these artists don't fit within dominant racial or heteronormative categories they must find a way in art that is premised on Anzaldua's concept of *el conciemento*—oppression is resisted or disassembled during the process of restoring one's identity. Harmony Hammond, a curator and arts activist, operates with this ethos, writing, "accumulation, layering, and connecting gendered fragments initiated a 'survivor aesthetic' that informs my work to this day. These pieces could be touched, retouched, repaired, and like women's lives, reconfigured."[42] The fragmentary, as suggested by Achtenburg and Hammond, is the substance needed to define craft consciousness and what artists make of the remnants when their identities as members of a diasporic community or as LGBTQ identifying artists or as women. The *survivor aesthetic* defined by Hammond is another way to conceive of the task: How do artists repair legacies of domination through reconfiguring their approach to process and the practice of teaching developing artists?

In a time of a global pandemic, violence against Black, queer, women's lives, political maelstroms, environmental disaster, and class inequities of historical disproportion, a survivor aesthetic benefits from a collective wish: *survival*. At the intersection of marginalized communities, survival and the "reconfiguration" of an artistic identity comes in the wake of, and is necessitated by, fragmentation and violence. The alienation felt through dominant craft is a manifestation of the racial, classed, gendered, heteronormative, or abled oppression experienced by marginalized artists. When writers consider the powerful nature of a coalition in craft consciousness, they empower collective ways of making that are authenticated by the artist who aspires to represent their world to the viewer, the reader, and to those cultures whom they love and cherish. Craft consciousness is defined through collective survival at the same time it synthesizes ways of making that are subversive and are aimed at resistance to the domination that is particular to each artist. Craft philosophies challenge dominant modes of production, that is, industrialization, and in the case of creative writing, the question might shift: If a marginalized artist survives cultural oppression in all its forms and matriculates into an MFA program creative writing, how will they, then, survive under the conditions of institutionalization (in dominant craft) and formalist specialization (in literary genre)? Under these conditions, the artist is implicitly assimilated and instructed to separate from home communities, making traditions, and family origins in order to meet the clear expectations foisted upon them by institutionalization, standardization, and/or specialization. Although these abstract processes seem at remove from the creative writing student, I argue that these amassing conditions affect the process philosophies they are building. Constructed on dominant craft, aesthetic, and literary traditions, the MFA program does not serve a survivalist's needs when it is designed on an exclusionary model. For the writer "out of category," the model limits the leaps between genre/form/medium and the experimentation and exploration in process necessary to become an artist.

In her chapter "Marginalized Aesthetics" from *Toward an Inclusive Creative Writing*, Janelle Adsit discusses how dominant craft dictates the terms of production. "Craft, that which the workshop is set up to teach, is a canon of taste-making principles … saturating the curriculum in creative writing, craft pedagogy mobilizes a set of aesthetic standards that are framed as heuristics for composing and revising literary texts."[43] Adsit continues by illuminating the ways that *taste*—mobilized through craft pedagogy in workshop—determines the nature of what gets produced—by whom and for whom. "Rather than teaching students to be responsive to a diverse range of aesthetic situations—and to assess and negotiate the complex demands of tradition, convention, innovation, reader-response, artistic intention, and the organicity of texts-in-process—craft pedagogy and its accompanying handbooks exist to teach the conventions of 'sophisticated literature.'"[44] If MFA programs arrest "the organicity of texts-in-process" and the complex network of aesthetic and cultural traditions artists rely on, they serve the institution more than the writer. And Adsit's intervention echoes Dawson's concept of sociological poetics discussed in Chapter 1 and the recognition that aesthetic choices are always already political and ideological choices. Adsit and Dawson frame aesthetic choices by an artist as a complex negotiation *between* choices that have personal, political, and rhetorical dimension. Artistic decisions serve as political interventions or as cultural reclamations or, more simply, as strategies for personal survival. MFA programs in creative writing define literariness through workshop protocol, course readings, guest writer invitations, visiting and permanent faculty appointments, literary journal editorships, and summer fellowships, and these opportunities can define literariness through a narrow set of aesthetic principles. As Adsit suggests, aesthetic range becomes compartmentalized when it reflects those that are already enfranchised through literary tradition and curricular design; she writes,

> Because the creative writing curriculum lacks a thorough or critical engagement with a diverse set of aesthetic range and a nuanced understanding of how texts move in the world, the student-writer becomes compartmentalized. A writer's sense of belonging comes to be structured around over-simplified notions of what it means to produce a literary text.[45]

When the terms artistic production are limited to culturally, socially, and aesthetically determined conditions, developing writers have their process and practice dictated to them. Producing a literary text is not a process that can be universalized, but this doesn't mean it cannot be taught, rather, I argue that intersectional aesthetic traditions from outside of writing can bring process philosophies to the center and displace a reliance on dominant craft discourse. To define this alternative in terms of craft consciousness, this second thought experiment imagines process thinking as a transdisciplinary space that allows artists to pivot, reconfigure, intervene, and transgress aesthetic traditions as they become experienced in their medium. In order to shift from an *aesthetics of taste* to an *aesthetic of intersection*, it's necessary to imagine craft as a vehicle for thinking through the most deeply held beliefs in creative writing. Are creative writers willing to reexamine craft traditions through the lens of intersectional aesthetics and process philosophies outside their current medium? Can they provide a pathway for writers out-of-category to intervene in cultures of domination and find liberation for themselves? These questions are large. They encompass even larger questions for developing creative writers who must navigate MFA programs in two to three years; nonetheless, professors and administrators are positioned to reexamine their most deeply held beliefs about how we educate writers. These departures from tradition are fundamental to a professional writer's evolving practice, and as we will see in Chapter 3, they allow the artist to transgress the expectations of their art forms.

As an example to illustrate my point, one of the dancers I interviewed, Jasmine, discussed eliding Western traditions in dance and *breaking proscenium*. Proscenium is a real and metaphoric concept—an imagined and physical space—that encircles the dancer on stage. It is the constructed space between audience and performer, and it exists as an expectation similar to the fourth wall in cinema, where the performer remains separated from the audience through an invisible threshold. For Jasmine, participation in non-Western African dance traditions in Guinea allowed her to see the artifice of proscenium. Dance in Guinean tradition is a community-based activity where everyone is a performer. Audiences can *watch* dance—albeit passively and stoically—or they can *dance*. If we conceive of dance through a Guinean lens as Jasmine did, aesthetic parameters move from the soloist to the community of dancers participating in a shared movement. Jasmine's composing and choreography process was radically influenced by her visit to West Africa, and she came to understand dance from a fundamentally different foundation—as a collaborator, not as a soloist. Our sense of collectivity is malnourished in Western art. Breaking with proscenium serves as a metaphor for the ways craft consciousness invites creative writers to explore intersections in aesthetics and processes for making from outside the West. In this migration away from Western aesthetics, ways of knowing are not singular and separate but multiple, and the soloist is displaced by more collective ways of making.

Through viewing the artist as a collaborator rather than a soloist, craft consciousness also initiates a reconsideration of Platonic legacies separating craft and knowledge. Plato's separation of techne and episteme, as discussed in Chapter 1, is displaced by non-Western aesthetics where there is no separating art from craft or knowledge from art. By challenging these separations, craft consciousness defies tropes in making by redefining *who* makes art and *how* they can make it. In *Disability Aesthetics* (2010), Tony Siebers presents a point relating to *who*, arguing that disability aesthetics must include those otherwise not be seen as fitting subjects or arts practitioners. He writes,

> Traditionally, we understand that art originates in genius, but genius is really at a minimum only the name for an intelligence large enough to plan and execute works of art—an intelligence that usually goes by the name of "intention." Defective or impaired intelligence cannot make art according to this rule. Mental disability represents an absolute rupture with the work of art.[46]

Siebers "establish[es] disability as a critical heuristic that questions the assumptions underlying definitions of aesthetic production and appreciation."[47] Through questioning basic assumptions of aesthetics and artistic production, Siebers sees disability as a *heuristic* that does not define art as the ideal artists representing the ideal subject. His sentiments parallel the ways craft consciousness can serve as a heuristic that revolutionizes how artists are trained to think and modify their process and practices. If their process is not directed toward emulating canonized models in a medium, craft consciousness legitimizes the fragmentary, the diasporic, the placeless, the out of category, and the otherwise invisible or marginalized. To move more fully to a process model for craft requires writers to see the identity of artists *and* their processes as flexible, intersectional, and transdisciplinary. Aesthetic diversity is less plausible when models for training writers are built from genre specialization, literary formalism, and the institutional drive toward standardization, assessment, and verification.

Dominant craft discourse simply cannot sustain the intersections in marginalized aesthetic traditions because it is built to exclude. These exclusions in dominant aesthetics benefit from a collective resistance, and through collaboration, boundary jumping, and the host of techniques artists use to undermine subjugation, creative writers can view themselves as fluid, as perpetually becoming something new. The self is a reimagining. And through the reimagining described by Gil Scott-Heron, the artist becomes someone different, someone they want to become. This second experiment in defining craft consciousness is premised on letting go of dominant craft traditions by embracing an aesthetics of intersection and coalition. This definition is based in process philosophies that see the artist's thinking and metaphysical reality as based in *process metaphysics*, on *perpetual change*, and not on specialization. MFA programs in creative writing could focus on determining the taste of contemporary literature; however, I argue that they do so to the detriment of helping writers to build a lifelong practice that they can carry in their heart and minds. In the collective estrangement from dominant craft, power is reclaimed through collectivizing and through disrupting forces that seek to limit artistic production to only the few. From this second definition of craft consciousness, Experiment 3 searches out those theoretical frameworks that are built on separating artists—and in its place—the experiment shapes an alternative to the oppositional discourse currently defining craft.

Thought Experiment #3: Craft Consciousness ...

... frames consciousness as thresholds or formations that displace theoretical and philosophical traditions that define craft as oppositional to art (or knowledge).

Experiment 1 described the challenges that materialized when craft was assimilated into the academic field of composition and rhetoric studies. Like Experiment 1, this third experiment identifies the ways that craft has been curtailed. Unlike the first experiment, it begins to build toward a definition for craft consciousness by building in a different way than what AnaLouise Keating terms *oppositional consciousness*. To offer a definition, oppositional consciousness represents the impulse that appears endemic to intellectual and artistic debates alike, whereby two ideas are held in contrast to one another in order to define them. For example, oppositional consciousness separates craft from knowledge, craft from talent, and craft from art. Dominant aesthetics from Plato to Immanuel Kant create hierarchies in oppositional consciousness that impact creative writing, that is, craft cannot be art, cannot be knowledge, cannot be politically or culturally engaged, or cannot reflect process.

In Experiment 3, I seek out a non-oppositional definition that understands craft as *thresholds* in consciousness that the artist traverses as they *become someone new again and again* in the spirit evoked by musician Gil Scott-Heron. Contemporary theorists AnaLouise Keating, Sandra Corse, and Howard Risatti challenge oppositional definitions and craft's association with functionality (Kant) or a static sense of artistic being (Heidegger). From Risatti and Keating, craft consciousness pushes beyond the impasses that marginalize craft as functional and the artist as a trained specialist. Craft consciousness constructs thresholds rather than oppositions, and in this conceptual shift, the internal processes of the artist become more critical than external criteria. Interior spaces, as mentioned by photographer Dawoud Bey, are not always permitted to marginalized artists and their subjects; and given this fact, the experiment serves to strength the trajectory of Experiment 2 toward a coalition of writers interested in making interior processes and intersectional aesthetic exploration foundational to their practice and teaching. Thresholds reframe the way writers think of craft, and I argue that objects must be seen as manifestations of consciousness, not as simple outcomes.

Victor Vitanza, an innovative scholar in composition and rhetoric studies, embodies the pursuit of writing through consciousness and exploration, and he resists domesticating language through standardization or professionalization. In his essay "Abandoned to Writing: Notes Toward Several Provocations," Vitanza exemplifies a radical approach to process whereby practitioner and medium are "full of questions of becoming" and where institutional forces are undermined by serious play; he writes,

> There is the impotentiality (*atechne, adynamis, potenza*) for such a conversayshun, but I often doubt that my colligs [*sic*] can allow for themselves to be in such a relationship with the question, that is, With Language (*Logos*)! The full question becoming, What is it that language wants? With me? Now that the horizon by which we write is disappearing, being taken as place (writing space) from writers? ... Perhapless, there are two possibilities here: "We" can start teaching writing precisely as the university needs it taught. Or "we" can attempt "to teach" writing the way "we" want. But there are, let us not forget, third (interval) *wayves*. And therefore, "we" should ask: **What is it that writing wants?** I suspect that "writing" does not want what either the uni-versity thinks it needs nor what "we" think we want. (Vitanza's use of **bold**)[48]

Vitanza characterizes writing as the interaction between writer and text, and his focus on the autonomy of the medium provides an alternative to institutional and professional impositions on writers. Subdued by institutional or professional outcomes like those described in Experiment 1, Vitanza describes the incongruity between what we want and what the university or academic field wants. Vitanza draws writing (and the teaching of writing) toward interiority and the dynamicity of the text. In the case of the writer *and* their language, he envisions a non-oppositional arrangement where both writer and text are on a continuum of becoming; this suggests that teachers must consider the will of the developing writer in relation to the changing nature of text.

Maurice Blanchot's description of Friedrich Schegel, which Vitanza references in his essay, makes the point clear. Vitanza writes, "What Schlegel says of philosophy is true for writing: you can only become a writer, you can never be one; no sooner are you, than you are no longer, a writer."[49] If *becoming* a writer rather than *being* a writer is the objective in creative writing, then one never arrives fully in the identity of writer, rather, they persist in the activities and processes associated with an identity that's constantly transforming. To be a writer is to get stuck in the trappings of being. Being an artist, as described by songwriter Gil Scott Heron, is like "shedding plates like a snake" and his sentiments describe the difference between being and becoming; he says, "I did not become someone different that I did not want to be. But I'm new here, will you show me around?"[50] Becoming is a fluid state. The artist feels simultaneously like a master craftsperson and a perpetual newcomer. Vitanza and Heron present the material of art as organic and living, and these characterizations extend into the ways they describe identity through multiplicity and transformation. Each writer understands the position of the artist as more than prescribing a method or accepting a label. Neither a label nor an endorsed method can make someone an artist, and in place of these tropes of permanence, Vitanza and Heron present the processes and identities associated with making as thresholds that are crossed and recrossed in the mind.

In *Transformation Now!: Toward a Post-Oppositional Consciousness* (2012). AnaLouise Keating builds upon Heron and Vitanza's sentiments by using the concept of *thresholds* to displace intellectual and artistic norms built upon opposition. Oppositional consciousness, in Keating's argument, situates interlocutors in an us/them binary. The underlying assumption of oppositional consciousness is that one can either/or but not both/and. In her overarching theory, there is the potential to treat consciousness as more than its oppositions. As it applies to craft consciousness, non-oppositional consciousness can be framed through thresholds rather than binaries; she writes,

> *Thresholds* represent complex intersections among a variety of sometimes contradictory worlds—points crossed by multiple intersecting possibilities, opportunities, and challenges. Like thresholds—that mark transitional,

in-between spaces where new beginnings, and unexpected combinations can occur—threshold theories facilitate and enact movements "betwixt and between" divergent worlds, enabling us to establish fresh connections among distinct (and sometimes contradictory) perspectives, realities, peoples, theories, texts, and/or worldviews.[51]

The threshold is a more precise metaphor for the "transitional" and "in-between" spaces that living artists occupy in their practice. In fact, it's more difficult to imagine examples of artists occupying one genre or medium than those who remain locked within a single medium or tradition. Think of Picasso bridging thresholds between African mask traditions and Modernism. Think of Ray Charles occupying a threshold between the sacred and the secular in the development of rhythm and blues. Think of Ruth Asawa recrossing thresholds in sculpture, Mexican basket-weaving, and land art. To my point, thresholds are transitional (and intersectional) spaces that allow writers to think about the ways that aesthetic traditions and craft criticism from outside of writing shift them away from specialization. Non-oppositional consciousness pushes creative writing past its current predicaments of craft, including those predicaments that arise from institutionalization *and* those predicaments that situate MFA training as serving a single function, that is, specialized training in a genre.

Oppositional consciousness influences the legacy of craft regardless of the art form. For creative writers, oppositions manifest in the ways that aesthetic traditions and genre specialization define (through exclusions) what constitutes the literary. Literariness is defined through oppositions separating literary fiction from genre fiction, lyric poetry from slam poetry, creative nonfiction from general nonfiction. These oppositions are formed through implicit and explicit directives of MFA program faculty and through the conversations of a workshop cohort. Cisneros and Harjo's experience in the Writers' Workshop marks the way male confessional poetry held sway over what constituted the literary. Literature produced under conditions of opposition, as was the case in Dowling's study, make the politically motivated or culturally embedded antithetical to the literary because they hazard writing toward the *functional* rather than the literary (nonfunctional). When literariness is defined through exclusions or the taste-making Adsit has described in dominant aesthetics, oppositional consciousness pushes developing writers away from making practices that may have a value to them. Function is a high crime in art; for craft, it is, perhaps, a higher crime, and I argue that politically motivated or culturally situated writing can often be treated as simply functional in workshop conversations. Creative writers who are moved to write about a marginalized community or motivated by a political justice cause are interested in straddling a threshold between art and lived experience.

Between functional (craft) and functionless (art), there is a long legacy of exclusion that lands squarely on women and other marginalized artists. As discussed in the introduction to this book, craft arts (textiles, woodworking, pottery) have historically been subordinated to the fine arts (painting, sculpture, architecture). The oppositions currently defining craft in creative writing have legacy in dominant aesthetics, and I argue in Experiment 3 that Keating's concept of thresholds draws the term toward process philosophies and non-oppositional consciousness. Before turning toward the ways that craft consciousness captures the processes and interiorities of the artist, it's vital to unpack how oppositional consciousness frames the aesthetic theories of Immanuel Kant and how contemporary craft theories complicate Kantian legacies. From this short discussion of craft theory, the experiment concludes by situating a definition of craft consciousness in thresholds rather than oppositions.

In *A Theory of Craft: Function and Aesthetic Expression* (2013), Howard Risatti traces the history of craft to R. G. Collingswood's *The Principles of Art* (1938). Risatti argues that craft is often judged "qualitatively," meaning, "if a work is inventive, creative, it is art; if not, he concludes it must be a work of craft."[52] Risatti provides other examples of such an opposition, but his argument focuses acutely on art forms that have legacies in functionality (such as woodworking or garment making). Collingswood's sentiments, Risatti points out, have a Kantian legacy and lay a foundation for twentieth century's valuation of craft arts. Risatti does not attempt to choose a side in the debate in what constitutes art; however, Risatti works (as with Tim Mayers's analysis of Heidegger) to identify the ways that craft represents internal rather than external qualities. The preponderance of technique handbooks in the arts (especially in the craft arts) dictates our understanding about what constitutes craft and how it distinguishes itself from practices associated with thinking. Risatti "examine[s] craft, both internally as a practice and externally in relation to fine art. Only in this way can one discover whether craft is the same as fine art or a practice unique unto itself."[53] For creative writers, Risatti provides a footing from which to conceptualize craft as an internal practice and the object as the *embodiment of consciousness* rather than a reflection of function.

For Immanuel Kant, in *The Critique of Judgment* (1790), art is defined through a teleological question based in function—what is the purpose for the artifact made? Kant frees the artistic genius to make the unpurposed, the functionless. Kant's characterization of art allows for an open play between imagination and expression, a higher ground than mere craft. His philosophies appear to say art is free and "craft is mercenary." Sandra Corse, in *Craft Objects, Aesthetic Contexts: Kant, Heidegger, and Adorno on Craft* (2008), points out that Kant's philosophies have been integrated unjustly into the marginalization of the craft arts.[54] Corse goes on to suggest that Kant utilizes multiple craft arts examples to illustrate how modernity can be integrated into the incommunicable, purposeless qualities of art. Corse points craft studies scholars toward the ways that Kantian aesthetics may be rehabilitated in order to render a more elastic, inclusive definition of craft, a definition that does not serve as justification for the categories separating the craft arts from the fine arts.

Sandra Corse's analysis of Kant echoes craft theorist Howard Risatti's argument that objects do not fit in discrete categories. Risatti argues in *A Theory of Craft* that the object reflects more than its materiality, and the object is better understood as a reflection of the mind: "In the conceptualizations that brought craft objects into being as physical entities can be seen the *workings of consciousness itself*. Making craft objects is one of its earliest tangible manifestations. Objects stand as concrete expressions of the power of human creativity to wrest a realm of culture from nature."[55] For objects, the categories in fine and craft arts reduce the imaginative space they occupy, often based on their proximity to practical use in the world. In a similar fashion, creative writers can find the space they occupy reduced through implicit aesthetic privileging within the cult of voice. Christine Smallwood argues in *Harper's Magazine*, voice can mark identity privileging. She writes, "There is no cult so fervent in contemporary fiction as the cult of voice ... Voice is inherently contemporary, the node of an interlocking web of other contemporary values: authenticity, personality, identity, speaking one's truth."[56] The authenticity ascribed to voice makes it a justification for those "who find their voice and those who don't" in competitive MFA/PhD creative writing programs. For creative writers at the margins, writer Kate Haake reminds us that space in consciousness is eliminated when others construct who we are for us; she writes, "[All] we really want is what everyone must want, a space to be and speak who we are, as we know us, our own selves. If the gaze that constructs us does not know its own self as a gaze, but perpetuates itself as both natural and true, then that small space is erased."[57]

When craft is naturalized as *technique* and voice is naturalized as *talent*, both terms become measures of one's proximity to literary privilege, a privilege bestowed on some through the sociocultural and aesthetic conditions of workshop and MFA programs. Sandra Cisneros's experience at Iowa serves as one of many case-in-points, and Dowling's analysis demonstrates how many creative writers succumb to pressure; he writes, "Such adolescent fare was indicative of the conformist tendency to 'write for workshop,' calculating attempts to produce material 'with the greatest change of receiving approbation.' Such writing epitomized how students responded to the escalating pressure of the world's most prestigious program."[58] To "write for workshop" is to write for endorsement in a context where submissions become artifacts to be read objectively, apolitically, and under the auspices of literary tradition. Literary traditions are based in dominant aesthetic traditions privileging the purposeless and the assumption that the author is a static being cloaked in genius.

I have argued throughout this third experiment that oppositional consciousness limits the space developing creative writers require to conceptualize and create. Through viewing the object as a manifestation of consciousness—rather than as an object of a category to be assessed by dominant tradition—faculty working with creative writers should see workshop submissions as just that, the work of consciousness. Surely, a traditional workshop method based in literary formalism will be insufficient and creative writing faculty will need to view submissions through the lens of consciousness. What does this mean? If submissions are objects of consciousness, they must not be evaluated through opposition to the literary tradition or dominant aesthetics alone but, instead, understood through the dimension of the processual. Process conversations in writing workshops are oftentimes reserved for the postscript of conversation when the author volunteers a few obligatory words in reference to their submission. Creative writing maintains this procedural tradition despite the fact that MFA programs in the arts require artists to contextualize their work before critique conversations about a submission.

In lieu of an emphasis on a submission's relation to categories or traditions in literature, process philosophy presents the function of workshop in a new way: to support the writer building work between thresholds of consciousness. The forensic evaluation of a submission by peers propagates competition more than collaboration because it is object focused, and I argue that this is because oppositional consciousness dictates the evaluation of the artifact based on dominant traditions in literature and aesthetics. Centering on *process* rather than the artifact requires a new definition for craft in consciousness, new procedures in workshop, and new design in MFA/PhD programs. For now, I will save the discussion of workshop procedure and program design discussion for Chapter 4; and, in this third experiment, it is enough to see oppositional consciousness as an obstacle to defining craft consciousness. Moving from oppositions to the concept of thresholds allows for at least three significant shifts in our thinking about how creative writers conceive of craft. First, craft has more often served to authenticate writers already privileged by dominant literary and aesthetic traditions. This fact is not a problem for writers endorsed through workshops, namely the white, cis-gendered, able-bodied, however, the forces of market competition, editorial objectivity, and traditions have a way of detaching folks from the identity of "writer" and marking their craft as cultural or political—both shorthand for making that is simply *functional*. Second, and related to my first point, oppositional consciousness pushes the writer toward standardization and specialization—both institutional processes that are inimical to artists from nondominant traditions. For those artists who may see their work as developing from communities where writing remains a vehicle for resistance to violence or political movements, dominant craft discourse is simply the wrong tool for the job. Third, and finally, in order to create a framework for mentoring developing creative writers, a philosophy based in process rather than genre is critical for mentorship. Artists are non-static beings that transform alongside the materials they engage. By working from Victor Vitanza's notion of writing as an interaction between artist and medium, craft becomes a series of thresholds in consciousness rather than a simple reduction or opposition to fine art.

AnaLouise Keating's concept of the threshold is more than a handy working metaphor, and it is a direct challenge to the epistemological and ideological assumptions carried through craft in creative writing. Oppositionality structures how craft is defined and deployed in creative writing, and Keating offers another way for conceiving our work as educators, namely through removing the barriers to open artistic and intellectual debate that is not based on antagonisms. In Experiment 2, I presented the way to conceive of the thresholds across and between marginalized aesthetic traditions, and though I may be accused of sparring with literary formalism and dominant craft discourse, Keating offers an alternative ontological path that is less antagonistic. Threshold theory is built upon commonalities, intersections, and in-betweens, and in the case of craft consciousness, it facilitates a non-oppositional, non-antagonistic understanding of the creative writer. The writer is always at the crossroads between composing practices and new material explorations. Through their transformations, they become someone new, someone different. The difference I am interested in illuminating in craft is post-oppositional because as Keating suggests, "oppositionality saturates us and limits our imaginations; we define 'self and society' in antagonistic, conflict-driven terms that prevent us from obtaining a more ample awareness of the realities of the universe and our connections in it."[59] As it will become obvious through interviews in Chapter 3, artists are interested in the liminality, ambivalence, and transformative potential of thresholds as they relate to their practice and thinking through process. Thresholds operate apart from the hierarchies of oppositionality, and in the case of craft consciousness, thresholds represent how artists think and adapt their composing practices. In Experiment 4, the discussion of threshold theory expands into the writing of Buddhist philosophy and those consciousness studies scholars working to understand the interaction between the modes of consciousness defining craft.

Thought Experiment #4: Craft Consciousness ...

... traverses material, phenomenal, store, mind, and access consciousness and reflects a dynamic, inclusive understanding of "what it means to be an artist."

Experiment 4 ventures toward an understanding of consciousness by examining how theories of the concept integrate with a new definition of craft. This thought experiment will inevitably disappoint philosophers, neuroscientists, psychologists, and humanists interested in solving the *hard problem* of whether or not consciousness exists. The hard problem of consciousness engages with how the material world correlates with the ineffable, subjective experiences (called *qualia*) we have a difficult time understanding in life.[*][60] We cannot simply attribute all experience to the physical or material. I align with mysterians and idealists in philosophy, who see the matter of whether consciousness exists or not as indeterminate. Experiment 4 supports Ned Block's sentiment that there are "a number of different consciousnesses" constituting reality.[61] And building upon AnaLouise Keating's idea of thresholds from Experiment 3, this section defines craft consciousness as a mental awareness understood through Thich Nhat Hanh's concept of *formations*. Formations are defined in Thich Nhat Hanh's philosophy as physical *or* mental (what Nhat Hanh refers to in Sanskrit

---

[*] In philosophical terms, the concept of *qualia* refers to the subjective experience of something, the brightness of the sun, the purr of a cat, for example. The term is complicated by the more ineffable and less articulable dimensions of subjective experience, such as the feeling of déjà vu or the essence of a family picnic. For Susan Blackmore, *qualia* are what we are left with in our daily lives; she writes, "these experiences seems real, vivid and undeniable. They make up the world I live in. Indeed they are all I have" (Blackmore). From the essence of qualia, we must recognize the ways that material interactions or physical elements alone cannot fully define what craft is.

as *Samskara*). Material like paper is a physical formation just as happiness is a mental formation. Defined as a formation within our internal faculties, craft consciousnesses overlaps both the mental *and* the physical, a space where practitioners negotiate across thresholds in consciousness. If thresholds represent lateral *movements* across the mind, this experiment discusses how formations, mental or physical states, inflect upon the vertical depth of practice. In order to understand these formations, I discuss the four kinds of consciousness in Thien Buddhism—mind, sense, store, and *manas*. From Thich Nhat Hanh's discussion of Buddhism, the experiment also integrates scholarship from consciousness studies scholars and philosophers Susan Blackmore, Ned Block, and Thomas Nagel in order to argue that material, phenomenal, and access consciousness influence writers' understanding of process and art.[62]

Defining craft consciousness as a *formation across multiple thresholds in consciousnesses* serves two important objectives. First, it identifies how an artist can put a more complex understanding of practice into action as they navigate the material *and* experiential spheres of consciousness. Second, the examination of multiple consciousnesses demonstrates how a focus on materialist ideologies (in formalism) may limit writers' process and practice to a physical manifestation. Material consciousness, or an awareness of physical formations in literary texts, represents only one register of consciousness and one that must be integrated with other forms of consciousness. To understand *what it is to be an artist*, we have to examine how sense and mind consciousness develop into *store consciousness*, a deep-seated state of consciousness that is "fed by the consciousnesses of others" in the Buddhist traditions described by Nhat Hanh. Store consciousness works toward a collective understanding and away from "the artistic self" as a stable, independent entity. The instability of self, what Nhat Hanh refers to as the *manas*, allows the artist to explore the formations of consciousness for themselves. These formations are activated in craft consciousness and as an artist puts into motion material, experiences, processes, and concepts or ideations that drive them through the exploration of a project (Figure 1).

Materialist ideologies present matter as fundamental to nature; all elements can be explained through physical phenomenon. The hard problem of consciousness reflects that fact we cannot fully account for the ways that much of our understanding of the world operates beyond the material. To teach craft in creative writing through a materialist lens is to conceptualize the literary text as the means and ends of one's education as a writer. Experience in reading and writing stories, poems, essays, nonfiction, or dramatic work requires writers to examine a genre through its constitutive parts (plot, character, setting). From

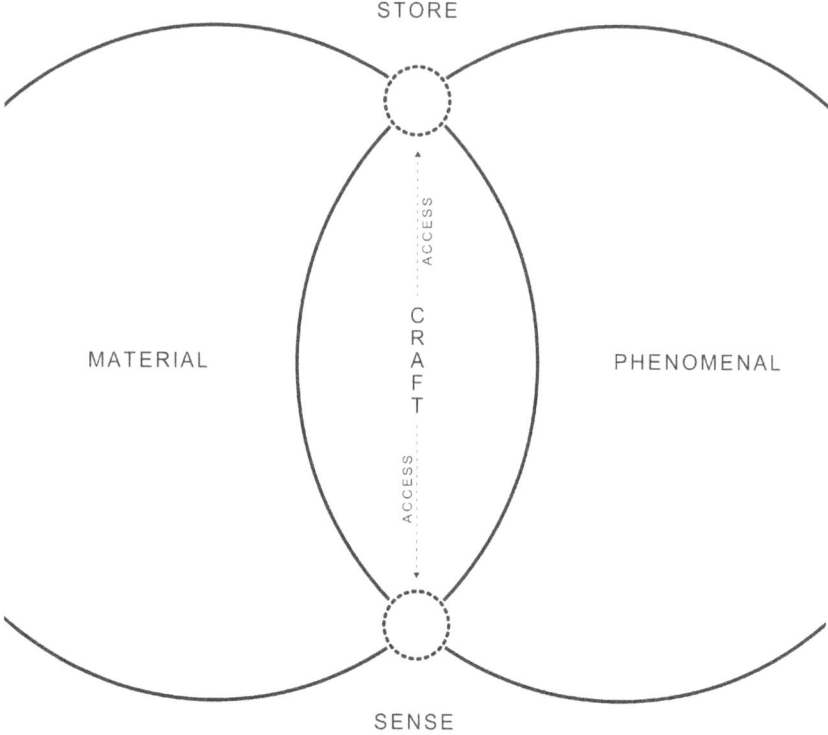

Figure 1 Thought Experiment #4 (in collaboration with John Francis Walsh).

these parts associated with formalist conceptions of the short story, in the case of fiction, the developing writer practices assembling their own artifacts. The creative writing textbooks written for an audience of undergraduates operate on materialist doctrine and the presumption that learning a genre involves building inductively from parts. For the uninitiated, this method of instruction codifies writing by defining what constitutes a literary genre based on external criteria. As seemingly neutral criteria for construction, craft can be disseminated in a manner that belies the principles of exclusion in play. Writers in undergraduate and graduate programs learn early on what material and methods to exclude from their practice; genre fiction (romance, science fiction, fantasy) is generally a *no-no*, magic realism is a *maybe*, spoken word is a *no*, performance art is a *"huh?,"* and confessional (or narrative) poetry or realism is a sturdy *yes*. Between the choice of subjects and methods there are in-betweens, but these interspaces are eliminated through congealing principles of dominant craft and the way genre criteria become based in exclusions that affect a writer's ability to bring all of who they are to the work.

Material consciousness presumes that the medium behaves the same for each artist, and it can move educators to elide phenomenal consciousness in the process of making. Although marginalized writers have a complex relationship to formalist criteria, guidelines can appear dissonant with lived experience, what I will later refer to as *phenomenal consciousness*. Unlike mass-market textbooks on writing, craft criticism integrates moral, cultural, political discussion of craft with attention to phenomenal consciousness. Nonetheless, memoirs on the writing life and craft textbooks operate to commodify craft and buttress obsessions with the experience of the laudable few celebrity authors. Janelle Adsit provides an extensive list of exclusionary textbooks and craft criticism in *Toward an Inclusive Creative Writing*, and her research references the *VIDA Report: Women in Literary Arts*, which tracks the exclusions of women, people of color, nonbinary, and other marginalized writers in publishing markets and literary journals.[63] The list and data from VIDA point to what is more visible in the promotion of online workshops like *MasterClass*, namely that technique lessons by marginalized writers have not been as marketed. Craft criticism by marginalized authors often stretches beyond materiality and toward intersections between cultural and phenomenal consciousness. The published craft criticism by Toni Morrison in *Source of Self-Regard: Selected Speeches, Essays, and Meditations* or Charles Johnson's *The Way of the Writer: Reflections on the Art and Craft of Storytelling* or Sherry Quan Lee's anthology *How Dare We! Write: A Multicultural Creative Writing Discourse* demonstrates that materiality can be less vital than the connection between phenomenal and cultural consciousness.[64] Conspicuously, craft criticism by authors of color appears less focused on technique. They turn toward the phenomenal consciousness informing the practice of marginalized writers, that is, they focus on the identity of the artist, dominant literary traditions, and discussions relating to the oppressive structures in art more broadly.

The section titles of Morrison, Johnson, and Quan-Lee's books bear out this observation: "Who Is the Writer?" (Johnson); "The Tyranny of Grammar" (Quan Lee); or Toni Morrison's "Arts Advocacy" and "Unspeakable Things Unspoken: The Afro-American Presence in American Literature." Among these examples of criticism by authors of color, craft questions intersect with phenomenal consciousness insofar as they concentrate their energy on the social, political, racial, and theoretical dimensions of craft rather than technical matters. This is no accident. Matthew Salesses points to the experience of reading craft criticism by writers of color. What seems like a disregard of "pure craft," he argues, is not a matter of neglect of literary techniques, rather, it serves the cause of enfranchising new craft definitions. He writes,

> When writers identify race and gender and sexuality, etc., as central concerns of writing, it isn't because they have nothing to say about pacing or space breaks. They are doing the hard work other writers avoid, in order to shed light on the nature of craft itself.
>
> They are:
>
> a. reacting to a history of craft as "just craft" and even trying to correct it,
> b. catching up writers outside of dominant culture by teaching the cultural context that goes most unexamined, and
> c. making sure that they do not participate in the erasure of their own difference.[65]

Salesses's observations draw phenomenal consciousness to the fore, and his argument suggests that teaching pure craft (material or technical considerations) apart from context is to participate in an erasure of difference and a writer's experience in culture. Phenomenal consciousness provides the impetus for analyzing the relationship between text and experience. Dominant craft discourse frames formalist, material consciousness as the primary, if not exclusive, method for training apprenticing writers, and it severs experience and culture from textuality. The materialist focus in dominant craft serves a narrow group of writers, and without phenomenal or cultural consciousness in practice, the artist is constrained and limited in their process. Rather than insisting upon a formalist understanding of creative writing, professors and students must consider ways to push at the edge of materiality, experience, and form. South African artist William Kentridge has spoken of this sensibility among living artists, saying, "But of course we have to resist the form and to encourage hesitation, the repetition, the deviation, as it is only on the edges of the straight line of thought where we are actually going to find something new."[66]

Formations in phenomenal consciousness are neglected or rendered invisible through fidelity to material consciousness alone. Artists out-of-category (to use Achtenburg's term) become visible through craft criticism forms such as oral histories, artist collectives, and other non-published forums. Grassroots efforts to collect and publicize craft criticism by people of color exist in the *decanon: a visibility project* and the "Writers of Color Discussing Craft—An Invisible Archive" and *BOMB Magazine*'s oral history archive. And these archives disrupt technical, materialist legacies and the textbook versions of craft that are written by white writers for white readers. The colorblind ethos of textbooks obscures the ways that craft has been whitewashed and ascribed a value that is determinately apolitical and neutral. For artists implicitly endorsing dominant craft discourse through their workshops, the world is rendered objective, apolitical, racially neutral, heterosexual, able, and technically standard. By concentrating on non-published conversations on process by artists out-of-category, the conditions are created for making other artists' phenomenal consciousness visible.

In the anthology by creative writers *How Dare We! Write: A Multicultural Creative Writing Discourse* (2017), material consciousness is integrated with the phenomenal, spiritual, and cultural consciousness negotiated by marginalized writers. The anthology blends spiritualism, formal experimentation, personal narratives, and a collective ethos of resistance that highlights how experience shapes writers through (and sometimes despite) the discourse shaping the writer. In their essays for the collection, Jessica Lopez Lyman and Sherrie Fernandez-Williams speak to the ways that dominant craft discourse alienates writers of color. Lyman describes her state as an outsider: "Ontology, phenomenology, epistemology. Early on, it becomes evident in your graduate seminar these words are borders. They divide the perceived intelligent from the masses. You try them on like mama's bracelets and dad's dress shoes. Loud sparkly you shuffle around awkwardly with your new vocabulary hoping no one will recognize you're playing dress up."[67] Lyman's alienation and precise analogy reflect the boundaries between academic and non-academic discourse. Lyman's essay, "Imposter Poet," also highlights the ways that the MFA programs weaponize a neutral sense of craft in order to present literature as an endeavor severed from the lives of real folks. In her essay "A Case for Writing While Black," Fernandez-Williams describes the implicit pressure and more explicit oppression framed within Lyman's description of academic discourse. Fernandez-Williams writes,

> The goal was clear to me: Do not make any attempt to sound moralistic. If there is an agenda behind the writing, we must disguise it, or dilute it. However, it did not occur to me until very recently that while it is true that we might alienate some of the conveying a certain point of view and exposing what we to be systematic institutional oppression, power and privilege, microaggressions, white supremacy and other such concepts that makes some roll their eyes, by not disguising our truth, we actually be more successful at drawing our true audience toward our work. Our true audience does not want watered down truth.

Alienation from craft and academic discourse serves to communicate *who is and who is not an artist* in graduate programs in creative writing. Fernandez-Williams and Lyman surface the ways that writers of color are subjected to aesthetic pressures that appear acultural and apolitical. Dominant craft discourse serves as an instrument to control the discourse of certain bodies when it separates from cultural consciousness, and it can be served cold through programmatic and aesthetic exclusions. The wisdom of dominant craft dictates that creative writing remains depoliticized and deracialized through instruction that appears detached, audienceless, when in reality, this façade of politically neutrality and colorblindness serves an elite white readership. The effect of teaching through dominant literary traditions, prescribed workshop procedures, and mass-market creative writing textbooks obscures a narrowing in consciousness.

In his essay "The Student of Color in the Typical MFA Program," David Mura presents the dilemma in terms of consciousness: "I am arguing that what the MFA student of color experiences in a predominately white institution is not simply an obscure or numerically insignificant occurrence. Instead, it is symptomatic and revelatory of the ways the voices and consciousness of people of color are suppressed in our society."[68] For Mura, Fernandez-Williams, and Lyman, the direct assault on the writer of color comes through many forms: academic discourse, workshop experiences with privileged peers, and presumptions about whose reality will reach an audience. Under these strictures, Mura reflects Richard Wright's position that white and Black people are fundamentally in a struggle for control of *a representation of reality*. My own undergraduate literature professor Dr. Joseph Young said that, in referring to the protagonist Fred Daniels in Richard Wright's "A Man Who Lives Underground," Fred hopes for "an uncontaminated ontology."[69] Systemic structures in MFA programs (curricular design, classroom conversations, reading series invitations) are guided by presumptions about who is a writer and whose consciousness is validated. What reality of the writing life is being constructed through graduate creative writing programs? How can creative writing programs be restructured to integrate the phenomenal consciousness of writers outside dominant craft? These questions are foundational to determining *the good* of craft and the future of creative writing education. In order to begin to answer these questions, the second half of this fourth thought experiment is devoted toward examining formations in consciousness beyond the material. Through understanding phenomenal, access, and store consciousness, creative writers can expand the purview of craft consciousness and see the term as a bridge between those processes and ways of thinking that impact their practice and fluid identities as artists.

Phenomenal consciousness was famously defined by Thomas Nagel and his thought experiment: "What is it like to be …?" His thought experiment clarifies the question and involves an example from a small mammal: the bat. Nagel determines consciousness through the probing question: "What is it like to be a bat?"[70] If the answer, in the case of the bat, is that there is *a way to be* a bat then the organism is *conscious*. Consciousness is determined by a creature's ability to perceive feelings, sensations, and experiences they encounter in the world. Phenomenal consciousness pushes us to ask an elemental question of creative writers: "What is it like to be an artist?" or—more pointedly—"What is it like to be an artist within a particular social, cultural, or political context?" In workshops, seminars, and literature courses in graduate programs, questions of phenomenal consciousness are uncomplicated, or more accurately, they can too easily be left at the classroom door. Nagel's thought experiment serves to determine whether a being is conscious, and extending his experiment to a more precise line with artisthood allows us to ask: How does a writer think through their practice? The answer to this question, for the individual writer, creates a complicated series of dilemmas, and for a cohort of writers, this question becomes further complicated by the dynamic, innumerable ways each writer might answer. But, I argue it's the right question. Because it requires more than analyzing common texts or exchanging writing, the question opens Pandora's box, as it allows a group of writers to determine how experiences and assumptions intersect each other.

It seems implausible for James Baldwin and Norman Mailer to answer this question the same way—what is it to be an essayist? Each author's phenomenal consciousness would inflect on the way they answered; nonetheless, the question serves a vital function in making visible how the pursuit of the essayist may be similar or different. Their answers serve the greater cause of surfacing phenomenal and sense experience in the world, and for a cohort of writers, it builds new thresholds for understanding the role of the artist in the world. This dialectic about the role of art/artist in the world may be a by-product of the most engaging workshop discussions; however, I argue that it should be brought into parity with thresholds of consciousness in material, sense, and one's corporeal, mental, and spiritual sense of the world. Phenomenal consciousness, also called sense consciousness in Buddhist thought, does not differentiate what the body smells, tastes, sees, hears, and what we comprehend or sense about an object. In the words of Thich Nhat Hanh, sense consciousness is inextricable from our bodily consciousness; there is no split between mind and body.[71] Phenomenal and sense (or bodily) consciousness differentiates writers from one another, and the objective of a creative writing education must better support formations in consciousness and approaches to process from diverse artistic traditions. Once craft principles materialize in a literary form, they can become standardized through institutional programmatic mechanisms or through dominant aesthetics. In this scenario, a situation chronicled in Experiments 1 and 2, the artist is separated from the object in the name of standards preferred by academic fields or in the name of aligning the creative writer with endorsed aesthetic traditions. What happens in an unexamined fidelity to technique and literary or aesthetic traditions creates a narrowing of consciousness and a focus on material outcomes. Unfortunately, *what it's like to be a writer* may have little to do with *process* or thinking as an artist and everything to do with genre-focused workshops and literature curricula that make artists out-of-category "electives." The structures of creative writing are based on preoccupations with material outcomes (publications, fellowships, professorships) that reflect a social, material, and aesthetic imbalance that favors the already privileged.

Perhaps James Baldwin might ask the question in this way: "What is it like to be an artist in a world constructed to silence?" To overcome silencing, intended or not, requires us to ask questions about how phenomenal consciousness and sense consciousness reinscribe craft consciousness with a more inclusive, variegated conception of what it means to be an artist. What it's like to be an artist is a culturally embedded question. Xánath Caraza, in her essay "Writing Is as Necessary as Air to Me," presents the imperative I describe; she writes, "I feel that I need to respond to the world in the form of a poem or short story about what I have seen, experienced, or witnessed. Our writing is part of human history. It reflects our times, our life, the political atmosphere, the beauty of a sunset, but also a war and its effects."[72] In her description, Caraza integrates physical (sunset, poems, stories), mental (beauty, bearing witness, effects of war), and sociocultural elements (history and politics). The formations in consciousness Caraza captures represent more than material formations. By synthesizing material, phenomenal, and cultural elements in her description, the artist uses writing to articulate the experience of connecting the otherwise disparate—the beauty of the sunset and the effects of warfare. She understands writing as non-oppositional (not political writing vs. literary writing) and the expression she gives to writing is analogous to an ecosystem within consciousness. As discussed in Experiment 3, oppositional consciousness does not capture how craft activates in the mind of the artist. Formations in consciousness create a foundation for craft consciousness, and these multiple modes of consciousnesses, what Nhat Hanh calls *formations*, are intersectional rather than oppositional. Creative writers cross thresholds in consciousness, working within material conditions and mediating or integrating the dimensions of cultural experience into their work.

Given all the warnings I have provided against a solely materialist approach to craft, how can writers support the development of craft consciousness and put material and phenomenal consciousness into action? Ned Block, a philosopher and contemporary of Nagel, distinguishes phenomenal consciousness from *access consciousness*, and though the concepts overlap in his theoretical discussion, Block defines artists' abilities to draw experience into actions. Access consciousness is defined through "the *availability* for use in reasoning and rationally guiding speech and action."[73] Access consciousness, according to Block, is different than our phenomenal experience, or self-consciousness or what he calls monitoring consciousness. It is defined by our ability to put into action what we perceive. Access consciousness allows us to take phenomenal experience (I smell smoke) and put it into action (getting a fire extinguisher or calling the fire department).[74] Access is action and it signifies craft consciousness as more than an experience to have, a material to know, or a threshold between consciousness formations. Action is practice. The thoughts of an artist are a negotiation across processes during a project; it requires them to ask "What is needed to move this project forward?" Exploration through a project requires bridging the conceptual and actionable. Block's concept of access consciousness is closely related to Thich Nhat Hanh's characterization of mind consciousness or "the 'working consciousness' that makes judgment and plans; mind consciousness is the part of our consciousness that worries and analyzes."[75] Nhat Hanh's concept of mind consciousness (the sum total of our mental formations) also represents the deeper sources of thinking for the artist, what he calls *store consciousness*. Store consciousness does not contain the same obstacles and anxieties associated with mind or access consciousness, and it reaches depths that affect how we might think of craft consciousness, as an engagement in process that lasts a lifetime. In Nhat Hanh's interpretation of Buddhist thought, store consciousness is embedded in the spirit, a site of groundness *and* fluctuation. He writes,

> There are many names for this kind of consciousness. Mahayana tradition calls this store consciousness, or *alaya*, in Sanskrit. The Theravada tradition uses the Pali word *bhavanga* to describe this consciousness. *Bhavanga* means constantly flowing, like a river. Store consciousness is also sometimes called root consciousness (*mulavijñana* in Sanskrit) or *sarvabijaka*, which means "the totality of the seeds."[76]

Nhat Hanh discusses the dynamic nature of store consciousness and its value in Buddhist beliefs, and the term may be associated with the preservation of ideas (as in storage like seeds) and the complementary *bhavanga* or "the sense of processing and transforming." Store consciousness requires less processor speed across the mind's motherboard. It remains open and committed to curating, preserving, and synthesizing the information and consciousnesses that we contain. Store consciousness operates on a free-flowing nature and is less focused on the mental formations of mind consciousness or the purely material. Store consciousness does not have the *intentionality* of mind consciousness (or mental formations) and it presents consciousness like a delta built by accretion and the flow of waters through the artist.

In Experiment 3, Victor Vitanza reminds composition and rhetoric scholars of their tendency to push writing toward outcomes. If *intention* drives the mind and our access consciousness, then *unintention* may sustain our store consciousness. Store consciousness is the garden not the gardener as Nhat Hanh says, and it remains important as a site of accumulative knowledge in craft. In order for craft consciousness to operate in the tradition of store consciousness, insights are "collected like seeds" from phenomenal, material, sense, and mind consciousnesses.[77] Nhat Hanh's description of store consciousness is not without complications, and he points to the concept of *manas* that cling to a notion of a *stable self*. Unstable concepts of self-trouble may trouble our store consciousness, and Nhat Hanh expresses the predicament of store consciousness through the manas, which suggests that *there is no true self* or no self to cling to. The idea of the self inhibits clarity of thought. Store consciousness is not only self-focused, and it becomes in Nhat Hanh's interpretation a foundation from which a definition of craft consciousness emerges as a *formation* across consciousnesses. If the self is unstable and fluid, then the mind is more than a storage site for material or experiential knowledge. In practice, neither phenomenal nor material consciousness alone serves the writer. Together, it's the thresholds *between* consciousnesses that the artist needs to sustain as the bridge between concept and action.

By integrating theories of consciousness from philosophers, spiritual leaders, and artists, consciousness grows from material consciousness to the registers of phenomenal and access consciousness and to the four dimensions of consciousness in Zen Buddhism (mind, sense, store, and *manas*). These formations serve as a network that remains incomplete because, as Nhat Hanh suggests, store consciousness defines the self as irresolute and evolving. Applied to the creative writer, the question of *what it means to be an artist* remains an open one throughout their education and afterward as they develop as a working artist. Craft consciousness must be defined by the overlapping thresholds of material, phenomenal, sense, access, and store consciousnesses; it cannot be limited to any one register of consciousness. The process of becoming a writer requires a negotiation across thresholds of consciousness *and* an examination of formations neglected by an exclusive study of material consciousness.

If craft continues to be ratified by formalist, materialist approaches in creative writing, it will neglect formations of consciousness that operate internally and from within writers' home and cultural or personal experience. When we take Nhat Hanh's concept of *formations* as a model for craft consciousness, oppositional consciousness is replaced with an intersectional model of craft, a model that invites writers to integrate processes, practices, and knowledge from the thresholds of other art forms and traditions. Craft consciousness represents an internal heuristic that has radical potential to resist the subjugation of dominant craft and the predominance of oppositional consciousness as the defining factor in determining what is art. Although it has been discussed only briefly in this thought experiment, Nhat Hanh's definition of store consciousness will serve as a critical lens for Experiment 5. For now, and before moving toward Experiment 5, craft consciousness has been defined through Experiment 4 as the thresholds that artists traverse in practice. In the delineations of consciousness described in this experiment, writers who mentor must consider how lived experience and culturally embedded knowledge characterizes *what it is to be an artist*. In Experiment 5, the conversation shifts toward women artists, and it seeks to build a new definition of craft consciousness in order to counter the oppressive historical, cultural, and gendered forces that have marginalized art created by women.

Thought Experiment #5: Craft Consciousness ...

... shares a lineage with the labor of women and those who have had to renegotiate their identity in the face of colonialist, gendered, racialized violence.

Craft has been a label foisted on women and other marginalized artists, and it has served as a rationale for gendered and racialized subjugation. Women artists have had the mediums associated with their labor diminished and oftentimes categorically dismissed as *craft*. Women artists, for these reasons, have often avoided the signifier craft because it removes agency from them categorically, technically, and by virtue of a definition of art that makes *functionality* oppositional to art. As an example, my cousin Jenna is an exceptional crochetist who learned from our Grandma Bunny. Jenna's art, which she posts to Instagram, is both functional and aesthetically exceptional. Her practice is a pursuit she undertakes as a mother of four, a homeschooling parent, and a partner completing the majority of the domestic labor. It is in the invisibility of gendered labor that art resides, and to see Jenna crocheting is to see how practice remains an interior vision of how to find spiritual and artistic wholeness. Categorical labels don't capture what Jenna does or how she thinks, and it remains clear that prescriptive definitions of technique deprive women of a sustaining practice and the consciousness their work embodies. This thought experiment draws into focus the ways that women artists are affected by the diminished standing ascribed to craft.

Feminist craft studies scholars, creative writing studies scholars, and all artists from outside of the academy must form a coalition that can disrupt these historical tendencies. Through redefining the labor, processes, and identities associated with the term, Experiment 5 builds upon the scholarly models in feminist craft studies. For the past decade, craft studies scholars have recovered craft as a signifier of objects and identities associated with women artists. Jenni Sorkin, T'ai Smith, Sandra Alfondy, among others, have drawn craft into conversation with *embodied* practice and the ways of knowing and making associated with women's artistic labor. Experiment 5 builds upon the precedence of craft studies scholars while revisiting theories by Gloria Anzaldúa and Thich Nhat Hanh, both of whom destabilize Western conceptions of what it means to be an artist. Artistic identity is marked by instabilities, fluctuations, and transformations, especially for those who face systemic oppression and gendered violence. This experiment uses feminist craft studies and craft criticism to lay out a transformative conceptual space for artists to claim agency and redress old labels.

Artists who face oppression often move into liminal spaces, in what Anzaldúa would call *nepantla* (in-between), and where the woman artist ruptures into the realization of the violence and cultural oppression she has faced.[78] *Nepantla* is a space that allows for reconciliation between the past traumas and future healing. Our own *instability as beings* requires us to first attempt to heal and later to seek transformation from those oppressive forces that control one's sense of being. As discussed in Experiment 4, Thich Nhat Hanh discusses our instinct to cling to self (*manas*) in a manner that does not allow people to find grounding, and he says that self-obsessing in consciousness leads people to suffer. For Anzaldúa, racial, colonialist, gendered violence and oppression cause trauma and require women to occupy a third space of "gentle reassessment." To seek a reassessment of self means, first and foremost, to attempt to heal from the past and present violence perpetrated against women. During the healing process described by Anzaldúa, the artist enters a mediating, contemplative space of reflection, and one Nhat Hanh would associate with "thinking without the thinker." Nhat Hanh sees the "no self" as the space for transformation and it parallels Anzaldúa's concept of *nepantla*, where the artist seeks healing through an action of recovery of mind, body, and spirit. From the insights developed in Nhat Hanh and Anzaldúa's writing, craft consciousness is a process of renegotiating agency. Through a transformative healing process, identity becomes non-static as it seeks physical, emotional, spiritual, and philosophical liberation. This is not a space for dominant craft where outside criteria dictate or determine what it is to be an artist; in contrast, it's a continual transformative space that conceptualizes the self as emerging from *past selves* or *no-selves* or *new selves*. Nhat Hanh describes meditation as a similar space where the self dissipates; he writes,

> When we meditate, we practice looking deeply in order to bring light and clarity into our way of seeing things. When the vision of no-self is obtained, our delusion is removed. This is what we call transformation. In the Buddhist tradition, transformation is possible with deep understanding. The moment the vision of no-self is there, manas, the elusive notion of "I am," disintegrates, and we find ourselves enjoying, in this very moment, freedom and happiness.[79]

Based on Nhat Hanh's description, art practice, like meditation, might not just be grounded in establishing a sturdy sense of self in art. To define craft consciousness as a radical feminist intervention, writers must integrate the philosophies of Nhat Hanh and Anzaldúa and frame art as a form of healing and transforming the self and community. Both philosophers draw on writers to consider how artists migrate toward *new selves* or *no-selves* in a process that presumes transformation as a more natural state. Anzaldúa and Nhat Hanh disrupt boundaries of self, and their philosophies push artists to consider how coalitions across fields in scholarship and art can challenge institutional boundaries. Self*less*ness flies in the face of the professionalization dictating genre distinctions for creative writing faculty and the institutional parameters thrust upon developing writers. In Experiment 1, these constraints were discussed in relation to composition and rhetoric, and for this experiment, I shift from theory toward prominent examples from women and indigenous artists who renegotiate their identities and the labels circumscribing their gender, their cultures, and their process.

Craft studies scholars T'ai Smith and Jenni Sorkin analyze the ways that women transform the concept of craft in practice and as they navigate repressive educational and institutional structures. Smith and Sorkin's scholarship expands definitions of craft to include *performative* and *intermedium* modes of practice.

Smith's analysis of Anni Albers and Sorkin's analysis of twentieth-century women potters demonstrates how women artists navigate separations between spiritual, academic, and artistic identities. Labor in art is not always separated from spheres of domestic labor and the responsibilities women complete in the home. To create and maintain an artistic practice, women transform identities and seek spiritual grounding as they traverse domestic responsibilities and face institutional, cultural, or gendered oppression. Building from Nhat Hanh and Anzaldúa's theories of spiritual rebirth, craft consciousness offers a mechanism for freeing women, nonbinary, and indigenous artists. Dominant craft discourse appropriates and tokenizes ways of being through the lens of oppositional consciousness and the historical precedence of aesthetic and literary traditions. If this pattern of dominance is to be challenged, craft consciousness must be centered on radical self (and community) transformation; it must be built on coalitions and collectives that are transdisciplinary and predicated on liberation for women and all marginalized artists inside and outside the academy. For women artists in particular, German weaver Anni Albers's story provides a blueprint. Her experience at the Bauhaus and Black Mountain College illuminates a method for resisting marginalization through intermedium exploration, and her work at the intersection between writing and weaving shows how intersectional approaches to process can begin to free the artist.

Anni Albers, an early twentieth-century textile artist, lived in the shadow of her partner Josef Albers (a pioneer of color theory) at the Bauhaus and Black Mountain College. In *Bauhaus Weaving Theory: From Feminine Craft to Mode of Design* (2014), T'ai Smith traces Albers's work through the history of the German Bauhaus (1919–30) and the artist-educators who defined the value of each medium in the famous Weimar school. Mediums were carefully theorized in the Bauhaus, according to Smith, and formalized to exclude women from participating in fine art. Smith references Anja Baumhoff's description of the three-tiered system: fine art (*Kunst*), including painting and sculpture; arts and crafts (*Kunstgwerbe*), like pottery and weaving; and handicraft or craftsmanship (*Handwerk*), such as carpentry.[80] Led by expressivist pedagogues Walter Gropius and Johannes Itten, the Bauhaus treated craft in a manner that echoed Morris, Ruskin, and Roycroft: a utopian ideal of the lower order than fine art or craftsmanship. Craft's integration into industry promised to offer authentication and a utopic ideal that did not pan out in a reality dominated by hierarchy and prestige at the Bauhaus. Ironically, and as craft was integrated into the Bauhaus, Anni Albers avoided labeling her work on the loom as craft. Instead, and as Smith notes, "[Albers] considered terms like *medium* and *design* as they integrated and, in postwar America, increasingly eclipsed the work of *craft*."[81] Smith describes Albers's weaving and the work of other women through the lens of intersectionality. Smith quotes Foucault to make the point:

> [Weaving] is as much a craft and medium as it is an apparatus (*dispostif*), in the Foucauldian sense. It is as much a specific practice (materials, tools, and way of putting things together) as it is a "heterogeneous ensemble consisting of discourses, institutions, architectural forms ... propositions—in short, the said as much as the unsaid." Weaving is at once *this* particular technique as opposed to *that* one (say, painting or architecture), and also the network that in various concrete, practical, and theoretical modes links together the competing discourses of modernism.[82]

Craft is a "heterogeneous ensemble" or "an apparatus" or a "medium," and it demonstrates how Albers, in Smith's characterization, sought to avoid the limitations prescribed to women weavers and textile artists at the Bauhaus, including Gunta Stölzl, Benita Koch-Otte, and Otti Berger. As discussed in Chapter 1, the idyllic nature of craft at the Bauhaus had the by-product of gesturing toward the utopic while cordoning off women artists from fine art. Smith describes the ways in which Albers used weaving to theorize what Stölzl would call "a picture made of wool."[83] Stölzl and Albers were drawn toward intermedium representations of their process and sought to disrupt the categorical marginalization of their work. These efforts lead Smith to ask: "What does it mean to use the criteria of one medium (namely, painting, as defined by the rhetoric of expressivism) to define the parameters of another (weaving)? ... And finally, why, or how, does this craft accrue a gendered value?"[84] For Stölzl and Albers, craft was gendered and not viable for defining their process or identities. Shifting their vocabulary toward definitions in medium or design provided both women the opportunity to traverse institutional and material structures that subordinated them.

The gendered nature of craft cannot be elided or ignored. Critiques of craft play upon old hierarchies and categorical dismissals of the work created by women artists. It would seem craft is easily labeled as "women's work" unless its craft*man*ship, in which case it becomes elevated and honored as masculine labor. Smith identifies the "accrued gendered value" of craft and it's notable how craft in the hands of women or traditional cultures and indigenous peoples is seen somewhere below fine art *and* craftsmanship. Albers's rejection of craft is instructive, but more importantly, her thinking through process on the page allowed her to explore material intersections and articulate the challenges in defining weaving. Smith writes, "weaving's identity came out of *struggle* between different material disciplines associated more or less with the arts—this craft simultaneously took on and rejected lexicons of painting, architecture, and photography."[85] By taking on oppositional definitions, Albers resisted her silencing as a weaver and developed an interdisciplinary process: thinking became weaving became writing. Understood in light of oppositional consciousness in the fine arts, craft consciousness is a feminist method for resisting the marginalization of women artists *and* it can be a space for building across thresholds in consciousness; Smith writes,

> The act of writing thus provided Albers with a possibility of articulating her goal of bringing material practice to the fore of education, but it was also here that she had to negotiate the impasse brought on by a certain incommensurability: that between (physical) practice at the loom and writing, or "touching" material and touching on its ideas.[86]

Albers's movement to the page illuminates the ways that embodied knowledge of material can be communicated to the page. Anni Albers's writing is a gesture that demonstrates how craft consciousness resides in an intermedium space between the material consciousness of the loom and reflecting that phenomenal consciousness out onto the page. To cross thresholds in consciousness, Albers moved between the page and the loom to externalize her thinking and explore the relationship between material, phenomenal, and store consciousness. Albers's adoption of writing as method for theorizing her practice offers a case in point for the ways that material exploration (fiber and text) leads to (and from) new explorations of phenomenal consciousness. For Albers, writing served as a resistance to her marginalization as a weaver and it demonstrates how craft consciousness (and its formations) allows artists and their communities to renegotiate the identities, processes, and values ascribed to them.

In her book *Live Form: Women, Ceramics, and Community* (2016), Jenni Sorkin collapses the binary between subject and object in ceramics. Sorkin presents ceramics as bound less to material outcomes and she argues, instead, that midcentury ceramics was a *performative act of social engineering*. Midcentury women ceramicists sought to imagine alternative, liberatory social spheres for women. Through her analysis of Margueritte Wildenhain, M. C. Richards, and Susan Peterson, Sorkin argues that "the complexities of *live form* as a heuristic tool that has implications beyond individual artistic production, in that the 'revelation contained in the act' is a process not just of art making but also of learning ... Women ceramicists improved upon formalism's use value, transforming the standard hegemonic discourse into a necessary life skill."[87] The term "live form" is borrowed from Wildenhain's phrase for a *Life Magazine* profile, and live form captures the process metaphysics of performance rather than the material outcomes of a substantive metaphysics. For the ceramicists Sorkin analyzes, the live form is haptic, process based, and less engaged with formalism or labels of *functional*.

To Sorkin's point, women's labor is disembodied and objectified through formalism and through separating an object from the processes of its making. A superficial reading of ceramics, then, would detach "live form," "performative acts," and "haptic identities" from the processes of production. Midcentury women ceramicists were marginalized as popular television personalities, and to Sorkin's point, the detachment of performance in ceramics misses the profound ways that Wildenhain, Richards, and Peterson reframed ceramics and the material conditions of women through their work for television broadcast. By reframing ceramics as social engineering, not object production, Sorkin aligns artists with a shift in agency. The embodiment of process that is *live form* represents a realignment in craft; craft consciousness, from this point of view, is not a metric for evaluation and it squares more appropriately with a version of craft that sees the artist as an embodied medium. Sorkin's analysis of midcentury ceramicists echoes Tim Mayers's observation that creative writers are mediums more than messengers. In *(Re)Writing Craft*, Mayers writes, "The poet, though, actually attempts to allow the language (an ontological category that encompasses all particular languages) to speak—or to be written—*through* her/him. Language is not the medium for the poet: the poet is the medium for language."[88] Referencing poet Joe Wenderoth's craft essay "Obscenery," Mayers writes, "Poets who attempt to establish—or to protect—a 'genuine' subjectivity in a 'genuine' realm of being, according to Wenderoth, are actually *fleeing* from poetic knowledge."[89]

Whether it originates in text, clay, or wool, embodied knowledge is performed knowledge. It disrupts the logic of formalism, which separates object from producer, and it locates art in the processes of the living. Through their historical scholarship, and its reassessment of neglected women artists, Sorkin and Smith outline feminist interventions that can define craft consciousness. Craft has served to delegitimize practices, processes, and materials associated with women artists, and any rehabilitation from this precedence requires the acceptance of four points made in this fifth thought experiment. First, intermedium explorations allow women and other marginalized artists (like Albers or Asawa) to resist institutional, disciplinary, or gender discrimination. These explorations integrate knowledge based in performance or other process-based approaches to making (Wildenhain, Richards, Peterson). This second point leads to a third and the observation that art is a socially, culturally embedded practice that arises from within cultures and communities. From this last point, I will argue in the next portion of this section that artists are framed by Western notions of the artist. The prevailing wisdom of creative writing graduate programs operates on specialization and it is oppositional to the transformative practice discussed by Anzaldúa and Nhat Hanh and illustrated by Smith and Sorkin's research. If we can conceive of artists as constantly transforming, then we can see beyond the "accrued gender value" of craft. Female artists and indigenous artists alike are not idealized in the way that white, male, able-bodied artists are. The fetishization and/or objectification of the craft arts is a symptom, I argue, of the desire to signify the artist and their practice through a gaze that is gendered and based in colonial domination.

Values in craft are gendered and racialized, and for indigenous artists this means craft signifies them through hypervisibility in the form of traditional crafts. This museum-like characterization of Native peoples and their art remains, ironically, ignorant to the ways indigenous cultures understand and apply practices and processes to their lives. If the dominant Western aesthetics demands an aloofness and remove from function, indigenous artists pull art in a wholly different direction and toward viewing craft as inextricable from cultural function. Daniel Justice proves the centrality of function of art to indigeneity, writing, "indigenous aesthetics is the essential taproot of Native art."[90] Dominant aesthetic traditions' fixation on the acultural or apolitical do not serve to reflect the ways art is culturally embedded for Native peoples. The ignorant wish, it would seem, is to perceive Native art within a time capsule where a colonialist gaze fixes both the artist and indigenous cultures. The ignorance that fixes craft to gendered value parallels the ways indigenous artists may fulfill a colonialist value wherein indigenous art serves as a historical artifact rather than a living practice that evolves with a changing culture. In discussing language's ability to move the artist and reflect movement within Navajo culture, poet Sherwin Bitsui captures this point, saying,

> Navajo is thought in motion, a very verb driven language. Everything is tactile; everything is about moving within the world or having the world move within you. [The Navajo] also have this ability within the language, its philosophy and worldview, to make the metaphorical very real … to make it literal in a way. Perhaps because we live in a ritualized, ceremonial space, our culture exists in an inner relationship with all things.[91]

What Bitsui describes does not fix Navajo language or culture in place. His description provides motion, tactility, and it serves as an expression of how the worldview of the poet reflects interrelatedness between language and culture. Indigenous artists, and rightly so, may reject the ways that colonialist language and institutions have subjugated and distorted indigenous craft. In his essay "Can I Get a Witness?" for the collection *Sovereign Words: Indigenous Art, Curation and Criticism* (2019), David Garneau suggests that indigenous art must resist the distortions of indigenous identities and the degradation of the ontologies and values of Native peoples by colonizers. He writes,

> Indigenous art ... what it hopes to stop is reproduction of the colonial, and the misguided idea that art, criticism, and identities are forms of revealed and universal truth, rather than agreements among similarly trained elites. It marks the end of distorted identities and Native people made invisible or degraded by an ontological hierarchy built to benefit its colonial designers.

Under conditions of subjugation and violence, the first action is to be made visible, and the second action is to disassemble the colonial project through creating a collective and social consciousness that supports Native artists. Garneau goes on to frame this perspective through the lens of consciousness, and he draws the connection between Aboriginal artists in Australia and Canada, writing, "Our ability to articulate [shared identities]—to have a self and collective consciousness—constitutes a different, an Indigenous mode of being. Indigenous is both a particular self-consciousness and a social consciousness. It is the continuous circuit of recognitions and performances by, for and among Indigenous peoples."[92] The "continuous circuit of recognitions" remains a phrase that bridges between *particular* indigenous peoples and *shared* indigenous consciousness and aesthetic traditions. Garneau articulates the point made by Justice and Bitsui that indigenous artists are interconnected through larger networks of indigenous peoples. Understood through the collective and individual, any definition of craft consciousness must avoid the co-optation and violence of colonialism and the marginalization endemic to patriarchal structures of the West. How can creative writers create a *space of evolving artistic practice* that recognizes individual and collective consciousness? Garneau offers a poignant directive in his essay for the collection *Sovereign Words* by suggesting that indigenous artists need more than anything a space that is not occupied by white, colonialist aesthetic or ontological values or modes of being and becoming.

In Experiment 2, I argue that craft consciousness can be defined through intersectional aesthetics, and it is vital now to suggest that intersectionality may also mean sharing resistance to patriarchal, colonialist craft discourse while avoiding the recolonialization or co-optation of indigenous artists. Understood through the lens of indigenous aesthetics and feminist craft studies, craft consciousness operates within an enlarging spirit that expands our understanding of who the artist is and how they evolve within specific cultural traditions. We are never absolved from reflecting on the gendered, racialized, and colonization that defines the artist. Trinh Min Ha reflects this need, writing, "*I am therefore at the same time: useless, useful, and instructive.*"[93] Dominant craft discourse fixes the identity of the artist. To disrupt the categorical dismissal of women, Indigenous, and other marginalized artists, we must understand consciousness to be the site for renegotiating an identity. The identity of the artist can reflect embodied performance, cultural embedded practices or traditions, and it invites an even more radical notion: *the instability of self*. This last point draws forward from Anzaldúa and Nhat Hanh to the process philosophies of Alfred Whitehead. Between the transition from a substantive metaphysics to a process metaphysics, artists and scholars must also pay mind to the co-optive, assimilationist practices in capitalism, and the next experiment analyzes how craft and creativity are defined and marketed through the machinery of late capitalism.

Thought Experiment #6: Craft Consciousness ...

... resists being subsumed or commoditized through a collective of practitioners that fights against the forces of capitalism, industrialization, and digitization.

In Experiment 6, the definition of craft consciousness gestures toward the collective in a way that echoes the terms "class consciousness" and "critical consciousness." From lyric essayists to sculptors, there is a common psychosocial, institutional, and cultural position shared as practitioners. Although Experiment 6 does not provide an in-depth examination of György Lukács's concept of class consciousness or Paulo Freire's term "critical consciousness," these foundational theories reflect the thrust of craft consciousness toward a practitioner collective who desires artistic liberation for one and all. In Gloria Anzaldúa's discussion of *conocimiento*, consciousness is framed as a resistance against colonialism and gendered and racialized violence. Critical consciousness, class consciousness, and *conocimiento* articulate the oppressive forces in capitalism that coalesce bodies into a common psychosocial position. Through their theories of consciousness, Anzaldúa, Lukács, and Freire diagnose the conditions of oppression and articulate the capacity of the individual and collective to make systemic and institutional changes. The spirit of craft consciousness has, to this point, been defined as an internal heuristic in the artist, and I argue, in Experiment 6, that this awareness extends into the collective. The awareness that frames craft consciousness is at once observable in the individual and in the collective, and it is the whole that can make foundational changes to the way craft is defined, practiced, and taught to writers. Materialism and formalist ideologies in creative writing detach the artist from the object and the individual from the collective through a free market rationale. All systems and mechanisms in the creative writing programs, including the writing workshop, echo a free market entrepreneurial philosophy that treats the individual and the collective as oppositional. Oppositional consciousness, then, serves to advantage already-privileged writers, dominant aesthetic traditions, and more insidiously, it packages *craft* and *creativity* as markers of individual talent rather than collective power.

In his book *Against Creativity* (2018), Oli Mould argues that *creativity*, like craft, has fetishized individual talent and been subsumed within market forces since the Enlightenment. *Creative* writing is a term of distinction in writing studies, and it isolates, linguistically, the idea of creativity in order to elevate and differentiate literary writing from scholarship or genres with popular commercial appeal like romance or mystery. Discussions of creativity have the potential to define creative writing and craft as oppositional, terms separating those of innate talent (creatives) from those who demonstrate proficiency (craftspeople). The separation between these two ideas, craft and creativity, gives rise to connotations that parallel the inequitable structures discussed earlier in the craft arts and fine arts. When artists are elevated above craftspeople and creativity transcends craft, individuation becomes paramount and antithetical to collectivization. I argue that creative writing graduate programs are built on marketing individuals, and in the most competitive and highly ranked programs, the individual is the commodity to be groomed for the publishing world. Growing resource scarcity, even in selective graduate programs, requires faculty and administrators to concentrate financial and labor resources on the individual in the form of stipends, fellowships, contact with agents, writing retreats, and recommendation letters.

Why are resources so focused on the individual writer in graduate programs? It would seem the natural state of creative writing to view the collective as oppositional to the individual writer who has to make their way through the world after graduation. Committees of creative writing faculty negotiate resource allocations and their labor in the name of mentoring individual writers rather than cohorts, and faculty labor is analogous to an investment in a start-up company, a handful succeed, but most fail. This is not a callous operation. It would seem the reality where student competition is seen as an inherent good for the whole—it may, even, lead to higher quality writing. One graduate of the University of Iowa Writers' Workshop captured this sentiment, saying, "we imagined there was a bookshelf that held only one book."[94] The one book and one author mantra, if it remains institutionalized, creates competition, suspicion, and an arrangement that directly parallels the competition embraced in free market capitalism. As with formalist separation of object and artist, creative writing is in danger of accepting the opposition of the individual and collective as a natural condition in graduate programs where shrinking budgets, faculty labor considerations, and student cohorts are built upon genre designations and finite resources. But imagine, for a moment, creative writing graduate programs that allocated material and social resources toward the collective good. Such an arrangement may advance collaboration among a cohort and diminish the competition that is inherently inequitable. At base, and within late capitalism, creativity and craft are concepts that invite co-optation and perversion in the free market, and it is the task of creative writing to determine whether craft will reflect this troubling phenomenon in MFA programs.

In our contemporary cultural moment in the United States, craft has been swallowed in the vortex of markets that see craft as a linguistic modifier like Velcro that affixes to anything you can hawk. From cocktails and wood toys to milkshakes and blue jeans, the label operates to suggest an *authentication* process, often invisible to the consumer, which preceded the object's presence in the world. Jenni Sorkin associates this expanding system in the art world as "craftlike" rather than "craft." In her essay "Craftlike: The Illusion of Authenticity" in *Nation Building: Craft and Contemporary American Culture*, Sorkin describes craftlike as "illusory and seductive" and part of an endless process of revival in the form of material or technique. Artists are drawn to the ways that "craft processes are interesting to artists because working a stringent structure that narrows choices and options feels bolder than facing the possibility of everything."[95] Sorkin goes on to analyze the ways that histories in the Studio Craft Movement have been eclipsed in ways that don't "[tie] the object to the maker from production to market"; this *reference* to craft (craftlike) allows some artists to "scale-up" production without *doing* craft.[96] Sorkin references the Studio Craft Movement that extended from the 1930s to the 1960s, and though she does not draw this disciplinary parallel, creative writing histories map onto the proliferation of MFA programs in other arts. Sorkin's research provides a backdrop for the question put forward by historians of creative writing: Has the field lost sight of its educational mission as the practitioner wing of English Studies (Myers) or has the field become a machine of political will (Bennett) or a capitalistic enterprise (McGurl) more than a site for training writers?

Creative writing in the United States has scaled up to more than three hundred graduate programs, and by sheer numbers, this phenomenal growth suggests that creative writing is no longer a site for small-scale literary production. Creative writing is multinational and ever-expanding in Europe, Asia, and Australia. In Chapter 1, I discussed the role craft plays in *authenticating* labor, and in light of Jenni Sorkin and T. J. Lears's historical research, it remains in question whether creative writing has *appropriated* craft as a means to authenticate its spread as a professional academic field across the globe.[97] One argument would suggest that "yes," the MFA degree, in particular, is no longer valued in capitalism and has become a marker of *privilege* rather than *authenticity*. This argument is leveled by critics of creative writing and it has become popular to present MFA programs as *inauthentic* and New York as the *authentic* centers for determining literary merit. Of course, this opposition does not take into consideration the ways that literary publishing is a poor judge of merit, especially given the historical biases referenced by previous VIDA Reports.[98] To state it simply, writers must ask whether they are doing craft or whether they are *craftlike*. As participants in capitalism and an economic value system that sells authenticity, craft, creativity, and the artisanal, creative writers must ask whether craft labels literary artifacts or whether it reflects the processes and conditions of practitioner knowledge. Creative writing becomes craftlike when it defines the term in a fashion that serves as a signifier for the free market or as a moniker for authenticating the individual's merits based in the biases and exclusions of dominant literary or aesthetic traditions. I argue that creative writers are *doing craft* only when they support the development of an *internal awareness* in developing writers and when they seek coalitions and intersections with other practitioners. Heaps and heaps of uncertainty accompany the developing writer through their MFA, and we do them a disservice when we treat craft as a label for markets or as a set of external, standardized criteria that curtails process thinking.

Programs become craftlike when they enfranchise dominant craft discourse and disenfranchise others based on race, gender, ability, sexuality, or class privilege. Creative writing becomes craftlike when it borrows the radical ideologies of craft to authenticate practices that are exclusionary. Under the banner of free market philosophies, craftlike or *craft-lite* suggests that we accept our position as a privileged creative class. In her essay for the *Nation Building* collection, Sorkin reminds us that craft is a network of individuals who collectively keep arts practices alive. For Sorkin, it is the workshop space that reminds us of the radical ideological intervention of craft:

> [Studio] craft is not all an object-based endeavor but rather a nonobject one, bound to a history of teaching the object and instructing the hand (students in all capacities) through pedagogical presence and performance of the maker. In other words, all craft instruction is live, which is its strength. Where craft is performed, the network or system stays alive. The power of the network alters the course of production, in its diversity of pockets, groups, and open circuits, far exceeding any individual maker or practice or even specific community.[99]

Sorkin argues that "networks alter the course of production" and the future of creative writing must take a path that is more "diverse" and "open" to reframing craft as a network and connected across a system of programs and workshops throughout the world. Craft consciousness represents a network of makers who are open, diverse, and unsettled by dominant craft and its craftlike mantras in formalist or capitalist principles. Ascribed to individual talent and codified in textbooks and workshop, dominant craft becomes the mythical lore that excludes some creative writers from developing across the networks of practitioners. I argue that writers must trace the term back toward collective histories, what Sorkin reminds us is our legacy: "The most important contribution midcentury craft made to American culture was a permeable and fluid network that has transferred community-based participation to the realm of pedagogy and connected a dizzying zigzag of university and arts schools and craft schools."[100] The practitioner network is creative writing's greatest strength; it has established a significant international collective of past and current students, writing faculty, and new or established graduate programs. The virtue of the field is not in cultivating individual talent, producing more publications, or fomenting formalism or dominant aesthetics into literary tradition. The practitioner network inside and outside creative writing can usher in a more radical shift in collective consciousness. Like craft, creativity has become inextricable from the ideologies of late capitalism, and writers must define craft *and* creativity through the lens of the collective, not capital markets.

It's hard to imagine a term that is more lauded than creativity, and it serves as a signifier of innovation or the characteristic trait of inventors or originators. If craft signifies authenticity, creativity serves as an even more flexible signifier for industry. For example, creativity applied to *creative* writing would seem to differentiate literary writing from academic prose or popular writing genres. Creativity would seem oppositional to craft, especially when the latter is associated with technique. Vlad Petre Glăveanu, in his chapter "Craft" from *Creativity: A New Vocabulary* (2016), points to the ways we mischaracterize creativity and craft as oppositional.[101] Creativity appears related to invention and original thinking while craft appears to correlate to technique or implementation. These mischaracterizations diminish creative writing and assume *creative* to be associated with the literary and craft to be associated with the technical and teachable. Separating craft from creativity or the artist from the object creates the conditions for assimilating the mission of creative writing with commodity production. Developing writers to become the relegated creative class means that they can be reassigned from one marketplace to another. Creatives can be moved into other sites where creativity becomes surplus and is repackaged for material consumption. When craft or creativity is defined in market terms, writers are surplus and their labor is not evidence of a network of practitioners; they're stimulants for free market capitalism.

Oli Mould, in *Against Creativity* (2018), suggests that creative labor is marginal labor because it is appropriated in markets where its purpose is to drive economic growth. Such an appropriation echoes Sorkin's suggestions that the craftlike carries expectations of the free market. Based in a capitalist model where creativity and craft are commodities, creative writers are symbolic entities rather than catalysts for redefining culture. Both Sorkin and Mould point to the ways that craft and creativity can be redefined through smaller "networks of production" (Sorkin) and "forge entirely new ways of societal organization" (Mould). The observations of Mould and Sorkin lead back to the series of questions discussed in Chapter 1. William Morris and other philosophers argued for a radical reconception of human's relationship to labor. For Morris, handwork was a response to industrialization and the hunger of capital markets. Philosophies of craft can become preciously superficial or augment inequities latent in the art markets of late capitalism. I believe a counternarrative is possible though. Creative writers can disrupt the forces appropriating craft and creativity; they can mobilize the growing network of graduate programs, retreats/workshops, collectives, and other programmatic infrastructure to resist late capitalism. Capitalism fosters a version of creative writing that makes workshop a theatre of the free market, based in competition among individuals, and it focuses the field away from collaboration across disciplines and away from equitable conditions for developing an artistic practice. Mould points to the ways that creativity is subsumed in capitalism through the idea that "everyone is creative." On the ground, however, it is the social and institutional conditions that determine who can and cannot be an artist.

Matriculation to a graduate program may temporarily validate a developing writer, nonetheless, it is within the MFA program where students are seemingly validated through competition and through their abilities to model creative being. Craft consciousness can serve as an intervention into aesthetic and pedagogical philosophies that exclude, for example, disabled writers. Mould discusses how dominant aesthetics can become more inclusive of other ways of being in the world; he writes, "By being radically creative in seeking out diffabled or minority ways of being, we can start to shake those foundations; the normalized identities of a white, able-bodied, and male creative class suddenly become very unstable. It is in this instability that new things can form; it is in this instability that we find the most creative people."[102] Dominant discourses on creativity like dominant craft allow for a limited view of the identity of the artist, and what has been a patriarchal, capitalistic rendering of creative writing culture. Mould's chapter on "Marginalized Creativity" points to the ways those new constructions of creativity lead to new understandings of both artist and subject. Applied to creative writing, craft consciousness expands ways of knowing and making beyond their associations with the able-bodied writer. Through the implicit acceptance of market philosophies in writing, there is the tendency to render invisible traditions and processes that are not located in the able-bodied. In his book *Disability Aesthetics* (2010), Tobin Siebers rejects disability as a simple theme and the disabled as subjects to be fetishized or mocked.

> It is more because disability is properly speaking an aesthetic value, which is to say, it participates in a system of knowledge that provides materials for and increases critical consciousness about the way bodies make other bodies feel. The idea of disability aesthetics affirms that disability operates both as a critical framework for questioning aesthetic presuppositions in the history of art and as a value in its own right important to future conceptions of what art is.[103]

Formations in consciousness must be open to diffabled writers and subjects. This openness not only creates an inclusive environment, it radically shifts the framework we have for understanding craft. Craft consciousness provides the internal awareness to critically examine how capitalism endorses ways of knowing and being that operate on the appropriation and marginalization of disabled bodies. Without reconfiguring craft and creativity, writers are bound to limit the ability of present and future artists to produce work. Siebers's discussion of disability aesthetics presents us with an alternative way of being and understanding of identities in art. As discussed earlier in this chapter and through the lens of access consciousness, writers and other artists are harmed and limited when craft is synonymous with ableist associations with talent, which then become prescribed through formalism, and especially, when it is activated through fostering competitive hierarchies among peers in MFA programs. To disrupt these mechanisms of ableist oppression, creative writers must actively redefine creativity, craft, and collectivity in the context of graduate programs. As a new framework for making, craft consciousness must be built on redefining the networked communities that are being run presently as market-driven signifiers. Sorkin, Mould, and Siebers remind us that alternative definitions for craft and creativity make possible new social and artistic realities. We are beholden as liberatory educators and imaginative artists to interrogate the boundaries we now abide in. Untested, unremarkable, craft is cast as a transparent, objective lens from which writers are made or unmade in their training. This ideological position, craft is craft is craft, binds us to ways of knowing that are exclusive. In the final section of this chapter, the six experiments are analyzed rhetorically in order to understand how they apply to writers.

Conclusion: Pushing Creative Writing toward New Formations in Craft Consciousness

These six thought experiments are not meant to arrive at a conclusive definition, and I hope they reveal the ways that creative writing's mission can be redefined through the impasses and potentials of craft consciousness. In this conclusion, I offer a short rhetorical analysis of the thought experiments in order to understand how they intersect and, inevitably, contradict one another. My objective is to summarize and frame how craft consciousness may apply to the work of living artists (Chapter 3) and the design (or revision) of new and existing creative writing graduate programs (Chapter 4). My exigence is, by now, clear—dominant craft operates on exclusions that limit the processes and identities associated with becoming a creative writer.

From the experiments, one rhetorical strategy that I employ throughout is to suggest that impediments to craft are dictated by dominant ideological principles. In the introduction and Experiment 1, materialist ideologies dictate a philosophy of craft that is grounded in formalism. Formalism, which arrives to creative writing through literary studies, works in conjunction with the drift toward institutionalization in higher education. Through the case study in composition and rhetoric studies, and the work of Kelly Pender, Tim Mayers, and Byron Hawk, I argue that the processes of institutionalization push craft toward verifiable standards and material outcomes. The dictates of materialism underpin formalism and the drift toward institutionalization for creative writing, and as a result, craft comes to separate the artist from the object. Severing artist from the object of their creation has the effect of building craft upon a bedrock of materialist and oppositional consciousness. Experiment 3 draws into relief the ways that oppositional consciousness complements a materialist definition of craft. Oppositional consciousness, as AnaLouise Keating calls it, offers a theoretical lens for understanding dominant aesthetic tradition and its legacies in dominant craft. Seen through oppositional constructions, craft is ascribed a value as functional and, therefore, antithetical to definitions of art by Immanuel Kant. Functionality becomes an indictment against craft artists, and women or artists-out-of-category in particular. Experiment 5 examines the research of feminist craft studies as they identify the ways that women's artistry is marginalized as functional or politically engaged. Gender and racial subjugation in definitions of craft are reflective of neocolonialist and late capitalist tendencies to commodify and appropriate craft and creativity in the name of economic growth. These signifiers reflect the necessities of the free market to brand creative writers and their work as goods to profit from. The experiments taken as a group, and by the description in this paragraph, are held together by processes that squeeze the revolutionary energy out of craft. Institutionalization leads to standards, formalism detaches artist and artifact, and capitalism treats craft as the signifier of consumer goods. These characterizations of craft are held together by the ways they serve select groups of writers already privileged through the discourses of literature and aesthetics. By upsetting this applecart, my hope continues to be for a disruption that makes craft consciousness a tool for redefining the mission of creative writing.

By shifting from a substantive metaphysics to a process metaphysics, my argument revolves around exploring new definitions apart from oppositional consciousness and the other impediments outlined in the paragraph above. Rhetorically, this means that identifying the impasses is not enough, and I have used the experiments to argue for a redefinition of craft through process philosophies, intersectional aesthetic traditions, and an understanding of practitioner knowledge as networked across a cross-section of living artists. Going forward, my argument centers on the ways that artistic identity is seen as stabilized and further fixed in place by institutional mechanisms or formalist associations with genre or materials. In Experiment 2, I draw writers toward the intersections between marginalized aesthetic traditions in the hope of providing a non-oppositional consciousness in craft. The second experiment operates through the idea of intersection and it feeds into the metaphor of thresholds suggested by AnaLouise Keating in Experiment 3. Non-oppositional consciousness reframes craft as a continuum bridging aesthetics traditions and process thinking from beyond creative writing. Experiment 4 extends the idea of intersections between marginalized aesthetic traditions and argues that consciousness formations are multiple. Between material, phenomenal, sense, access, and store consciousness, there are more ways to think about craft than material knowledge. Writers navigate thresholds across formation in consciousness, and I argue that craft consciousness occupies a unique position at the nexus between which the artist conceptualizes their process. From the experiments that are devoted to forensic analysis of the ways dominant craft fixes artists in place, the deliberative rhetorical moves in this chapter ask readers to consider how the term "craft consciousness" locates the artist—their identity and their practices—in processes that are dynamic and evolving within their minds and bodies. Craft consciousness serves an internal cause, and it must provide a framework for embracing home, family, culture, and spiritualism. Current approaches to pedagogy in writing workshops are in danger of weaponizing craft through a complex network of exclusions to those developing an identity and working practice. For marginalized writers, the MFA has become a site of implicit (and explicit) oppressions, marked by a privileging and classed model in specialization. This model, as we will see in Chapter 3, does not reflect the realities of living artists who operate on an ecosystemic understanding of craft where practice is an evolving, exploratory process. Artists study, get stuck, experiment with methods, get unstuck, find new materials, become exhausted, find a spark, then fan the flame with their life.

Living artists absorb a complex set of material and phenomenal stimuli, and we are remiss in seeing our task as teachers in materialist terms and in a context where inclusions and explorations are fundamental to becoming an artist. Artists are *perpetually becoming* something different and their subjects and materials remake who they are over and over again. Given circumstances in which there is an unstable notion of self, many artists don't cling to the *manas* of self as unchanging. Artists permit themselves a broad reach and the opportunity to make and remake their process and identity. Craft consciousness captures the ways that artists think through their projects and how those projects represent an evolving way of making, often beyond one material or medium. I argue that living contemporary artists can show us how to train creative writers by opening us to the spiritual, aesthetic, and cultural contexts that they integrate into their labor. Creative writers are artists, and lest we forget the heart of the endeavor, this means that we are preparing minds for a labor that is spiritually renewing and changes the culture they exist in. Creativity is ecosystemic, collective, and infinitely pliable, and the next chapter focuses on investigating how theories of craft consciousness are reflected in the words of living contemporary artists.

Through the interviews, craft consciousness is characterized by a dynamic relationship between the ways that artists' think and the methods they use to traverse material, generic, aesthetic, and spiritual forces in their work. In the twenty-five interviews, artistic process becomes a formation in consciousness more than a material or formal standard. Their consciousness informs artists' worldview and the conceptual frameworks they use in their daily practice. Artists do more than specialize in material and the conversations reflect the nuance of process philosophies that are networked and collective. Their philosophies are more like ecosystems that include the material, sense, and phenomenal consciousness that is craft consciousness. Sometimes artists specialize in one art form, but as we will see, even specialists in a medium are attune to intermedium and material exploration. Artists are gardens *and* gardeners and they gather what drifts and lands on the soil. As Robert Frost says, "they stick to nothing deliberately, but let what will stick to them like a burr where they walk in the fields." Artists are gardeners who develop a deeply reflexive sense of the world and remain attentive to the material and nonmaterial processes that allow them to explore ideas. To understand craft consciousness as an internal awareness, the six experiments contained in this chapter are given traction by conversations with living artists who practice and conceptualize process each and every day *what it means to be an artist.*

3

Radically (Un)Becoming: Qualitative Perspectives on Crafting an Artistic Practice

Introduction

If one wanted to orchestrate a vigorous debate among artists, I can think of no better way than to whisper a single word: *craft*. In his book *Cræft: An Inquiry into the Origins and True Meaning of Traditional Crafts* (2018), anthropologist Alexander Langlands puts it more pointedly and in light of the sentiments of David Pye and Sir Christopher Frayling: craft is "*a word to start an argument with.*"[1] Even among the affable and generous among us, our own ideas of craft often echo the degree of estrangement we feel from each other. One may even suggest that the person they are chatting with is too bound to their disciplinary position to see craft for what it is. What craft *is* depends upon an artist's perception of the ways material, aesthetic, and formal boundaries intersect. As the thought experiments revealed in Chapter 2, craft modulates across thresholds in consciousness, and it has the uncanny quality of creating *and* solving problems as craft scholars Glenn Adamson, T'ai Smith, and Matthew Crawford have written.[2] Conversations on craft with artists can be contentious or they may allude to craft's relationship to utopic communities, to a nostalgia for a more idyllic past, or to the powerful spiritualism or activism associated with the cultures of making. Between the historical analysis of the first chapter and the experimentation in definition of the second chapter, I surveyed panoramas from which to view the valuations of craft and the potentialities (and impasses) in defining craft consciousness. This chapter threads the historical and theoretical to the present and to the words of contemporary artists. By talking with twenty-five living artists from different mediums and disciplines, I collect perspectives from outside of creative writing in order to broaden understandings of craft consciousness for creative writers. I chose to interview a range of artists because I wanted to see how the definitions and conscriptions of craft compared between other fields and creative writing. In the chats that make up this chapter, artists discuss the fluctuating nature of materials, processes, and identities.

If the artist is a conductor, they direct processes toward ideations, they follow along behind without too much intention, pushing the orchestra toward crescendo or at least toward a form they hope fits the world they imagine. Cosmologies of craft are larger than creative writing, and through the comparative analysis of this chapter, creative writing studies scholars can reimagine the historical, pedagogical, and institutional architecture of the field. The mission of creative writing belongs in process philosophies that better reflect practitioner knowledge. Process philosophy has particular value to my research findings and interconnect with Alfred North Whitehead's cosmology of *dynamic change* and Thich Nhat Hanh's presentation of Buddhist conceptions of the *self as unstable*. No matter their professional status or material choice, artists' lives are premised on changes that are generative and ongoing. Process captures the metaphysical, cosmological, and spiritual dimension of making more than substantiative metaphysics or the oppositional consciousness that marginalizes craft.

Before undertaking qualitative research and conducting formal interviews, I had many chats with contemporary artists about craft. I meandered naively into these conversations, sometimes over a bite to eat, sometimes strolling across our campus. Other times, standing in their studio, I could feel the ground heave a little beneath my feet when I brought up the subject of craft; both sign and signifier were electrified. One abstract expressionist painter said to me, frankly, "*Craft* is what my professor told me *not* to do in art school." Another dancer turned to me, speaking candidly: "Well, what do you mean by craft?" Each encounter had the zest of a political debate, and I began to wonder why the concept had such potency. I should have known better. During my PhD in rhetoric and composition studies, I conducted a case study for a qualitative methods course taught by Dr. Roxanne Mountford. For the essay, I interviewed five writers from an MFA program in a large state university in the Western United States. From the interviews, it was clear that female writers were not as willing to label themselves as Writers in the *capital* sense, and I saw differences in the ways that men and women experienced workshops, craft seminars, and the MFA program. I spent more than one interview reminding my female peers of their writing accomplishments, but such a gesture could not overshadow the alienating, "toxic" workshops they reported on.

Conducting interviews from the MFA program for the case study gave me the first sense that some writers felt alienation and marginalization. In Kate Haake's *What Our Speech Disrupts: Feminism and Creative Writing* (2000), I found testimonials that echoed the women's experiences in creative writing programs.[3] Haake's book illuminates the ways that workshop pedagogy and conditions in MFA programs can operate with inequities and force marginalized writers further to the periphery and even away from writing altogether. I didn't have any radical desire to disrupt the systemic structures, nor did I have any idea how to make it more equitable outside of attempting to change how I taught workshop. In *What Our Speech Disrupts*, Haake experiments with melding autobiography, student anecdotes, critical theory, and writing studies scholarship. Her experimentation as a creative writing studies scholar gave me a hazardous measure of courage, and it allowed me to imagine creative writing as a coalition unifying feminism, writing studies, and art. Haake sees creative writers as artists, and as teacher-artist-scholar, she reminds of what is shared with our students. Process. Theory. Experimentation. Generosity. Courage. The book *What Our Speech Disrupts* and the research of Haake's close friend, Wendy Bishop, led me to see creative writing studies as a site for experimental and intersectional research. More than anything, this meant that research into craft's theory and praxis had to be in conversation with other artists.

The artist interviews of this chapter operate through the lens of a comparative analysis and what Malcolm Gladwell would call a "grand unifying theory." The unifying theory is craft consciousness, and as I have argued in Chapter 2, dominant craft operates on a substantiative metaphysics and material consciousness to its determinant and to the exclusion of writers who do not identify with prevailing aesthetic and literary traditions. Chapter 2 presented definitions of craft consciousness through the principle of intersectional aesthetics, thresholds in consciousness, and the knowledge that the marginalization of craft is redefined through process. Process unifies artists through the internal dimensions of craft consciousness and the external circumstances that shape their labor. In the sections that follow, creative writing is aligned with the studio arts and the wider histories of the MFA in the United States. To frame histories of creative writing and craft requires a wider swath of cultivation. The first section discusses ethnographic research into studio arts programs by Gary Alan Fine and Kim Grant's arts scholarship on process before moving toward qualitative research from creative writing studies. The chapter moves through these scholarly frameworks to discuss the design of the qualitative study and its methodological rationale. The findings that make up the second half of this chapter reflect the transformative nature of craft consciousness, which is embodied in the ways that artists reinscribe identities and change materials as they evolve in the processes that signify their living practice.

Through these conversations, artists shapeshift and evolve in their thinking as they traverse material, generic, formal, and institutional boundaries, and as with the story of Anni Albers, Ruth Asawa, Gloria Anzaldúa, artists sometimes reject craft because it marginalizes them and their labor. The findings from my conversations with artists, I hope, will stimulate creative writing faculty and program directors in graduate programs to revisit the virtue of the field. Currently, the MFA in creative writing in the United States aligns program design and pedagogical imperatives with genre specialization and coursework in literary studies. Literature may exclude marginalized cultural or aesthetic traditions when it is dictated by the imperatives of materialism and formalism. Through artist interviews, it's clear that restructuring creative writing will require us to make interdisciplinary, transdisciplinary, or even postdisciplinary approaches to artistic process central to educating creative writers.

MFA Programs in the Studio Arts and Process Scholarship in Art

Scholars are tasked with invigorating the virtue of creative writing through rethinking craft and the experience of the workshop and the MFA program. A comparative analysis of the ways nonwriters think serves this objective, and even more practically, it expands writers' access to alternative composing processes as it opens new ways for them to articulate their identities in the world. Creative writing studies scholars have neglected collective histories of MFA programs in the studio, performing, and fine arts. These family histories are far from symbolic or ancillary to creative writing MFA programs, and I argue that they represent our sister disciplines, the educational sites where practitioner knowledge is gathered and shared. Published histories of creative writing often link creative writing to literary studies, though, as Howard Singerman and D. G. Myers point out, writers and artists convened in arts colonies, craft schools, and university MFA programs throughout the twentieth century.

Creative writing MFAs, in fact, were preceded by, if not modeled on, BFA/MFA degree programs in the arts. For example, before creative writing programs the School of Fine Arts was established at Yale University in 1891 and conferred degrees for four decades, primarily to women, in drawing, painting, sculpture, and art history.[4] In drama, Yale conferred its first MFA degree in 1931, and in dance, Margaret H'Doubler opened a studio on the University of Wisconsin campus in 1921, developed a curriculum by 1924, and had finished her fourth book on dance pedagogy by the time the University of Iowa conferred the first MFA in creative writing in 1940.⁵ At the University of Iowa, Dean Carl Seashore developed scientific laboratory approaches to art appreciation and production in the early 1920s. Laboratory approaches in the Department of Speech included "debate, dramatic writing, production, sometimes oratory," and Seashore expanded initiatives integrating art and science. "Painters, sculptors, and graphic designers" were steered toward "projects and studies in which scientific principles characteristic of laboratory investigations would be brought into association with art creation, criticism, and the science and philosophy of art."⁶ Seashore successfully recruited like-minded scientists, and his influence at Iowa drew together fine arts such as music and poetry with those in psychology and science, a legacy that made "laboratory exploration" a formative expression of what would become the Iowa Writers' Workshop. The Workshop was not the creation of literary studies or the English Department alone; it was a confluence of artistic and cultural forces that brought the MFA to a campus where Theatre Arts conferred the first MFA.*

Histories of the MFA should be important to creative writing because they illustrate lineages in practitioner knowledge and experiential education, including science. BFA/MFA degrees in creative writing have been historically framed through literary studies, which elides models in the sciences and fine arts (dance, theatre, and music) and sites where writers collaborated with other artists in experiential education settings such as the Bauhaus (1919–30) and Black Mountain College (1933–57). Although it's beyond the scope of this book, future creative writing historians will want to more fully investigate how science and the fine and performing arts intersect with histories of creative writing. For this chapter I, draw less from published histories and more from ethnographic research into the studio arts and arts scholarship on the process-turn. The turn toward process in twentieth-century art, as Kim Grant argues in *All about Process* (2017), reveals that the objet d'art is not the artifact—it is the processes and the conceptual exploration that drives intellectual and artistic growth. The conceit at the center of materialism (and substantiative metaphysics) suggests that writers are the maker of things, when, in fact, it's the composing processes that are the center of the endeavor. I argue, through extending Grant's observations, that the artist is made through the

---

* The first MFA at University of Iowa was in the theatre arts department in 1939, entitled "An Actor's Preparation and Interpretation of Three Widely Different Roles in the Theatre" by Henderson Forsythe.

processes that compose them. More than makers of literary artifacts, creative writers make "who they are" through the processes they negotiate and which become their daily practice. The most tangible artifact in an MFA education, then, is the writer. To conceptualize what it means to be a writer, process metaphysics becomes reality and foundational to the academic mission of creative writing. Grant's research on process offers a scholarly framework that complements arguments based in process philosophies made in Chapter 2 and the ethnographic research by Gary Alan Fine into MFA programs in the studio arts. From Fine and Grant, process shapes craft consciousness through discussions of labor and the socialization of young artists.

Ethnographic research inside MFA programs in creative writing is very limited, and even self-described, "serial ethnographer" Gary Alan Fine was pushed away by creative writing program administrators before he began his two-year ethnography of MFA programs. Fine's book, *Talking Art: The Culture of Practice and the Practice of Culture of MFA Education* (2018), concentrates on the studio arts and it follows three university programs in Chicago while providing concrete analysis on four individual emerging artists who were students in the programs. As a sociologist, Fine offers observations and analysis of the "occupational socialization" of students working in different mediums in a two-year program. Fine observes that MFA programs are moving away from explicit technique-driven instruction and toward theoretical and conceptual work. By moving away from technique, MFA programs in studio arts differ from those in creative writing. For creative writing, genre and disciplinary boundaries are held in constant and restrictive for those hoping to cross into new genres or non-discursive mediums.

For Fine, the MFA program is a space of professionalization that is situated in a lamentable intellectual space where *beauty for beauty's sake* has been replaced. In place of this Romantic, bohemian ideal, students enact conceptual exploration through their practice and through social performances among their peers in the context of the whole-class critique. The emotionally laden space of critique parallels the creative writing workshop as it has been traditionally conceived whereby a student submits newly created work to the class for discussion. The critique in studio arts, however, is driven by the practice that the student must also say something or write something to contextualize their submission. In these written and verbal performances about their submission, the student in critique must discuss the concept, construction, and process they used. These performances align with Sorkin's "live form," but they stand in contrast with the submission protocol experienced by students in a writing workshop, where creative writers remain silent while peers and the faculty discuss their work.⁷

One way to read the mandated silence experienced by the student submitting a piece in a writing workshop is to contrast it with the studio arts where, according to Fine, "displayed objects, performed actions, and social commitments exemplify their ideas."⁸ The other way to read Fine's observations is to see creative writers as embodying craft through peer feedback rather than as creators providing commentary on their own artifacts. In both cases, the socialized space of workshop or critique is highly structured and high stakes. Fine suggests that theoretical domains, aesthetic posturing, and ideological alignments create a complex social community to navigate. Most students foster an anxiety about their professional lives after the program, and Fine reminds his readers that the MFA in studio arts is multidirectional and reflective of a complex art world where "making, theorizing, evaluating, mobilizing, socializing, and being in the world are the actions of contemporary art."⁹ Among these professional activities, Fine concludes that ideas have surpassed technical or aesthetic motivations, or put more simply, the *conceptual* has subverted the teaching of *technique* in a medium. Fine speculates about why professors ask emerging artists to offer rationale, and he concludes that institutional movements in "high theory" from the 1990s have led to an outcome: "ideas form the spine of the art world."¹⁰ Fine hedges toward a more fundamental reason for this pedagogical strategy among mentoring artists: young artists consider art to be an expression of self, more than a medium of cultural, political, and aesthetic connection with the viewer. His observations suggest that mentoring artists are interested in getting students to explore conceptual spheres and detach from their tendency to see art as based in technique or self-expression.

For creative writing, Fine's observations indicate that dominant craft's focus on technique and authorship may miss a more poignant consideration for students: art is about concepts, and cognitive as well as material processes, not techniques and fixed identities in artistry. Fine laments the absence of technique, and in the spirit of Ruskin or Morris, he is full of nostalgia for the loss of technical training. Material consciousness holds sway over the conceptual and processual in creative writing, and yet MFA programs in the studio arts have turned systemically in the direction of process. Fine's argument draws together two threads within the discussion of Chapters 1 and 2. First, his comments of lament strike at the feelings of the previous two centuries, namely that we feel the sense of loss as we move away from the material toward the immaterial through industrialization or digitization. Second, he points to the ways that professional socialization causes students in MFA programs to anticipate critique as a preprofessional context, a site where the social, conceptual, material, and processual meet. The artist performs in this space as an act of courage and as one expression of their identity. In the context of creative writing, the triangulation is different; it's made up of social, material, and aesthetic considerations in workshop. The conceptual or processual becomes *invisible* while peers enact the social rituals of workshop in the form of verbal feedback. For creative writing, the sacrifice of the conceptual and processual is meant to mirror the literary publishing market where editorial decisions are made on the material submission and the writer's literary reputation. The focus on workshop submissions fosters socialization of a different order. Creative writers socialize through material submissions rather than through shared conversations on the conceptual or processual, meaning the story or the poem becomes the thing, not the ideas or processes involved in making the story or poem. When peers speculate on writerly intent through their reading of a workshop submission, the undertaking turns peers into caretakers of social relationships and into defenders of literary or aesthetic traditions. Fine's research suggests clearly that creative writing has sacrificed the processual and conceptual in favor of socializing writers into a stewardship of the literary. In this configuration of values, the processes and ideas explored through the making of an artifact are diminished to the invisible.

Fine's qualitative research signals that the "process-turn" has already been integrated into the studio arts, and his analysis of studio arts MFA students aligns with Kim Grant's historical survey of the process movement in contemporary art. In *All about Process: The Theory and Discourse of Modern Artistic Labor* (2017), Grant discusses how the shift toward process was initiated by industrialization and made visible through Marxist theory and the Arts and Crafts Movement of the nineteenth century. By making *labor* visible, Karl Marx, John Ruskin, and William Morris also made *process* visible and central to craft. Grant's comprehensive survey points to the ways that process became associated with craft and displaced artifact-based valuations or art as a simple commodity to be sold. According to Grant, the centrality of process in twentieth-century art has shifted characterization of the artist away from the white, male genius, though Grant also uses prominent male painter and sculptors Cézanne, Matisse, Picasso, and Giacometti to make her point. These artists reflect the ways that process began to supplant the central focus usually given to the object or artifact itself. The movement toward process had the consequence of making visible the labor used to create, and it brought the internal and material processes of artistry into relief as an essential value.

The emergence of process integrated into arts education more broadly, and especially through early twentieth-century educator R. G. Collingswood who argued for a "model for the construction of a fully conscious and experienced mode of living" and a more expansive understanding of "the inextricable connection between the artist's process and the artist's life."[11] The consequence of the process-turn helped to establish the MFA in studio arts according to Grant, and she argues that MFA programs in the 1960s integrated process philosophies while resisting market forces; she writes,

> Like [Cézanne, Giacometti, Mondrian, and Picasso], the university-trained artist would not be unduly concerned with the creation of saleable commodities, but would be engaged in a creative process presumed to be of value in and of itself. Indeed, the establishment of artist-training programs on this model was a way to guarantee the self-sufficient value of the creative process. An MFA Program taught would-be artists how to be artists, far more than it taught them how to create art that would allow them to pursue financially successful art careers.[12]

Grant's analysis is consistent with Fine's observations; the mastery of technique became less valued than the immersive socialization in which the artist-in-training found value in the exploration of process. Here, it's worth pausing to note that craft can, if articulated as process, resist the commodification discussed in Experiment 6 in the previous chapter. Grant aligns her research with Oli Mould's claim that artists should subvert market-driven co-optation of craft and creativity. Process movements, then, make labor visible and make possible new characterization of who is an artist. Kim Grant, as with T'ai Smith and Jenni Sorkin in Experiment 5, points to how craft *and* process movements provide women artists a way to claim and articulate practices and identities in art. Grant's research suggests that process restructures the inequities in dominant aesthetics through feminism; she writes, "The expansion and centrality of process in contemporary art is greatly indebted to the development of feminism and its enormous influence in the art world. Process as conceived and articulated within the historical contexts of Western artistic discourse is dominated by ideas of the male artists, critics, theorists, and philosophers who set its terms."[13] Grant characterizes process as "an impetus for reconceiving art as a locus of, and means for, investigating social and cultural processes" and as a driver in a "reexamination of the artistic processes as embodied activity."[14] As with the popular women ceramicists analyzed by Jenni Sorkin in *Live Form*, Grant identifies Judy Chicago, Miriam Schapiro, and Carolee Scheneeman as changing the nature of art in the second half of the century by supplanting the object-driven with embodied, performance-based art.

If a process approach underpins the studio arts MFA, it should give creative writers pause and a moment to consider how a more process-oriented education might change current MFA models. At present, a product approach based in material outcomes (publications) forms the "good" of an MFA education in creative writing. The result of this materialist approach breeds competition, an undeniable good in market terms, but it primarily serves writers who identify with dominant literary traditions. Grant argues that conceptualization of art through process creates conditions for laborers to move beyond competition and "individualistic notions of artistic talent and genius."[15] Following a Marxist line of thought, divisions in art map onto divisions in labor and, therefore, create conditions of oppression for marginalized artists. A focus on process philosophies and the conceptual unifies working artists. Grant writes, "An elimination of division between mental and material labor in the arts would implicitly eliminate hierarchical distinctions between the arts and between different practitioners in the arts. Thought and action would be inextricably bound up with one another, creating a holistic form of productive/creative activity."[16] Hierarchies in creative writing are maintained through the elision of process and a focus on critiquing the artifact. This commodification of the submission in workshops, for example, operates to undermine process philosophies. MFA programs in creative writing shift process to the background and, in doing so, obfuscate the evolution of craft consciousness within the artist-in-training. Grant and Fine's research into process in studio arts training provides empirical and historical evidence for integrating craft consciousness into the material and programmatic structures of writing. MFA programs in the studio arts are not perfectly equitable either; however, the research by Kim Grant and Gary Fine suggests that process movements in artistic education have yet to materialize in creative writing. Although MFA programs in creative writing may not currently conceptualize craft as an intersectional, networked consciousness shared with other practitioners, Grant and Fine's research proves that the MFA program need not be driven by *technique* and "an economy of craft workers" and it should serve instead "the discipline of aesthetic citizens."[17] As a citizenry, writers in MFA programs are relatively unexamined from a qualitative research perspective, however, the emerging research in creative writing suggests that the *formation of an identity as a writer* is key to understanding the field.

Emerging Qualitative Research in Creative Writing Studies

Qualitative approaches to creative writing are limited to a handful of peer-reviewed essays and conference presentations at the Great Writing (the UK) and Creative Writing Studies Conference (the United States). A number of scholars, such as Gregory Light in the UK, have established a baseline for utilizing qualitative methodologies. In "From the Personal to the Public: Conceptions of Creative Writing in Higher Education," Light sets out to "present a structural typology of concepts of creative writing in terms of their defining features."[18] Light's work is significant in that it draws on interviews from forty creative writing students in the UK. In his discussion, Light identifies the ways that students understand creative writing to be more expressive and *personal* than other forms of *public* academic writing. Evaluating these perceptions of creative writing allows Light to define the ways that undergraduates in the UK see challenges transitioning between genres and how those challenges affect their identity. He writes,

> The relationship of the student's personal sense of identity to the public readership (academic literacy) associated with the discipline becomes a significant component of how s/he may understand the practice of writing within it. In some disciplines the relationship may lend itself more easily to the development of transforming/composing conceptions.[19]

Light draws creative writing studies scholars to the ways that disciplinary and genre cues affect how students understand themselves and the genres in which they compose. Light notes, in contrast to Fine's observations, that creative writing instruction delineates clear generic and disciplinary boundaries. The boundaries are not always clear to students of course, and their identity of the writer changes as they negotiate the world. The world, if it is to widen for the writer, requires disciplinary boundaries to become more flexible with their growth and exploration of material or conceptual spheres. Light's qualitative research suggests that writers negotiate impasses that are internal and external, and these impediments dictate their understanding of discipline, genre, and their identity. How might mentoring faculty pivot away from training in genre and disciplinary conventions in order to support the identities, languages, and cultures that the student brings with them to their writing?

Published qualitative research by creative writing studies scholars has begun to focus on the concept of identity as it relates to students' language experience. In "A Humanized View of Second Language Learning through Creative Writing: A Korean Graduate Student in the United States," Kyung Min Kim describes how L2 writers navigate a "fluctuating identity" as writers in creative genres. Kim utilizes translingualist practices and methodologies to draw together "second language learning, creative writing studies, and composition studies."[20] By bringing together creative writing studies and translingualist theory and scholarship, Kim demonstrates in the case study that languages are not experienced or reflected one at a time, in fact, they are experienced simultaneously and fluidly during the student's experience in writing. Kim's conclusion applies directly to creative writing insofar as it suggests that languages, genres, and identities are not fixed and cross-genre approaches may lead to more organic representations of students' lives. Kim suggests that poetry accesses the emotional desires and frustrations of students and that genres such as literacy narratives have a reciprocal and beneficial outcome for L2 learners in the context of both first-year writing and creative writing courses. If programs isolate creative forms from analytical forms, Kim and Light argue that the concept of genre leads to confusion or exclusions that are unintended and problematic for writers. Genres in the formalist tradition function through an oppositional consciousness that is premised on the notion that developing writers must identify with and assimilate to formal and genre conventions. Dominant craft discourse exemplifies the oppositional consciousness that stands in the way of writers, and in Kim's research we see how writers acquiring a new language benefit from a fluid conceptual space where they can construct new identities.

Kyung Min Kim's scholarship dovetails with qualitative research by Yan Zhao who studied fifteen L2 creative writers for her book *Second Language Creative Writers: Identities and Writing Processes* (2015). Zhao examines "the social constructive power in identity constructions" among L2 writers, focusing on their textual production and "think aloud story sessions." Zhao identifies the ways that multilingual writers use creative genres (both oral and written) to mediate and develop their literacy and enact "the process involved in transmuted ideas in creative expression."[21] Her study draws to the fore the ways that creative writers negotiate language, identity, and genres in a non-static orientation. The suggestion in Zhao's research pushes creative writing to consider how inflexible genre categories and a fixation on *artifacts rather than ideas* exclude writers who use genres to explore the self as a language learner. From Light, Kim, and Zhao's qualitative perspectives in creative writing studies, we can see how conceptions of identity are not fixed to category or genre, especially for multilingual writers. Identity formation as creative writers is not a linear progression, and the findings are reproduced through approaches to qualitative research, and increasingly, scholars are drawing creative writing studies toward activities that are non-disciplinary and marked by a complex understanding of what it means to become a writer.

In his essay for *Creative Writing Studies Journal*, "Bad Grades, Making Bank, and Hating Piano: The Divergent Trajectories of Two Creative Writers' Semiotic Becomings" (2021), Jon Udelson "examines how creative writers understand the circuitous pathways of writerly identity formation, as well as how extra-literate and extra-disciplinary activities contribute to this formation."[22] Drawing from a ten participant qualitative study, Udelson focuses his case study on two writers and presents analyses through the lens of Paul Prior's discussion of "semiotic becoming."[23] *Semiotic becoming* captures the "sociocultural dimensions of literate activity that account, historically and materially, for writers" professional and extra-professional development.[24] Udelson frames his analysis through using literacy studies and the "marked" and "unmarked" activities writers report as crucial to forming an identity as creative writers. *Unmarked* activities are those that are traditionally disciplinary based, and in the case of creative writing, we might consider workshopping, literary studies coursework, and even attendance at author readings as typical of unmarked activities. Udelson's findings reveal that *marked* activities, those deviations or contradictions in the linear progression of writerly development, such as piano lessons or rock climbing, for example, serve an essential function in identity formation as writers. Udelson's findings carry crucial implications for creative writing programs and pedagogy, and it suggests that writers "engag[e] with multiple, heterogenous systems of activit[ies]" and, in the rejection or deviation from unmarked activities, "allows them opportunities to re-identify themselves with regard to their writerly, artistic, and identity-based goals and seek out communities that nurture those goals."[25] Writers do not follow neat pathways of development, and instead, they "veer from these more direct and commonly assumed lanes tutelage, practice, mentorship, and professionalization."[26] In his case study, Udelson's findings are suggestive of concepts that map onto craft consciousness, namely that non-disciplinary, tangential, and processual traditions in art may hold the key to training creative writers. In the explorations of themselves, and during their *perpetual becoming*, writers need more than the unmarked, disciplinary activities currently institutionalized in MFA programs in creative writing. Udelson points to the convergences in disciplinary and extra-disciplinary contexts that should impact how we teach and design programs. I argue that these *convergences* of disciplines and activities, some visible and others less visible, become enacted through craft consciousness and making visible the processual traditions that are culturally situated in craft. Udelson, Light, Kim, and Zhao present qualitative findings that center on identity, and they reinforce Salesses's claim that *craft defines the audiences for literature*; it adds to these consequences that extra-disciplinary activities are foundational to building who we are as writers. How we are *socialized* as writers frames how we *identify* as writers, and these processes reach beyond the discrete, definable spaces of workshop or MFA programs. Udelson's findings complement and confirm the ethnographic work of Gary Fine in MFA studio arts programs and Kim Grant's scholarship on process. As a whole, these scholars in creative writing studies, social sciences, and the arts hold in common a perspective that draws together the processual and its implications for socialization. By focusing on concepts and processes in art making, Grant, Fine, and writing studies scholars provide a qualitative and theoretical geography to understand the MFA in creative writing as processes of socialization and identity (re)negotiation. Writers cross thresholds in consciousness as they acquire new language skills, and these thresholds as described by Keating describe how language, genre, and identity necessitate genre flexibility.

Craft consciousness intersects the thresholds in consciousness, and it supports an intervention that allows process to displace fixed identities, genre categories, and material outcomes that marginalize and alienate new creative writers. Zhao, Kim, Light, and Udelson illuminate the dimensions of the social and its impact on writers, and their conclusions take identity to be negotiable and changing with the languages, expressions, and activities internalized by the writer. Along with Fine and Grant, the scholars of this section provide a foundation for my qualitative research, which I hope will bring to light how practitioners describe process. The qualitative research in creative writing by Zhao, Kim, Light, and Udelson characterizes writers as perpetually renegotiating identities with language and knowledge acquisition. For my qualitative study, the objective was to expand qualitative research into a new population of study and to interview writers alongside other artists. By gathering data from outside of writing, I sought to analyze and corroborate the ways artists and writers talked about craft and the attendant processes and impediments they found in their practice. The next section provides details on the study design, methodological rationale, selection criteria for interviewees, and the questions I developed for the twenty-five artist interviews.

Study Design and Methodological Rationale

In order to expand the disciplinary and geographical diversity of my interviewee pool, I chose participants for the twenty-five interviews from an international group residing in or originating from Australia, United Kingdom, Italy, Senegal, and the United States. Interviews were conducted over more than a two-year period from May 2017 through February 2020. I chose these geographical locations based on conference trips to the UK and Italy and by traveling regionally in New York State from my home in Central New York. The study is a starting point, not an ending point, and it must be triangulated with contemporary craft criticism by diverse set of artists and future qualitative research by creative writing studies scholars. As researchers look for cross-disciplinary craft criticism, they will find value in anthologies like *Choosing Craft: The Artist's Viewpoint* (2009) edited by Vicki Halper and Diane Douglas, grassroots projects such as the *de-canon* archive, and interview archives, such as *BOMB* Magazine's African American artists' oral histories.[27] Oral histories, published interview archives, and craft criticism by contemporary artists, such as the *Queer Threads* collection, serve to further rewrite craft. The study I designed draws from a cross-section of artists and disciplines to interpret their understanding of material, craft, process, and their labor as artists.

Interviewees were selected based on referrals from friends and among those with whom I had brief chats relating to arts practice or teaching, though only one of the interviewees is a collaborator of mine (Erik). On some days, and as an extrovert's habit, I strolled into an artist's studio and began chatting before I asked for an audio-recorded interview. The data sometimes reflects this chance approach to gathering interview material, and I found it benefited the conversation through the element of casualness, which offered a more natural approach to the conversation. I achieved a gender balance and actively engaged in finding diverse set of interviewees, though I asked for no specific demographic information from interviewees. Additionally, and with one exception for the eccentrically visible Physics Bus founder, Erik, interviewees are given pseudonyms in this study because many interviewees asked for anonymity and because some would have rather had their name in lights. Artist interviews are a unique genre and magnify an artist's profile or promote their work; interviews create visibility, wanted and unwanted. In the process of conducting this study, a few artists expressed concern about how the interview (if their name was attached) may be interpreted by colleagues or, in the case of university artists, affect future prospects for tenure and promotion. Some artists were disappointed with the anonymity because it could not be used to expand their visibility, and other interviewees valued chatting without the pressure of a more public utterance.

In the study, interviewees are referred to by their medium(s) and sometimes through their institutional affiliation or artistic training. Although this study is focused on interviews from artists who teach, in some cases I chose participants based on their nontraditional training or the self-taught nature of their practice. In most instances, the interviewees had some experience with university training either as an undergraduate or as a graduate student. The interviewees did not necessarily follow the career path of their degree, and it was important to remain inclusive to both nontraditional and academically trained artists. I did not choose subjects who are part-time artists or devoted DIYers on the weekends. I focused on artists whose labor and compensation rested in large part on their ability to make or perform their art. Among those who run businesses related to selling art, there is one national brand and one couple that sells on Etsy and at a local farmer's market. Unsurprisingly, artists often synthesized identities as business owners, caregivers, teachers, scholars, administrators, life partners, and manual laborers. Interviews with self-taught artists were often the most engaging as they helped me to further locate craft conversations outside of the institutional parameters of MFA programs and creative writing.

I met artists in their homes, studios, workshops, campus offices, and academic conferences. When possible, I left the choice of location up to the participants, though I found that talking with artists in spaces where they worked or taught provided the opportunity for them to refer to material or spatial aspects of their work. In one case, a couple I interviewed preferred to treat, rivet, and sew leather while we talked. I found that the interview context very much mattered as a dancer stood to discuss a movement and a graphic designer sorted through a stack of sketches to discuss a concept she was explaining to me. Spatial considerations for the interviews affected the content of discussion, and I tried to accommodate or recommend spaces that would facilitate the conversation. Additionally, I found that one-on-one interviews in some cases evolved into one-on-two interviews in which a pair of collaborators (in the same art form or in different art forms) discussed their process with me. I believe this modification in method changed the data on practice to a more collective or socialized perspectives that was influenced by having two artists chatting together. I found that one-on-two interviews brought momentum to the talks, even when they interrupted each other or one lost their train of thought. Pairing artists for interviews created a reproducible method that appeared reciprocally beneficial for artists who may not have had a formalized opportunity to discuss their process with a collaborator.

Collaborative interviews, though not the impetus for this study, often became the most dynamic apparatus for discussing craft, practice, and process philosophies. I found that artists focused more on each other than on me, and it had the advantage of giving interviewees time to carefully consider answers. It certainly may have muddied the purity of their responses, and no doubt they were influenced by utterances by the other interviewee; regardless, at the level of energy, having more than one artist together provided valuable and compelling data. In contrast to Fine's approach in *Talking Art*, my overall objective was to devote considerable efforts to *enlarge the purview of craft in creative writing by looking outside our discipline*. My tendency was to gravitate toward those familiar with craft and its relationship to writing, and I tried to resist this implicit bias and recruit participants from a range of disciplines as well as from artists for whom a distinct medium was not apparent or categorical. In cases where an artist works across forms, mediums, and disciplines, I labeled them mixed genre or mixed medium, or I affixed identifiers based on their past and current work (i.e., graphic designer).

As evidenced in the first two chapters, I have sought to gather perspectives on craft that would benefit my study and fulfill five objectives: first, to gain historical, theoretical, and qualitative perspectives on the term; second, to dignify practitioner knowledge from a living source; third, to allow for pedagogical perspectives to emerge from arts practice rather than textbooks; fourth, to theorize a more inclusive, intersectional conception of craft; and finally, to identify disciplinary, programmatic, and institutional thresholds or impasses between creative writing and the arts. My biases are cemented around the speculations I had as a writer who traversed three graduate degrees in literature, creative writing, and composition and rhetoric studies. In my experiences as a student, I learned more from those sites where craft was configured by crossing genres, theoretical readings, art exhibitions, or conversations over drinks with other artists. These informal graduate program experiences led me to develop interview questions for this study that were based in practice and that evolved through the action of conducting interviews with participating artist-teachers.

> **Interview Questions**
>
> How did you come to art initially?
> How do you conceptualize craft as it relates to your practice?
> Where do you find sources to energize your artistic practice?
> How does teaching relate to your artistic practice?
> What is critical to cultivate in an artistic teaching space?

The interviewer's task is to get out of the way, and the qualitative research questions above were often adapted as interviewees began to draw their experience with materials or processes in a different direction. I found it best to listen rather than steer them back to the formulaic questions that stiffen the qualitative researcher to a prescribed template. Chatting with living artists meant that their responses were not imitable, which I found when one audio recording was lost after battery failure. I rerecorded a second conversation with the same artist and the path we traversed did not resemble the previous journey at all. Adaptability is not a formal research method in the clinical sense, but it is the trait that serves the qualitative researcher seeking to understand craft and *what it is to be an artist*. As I sat next to a creaking loom or watched hands busily hammering and riveting leather, I saw that living artists can express intimately the virtue of their practice through talks and nontraditional craft criticism produced outside published interview venues. The reward in these conversations came through patient listening and not through textbooks. It was remarkable how they sought to reconcile codified or institutionalized understandings of craft by describing how they negotiated practices across formations in consciousness. To understand craft, it is the lived experiences of artists that matter, and in my conversations, I listened for the ways that artists tried to capture the ineffable and what craft consciousness can be.

Findings: Thematic Correspondence across Craft Consciousness

I began interviews anticipating suspicion or resistance to conversations on craft, but what transpired instead developed into identifiable patterns that were enlightening. Discussing the nuances of their labor, artists animated the concept from the categorical or commoditized, and in fact, they often remapped the term through metaphor and anecdotes. Their more complex rendering of craft expressed internal processes, and more than erecting boundaries between forms, disciplines, genres, or materials, artists drew the conversation away from specialization at every turn. Professional artists did not talk much about inspiration or strike a precious tone as they rendered their identities. Art is exploratory labor. Their search was not articulated as simply material or as governed by designations in genre or other categories. They described their thinking as marine creatures might, moving by the tides of ideas and the currents that shifted within them and kept them spiritually fed.

Their consciousness of exploratory, holistic, and fragmentary processes did not allow them to cling to absolutes. They cycled through materials and methods as a condition of their labor and by the necessity of the idea they wanted to explore. The thought experiments of Chapter 2 capture the essence of the challenge. No interviewee could capture the denotative definition of craft, and it was more revealing how they employed iterative metaphors that circulated away from static definitions like the diagrams in Milton Van Dyke's *An Album of Fluid Motion*.[28] Based on their descriptions, process and practice were bound to an internal heuristic. They lamented (or resisted) renderings of craft based on external criteria because, in practice, they didn't settle in one material or one idea long enough to adopt the dictates governing dominant craft. Disabused of the need for external criteria, I came to appreciate Glenn Adamson's sentiment that "craft is subject more than a category," and artists often drew me away from terminology and toward processes that reflected thinking.[29]

Practicing art requires a vital engagement with thresholds across consciousness, and whether they spoke about material or phenomenal formations in consciousness, the driving heuristic was the internal exploration of ideations in a project. More than desiring isolation, artists often yearned for collaboration and the mutually enriching dialectic between one or the other art form. Ideas moved through their heads and the actions they took were dictated less by external criteria and more by the approximation of a scientist working out the logistics of a lifelong experiment. Because consciousness dictates the processes and practices they use, their identity was less fixed and more flexible. As general practitioners rather than specialists, they hovered perpetually between expertise and the knowledge they sought in a new idea, which, of course, required venturing toward a new material or new process. To this end, the patterns that emerged from conversations were reflective of a complex and nuanced understanding of process philosophy. Process metaphysical principles were evident throughout the transcripts and they were manifested through the patterns listed below:

1. Definitions and Disputations with Craft
2. The Artist Triangulates—Metaphor, Material Source, and Form
3. Conceptual Processes, Spiritual Awakenings, and Institutional Influence
4. Artists Out-of-Category and Metamorphoses within Craft Consciousness

The patterns above demonstrate the ways that conversations with artists migrate or become mobius, as one tries to marshal them into intelligible patterns. Descriptions of process by artists are transitory—they move between conceptual land masses—and to understand them through any one metaphor will seem incomplete. Artists circulate through materials, ideas, processes, and identities with alacrity and, often, deft tactfulness. Intentionality, like specialization or the more static tropes of craft, however, is not always the operating constructive principle at center. Accidents and unintentionality actually rule the consciousness of artists, and so, it seems odd to define craft as technique or through material, categorical, or generic formalities.

When we think of craft, we are thinking of what goes on between and within, not the thinking that stays put or requires specialized training. Cross-genre or interdisciplinary MFA programs exist in very small numbers in the United States, and the interviewees' comments suggest that MFA creative writing programs are outmoded in their design, in their fidelity to formalism, and in their exclusion of process as the foundation of arts training. The creative writers who make up 20 percent of the interviewees did not stick to a single genre, and most wrote in at least two genres, with two interviewees also exploring mediums outside writing. Far more typical among the interviewees were transitions across *multiple* materials, genres, or disciplines. Movements across material consciousness complement the action taking place across phenomenal consciousness. When one material is insufficient to bring an idea to fruition, artists are habituated to take another action, echoing Richard Sennett's remark "making is thinking." Formations in consciousness are not islands, and as with the discussion in the third thought experiment, artists move across thresholds in consciousness with an awareness of the categorical hierarchies in oppositional consciousness (craft vs. fine art), and interestingly, interviewees sought to circumnavigate definitions of craft that further marginalized them or other artists.

One way artists subvert hierarchies, beyond redefining craft itself, is to use collaboration as a method for discovery and evolution as artists. Collaboration was not ancillary, but essential and foundational to craft and consciousness. As part of the study, I interviewed four pairs of collaborators (eight artists in total). Even among the group that was interviewed with someone else, artists made reference upon reference to other artists or other disciplines where they found inspiration or conceptual traction. Painters talked about frame builders. Poets played electric guitars. Potters became leatherworkers. In these migrations, craft consciousness becomes observable and associated less with disciplinary boundaries or material constraints and more with the "networked individualism" associated with DIY and interdisciplinary explorations.[30] As a writer, I listened intently to the metaphors that artists invented in order to describe the processes that formed their philosophy or identity. Metaphors to describe art making fit with or echoed evocations of the natural world, and I was struck by how frequently artists spoke about nature as a point of spiritual interaction and invention. These references to the natural environment, coupled with the use of figurative language to describe process, allowed me to see awareness or more than a talent as the driver in craft consciousness. The findings reflect an undeniable fact, namely, that creative writing's fidelity to formalism and exclusionary teaching practices not only shut marginalized artists out, but they do not create conditions for the explorations, migrations, and dynamic change that underpins arts practice. Artists move across disciplines as wide ranging as weaving and found object art retain a commitment to a processism, to openness and potential across dynamic changes.

    In the findings section that follows, I draw patterns to the foreground, though, others patterns lie beneath the surface that a perceptive reader will see. To begin I analyze the discussion of craft as a concept before moving out toward the interdisciplinary migrations artists embark on. If migrations move horizontally from discipline to discipline or material to material, then artists also triangulate, meaning they use one thing to explain something else. Triangulating metaphor, material, and formal properties, for example, serves to articulate the action of craft consciousness as a node between multiple consciousnesses. Process cannot be articulated fully by rendering it as technique or material consciousness, so artists don't say "I employed this technique and that was that," instead, and as they describe their process, they may use a technique to explore a material they hope will express a concept they are invested in. Migrations across formations in consciousness capture the affair more than a single formation, such as material consciousness. By maneuvering between formations in consciousness, artists model behaviors and thinking that map onto who they are. They are nonspecialists who exist in the *instabilities* and *changes* that form their worldview and actions (or interventions) in the world. Understood in this manner, craft consciousness expresses movements that identify the artist as a thinker on the order of animal species that metamorphosize as desire or setting dictates. The findings and discussion section of this chapter set the stage for Chapter 4 and the application of craft consciousness to the programs and workshops within the field of creative writing.

I. Definitions of and Disputations with Craft

During my early interviews with artists, I led with a foolish question: How do you define craft? Interviewees, in most cases, balked over a formal definition, and it felt as though I was the teacher asking the student to report back the correct answer. The question was politically and aesthetically loaded and it was clear that the oppositions defining craft arts and fine arts put artists in an awkward position to respond. The stumbling for definition came through in the audio transcripts. The interviews showed that craft is a term freighted with expectations and antagonistic connotations. It had a leaden quality when I brought it up, and in our conversations, the spirit was thrown off and it academicized what was otherwise a pleasant chat. It made me want to hide the word under my chair cushion. For example, an art and architecture professor, Marian, who works in textiles and letterpress at a small liberal arts college, the term did less to clarify her practice and more to draw forward expectations in the academic sphere. The term was a moniker of authentication or precision that needed to be rendered with focused discourse. She said,

> The way I approach craft as a practitioner and as a teacher ... they're one in the same, so I sort of developed an approach to teaching design that's very invested in materiality and there are kind of different things that I'm just going to go *blahhh* and hopefully it all ties together for me ... I think it's hard to explain this stuff in a linear way.

Later in the conversation, Marian said: "Craft then ... I'm known in the department as someone who has very high standards for the execution of my student's models, and there's varying degrees of thought about this."[31] Marian sketched a series of definitions for craft beginning with handwork and sewing before gesturing toward "high standards" and the external forces of "linearity," both of which disrupted her response. A direction question on how one defines craft often brought mild stress or annoyance to the group of interviewees, and they either shirked it or resisted its connotations or flatly ignored it.

One novelist, poet, and children's book author, Kathy, who teaches at a large public university in Australia, said, plainly: "I realize that's your project. I'm sorry. I didn't mean to ramble so much ... some of it is serendipity. It has to do with what happens with your life."[32] There was a difference between the exact definition that I seemed to be fishing for at the start of the conversation and the one that emerged later, and in most cases the interviewee trusted definitions of craft that was given second. In reviewing the audio transcripts, I noticed that craft evolved with the conversation and their growing comfort. Lena, a French native and photographer and designer, put it this way: "Craft is literally the medium speaking different language, speaking different parts of self."[33] Riana, a conceptual artist working in silicone, sewing, and photography, said: "Craft is a very controversial term in art—in postmodernism, craft is dead—they're not interested. It's all about the idea. Other people argue craft is everything. The crafting of the end product, technology, method, skill. In some art there is no product. There is no physical artifact, so where's craft?"[34] Between the death of craft in postmodernism and Lena's suggestion that craft was "speaking different language, speaking different parts of self," I saw the oppositional configuration that would define craft. Was it an external criteria or what is an internal awareness functioning to express language and self?

Through sketching definitions of craft, interviewees also sought to follow Riana's line of thinking and engage with dominant aesthetics or the oppositions that marginalize craft. Nicholas, a leatherworker and potter, said:

> I've been a potter for 23, 24 years, and in pottery this is like a big debate. Art versus craft. No one really talks about it. I'm actually very comfortable. I'm just a craftsman; no one calls me an artist. It sets up this dissonance. And I never could really get it with the pottery either. I mean the fine artists. I know some fine artists. They're totally methodical about the way they paint, and music is the same way. You practice constantly. And it's all technical and I guess there's the deeper meaning behind it all, but I guess I don't really do that so much. For me, the deeper meaning is that it's cool that I can make something and then someone can use it and they're happy.[35]

Nicholas and other interviewees outline perceptions of institutional definitions of fine art as necessarily oppositional to craft. As a potter and leatherwork, Nicholas cedes authority in his practices to fine artists and their technical prowess, but in its place, he suggests that the functionality of his artifacts carries a value. Dissonance is created when craft is brought up in conversation, and the artists I interviewed saw it as a puzzling construct that restricted practice or their identity as artists. Nicholas's description, "I'm just a craftsman; no one calls me an artist," demonstrates the degree to which the artist often has to choose their side in oppositions between fine and craft arts. For Nicholas, who is a potter, leatherworker, musician, farmer, and virtuoso mechanic, the acceptance of non-art frees him to practice through a lens that isn't freighted with the expectations of fine art.

Charlotte, Nicholas's partner, trained as a leatherworker and taught techniques to Nicholas as he transitioned from pottery to leatherwork. She said about craft:

> The concept of art or craft or whatever is totally just a human construct. It's almost as if it's a parallel world that everything is as it is. Everything has its real form, like I'm Charlotte, but you wouldn't look at me and say, "Oh, she's art." If I painted my face silver and wore a silver dress that would be art. So, it can't be, it's slightly skewed. It's like a slightly skewed version of reality. You can speak to somebody and you wouldn't consider that art but they write a poem and that's art. Or a story or a song.[36]

Charlotte provides what at first glance appears to be a relativist definition of art, but on closer examination, she's actually deciphering the "human construct" or opposition between craft and fine art. Form plays a role in definitions of art, as she suggests, but it also means that definitions of craft and art may be arbitrary or ascribed value through institutional or other external criteria. Artifacts are ascribed value while other objects (poem, song, story, performance) are defined as art and others are viewed as simply functional. Charlotte adds to her comments the fact that performance or embodied art can be art, depending on the context and the expression. For Charlotte and Nicholas, institutional parameters have an arbitrary and marginalizing effect on how they view their art forms and their identities as artists. Nicholas accepts his position as a craftsman, which strikes me as undervaluing his work while Charlotte identifies the exclusionary and arbitrary nature of categories and forms used to define art.

Among the group of international artists I interviewed, a pair of collaborators, Sebastiano and Catherine, discussed their work in mixed media (sculpture, ceramics, painting, jewelry) as it relates to craft. For them, craft has an *elemental* nature and proceeds art. As collaborators on an abstract sculpture series, and natives of Rome, they described craft as a baseline for artistic expression. Sebastiano said in the interview:

> For me craft is the basic. If there is no craftsmanship, there is no art, I might sound a bit too strict but, in a century when everything is digitized, I think, at

the base, making art is a sense—and craft is a special skill. If you don't get your hands on something it's not a piece of art ... So I think craftsmanship is the memory of humankind and of artistic expression; there is no art if there is no craft.[37]

Catherine described an ebonist working in a small workshop in Rome and costume makers in the film industry in Italy, suggesting that craft was essential in labor and contained within artistic expression even if the artisan did not recognize their labor as art. She said:

Everyone who started to be an artist started with craft, doing something with the craft—it could be weaving or drawing or using wood, whatever ... a craft for me is a craft because you need creativity and you need *know-how* ... For me, an Italian, a Roman, you walk in the streets and you see the shops with the guy that is cleaning a frame and for me as I approach, I always want to be hands on.[38]

For Catherine and Sebastiano, craft pivoted back to handwork and interactions between material and the body. In the art culture and history of Italy, Sebastiano associated craft with traditions and "the old-fashioned" and suggested craft is oftentimes commodified, packaged, and performed as "amusements" for tourists in manners that are inauthentic, appropriated, or "misconceived."[39] Both artists saw the role of artists and artisan as neither mutually exclusive nor separate from one another. Artists and artisans were collaborators in expression even if the latter might be willing to sell their wares and "craftlike" qualities for mass consumption. Catherine had trained as an artist for the last few years in Brooklyn and said she saw the same consumerist craft being sold in New York City and through the lens of authentic "culture." In defining craft, interviewees often started with handwork, methods for making, attention to detail, and externalized criteria imposed on the artist. It felt as though craft was a set of criteria or disciplining of oneself according to models or forms of expression. For one violinist, Delia, she suggested initially that the Julliard method for practice was a craft, but later in the conversation, she spoke about craft as an internalized expression that deviated from or ignored outside forces.[40] In cases where a preliminary definition was provided by an interviewee, subsequent definitions traversed toward internalized concepts like "know-how" or toward the spiritual, emotional, and intellectual movements that went into their practice. Craft split apart in our chats, and I found that meanings for the term fragmented within the interviews.

Leslie, a graphic designer and sketchist, drew forward the fragmentary nature of craft by saying, "That word, if we looked it up again, what is the definition of craft? Is it fine-tuning something? Crafting, I could be doing that with food preparation, right? Crafting as a beautiful presentation or is it like just thrown on the plate? ... There's a lot of visuals. I think there's a sensitivity."[41] Chase, a Dyberry weaver, suggested that "craft is my obsession. And my compulsion to do it well. For years I was a printer."[42] Chase's discussion moved from the loom to the printing press, and he described "the dance" between three printing presses. "The loom is a machine," he said. Whether a *sensitivity* as described Leslie, or as a *compulsion* as noted by Chase, the trajectory of definitions in craft oftentimes extended from one medium to another, from the sketches in Leslie's studio to a chef's presentation or from Chase's loom to the printing presses he danced between. In response to my request for a definition of craft, interviewees were smartly evasive and they used analogies to describe craft in another medium or they settled on describing capacities or attitudes that came from within.

Definitions vacillated between external criteria and internal faculties as interviewees constructed definitions of craft. In practice, external or institutional factors played less of a role, and though artists offered preliminary definitions based on imposed factors, the definitions expressed later focused on process and the internal or embodied dimensions of making. Analogies and metaphors allowed for artists to experiment with definition, and these improvised linguistic constructions drew their thinking to complement with other art forms. Gestures toward related processes or other arts traditions happened very often, and I learned to avoid leading the conversation off with asking them to define craft. Without my request for a formal definition of craft at the outset of the conversation, artists built much more elegant reflections on the ways craft intersected their knowledge and processes of construction. More sophisticated definitions of craft emerge from thresholds and formations in consciousness than in oppositions or institutional definitions splitting craft arts from the fine arts. If craft consciousness builds upon the internal mechanisms articulated by artists, it has the potential to draw disciplines and artists together. The term "craft" has the habit of squirming away, and it should be treated as internal rather than external because the former functions as an actuator whereas the latter acts as an impediment against the artist. For creative writers, the internalized definition in craft consciousness shifts thinking away from technique or other external mechanisms. In its place, and as a condition which opens rather than closes processes available to the writer, craft consciousness moves toward bridges and synergies latent in artists' thinking.

II. The Artist Triangulates—Metaphor, Material Source, and Form

Artists want to think in capacities that expand an art form. The capacity of artists may appear to be determined by limitations imposed from the outside, but this need not be the case. Artists understand the process of making to be an internal heuristic that triangulates with, for example, material, form, and genre. Interviewees preferred to respond in analogies or metaphors when expressing what craft meant to them and their process. Interviewees' responses suggest that the best way to understand thinking processes were to draw upon relational or proxy relationships with other art forms like cooking, agriculture, writing, fashion, science, performance art, photography, printing making, and music. Figurative language or analogies express ideas about process that move beyond one's chosen art form, and this very common sentiment in interviewees demonstrated that artists attempt to translate their own work through understanding the work of others.

Traveling between these bridges of composing or thinking practices, from one art form to another, I found that interviewees were aware that I was a writer, and so they used a third art form to express their thinking. It was a kind of meeting ground for thoughtful expression. Oftentimes, this meant that in order to explain their practice they needed a third art form to build a conceptual space and communicate their understanding. People do this all the time of course, but the gesture in this context demonstrated the necessity of interdisciplinary knowledge. The capacity of an art form becomes stressed and productively distressed by the will of the artist. Negotiating craft definitions on these terms, on the neutral terrain of a third art form, provided a space where neither of us was an expert and where craft was less politicized or exclusionary. Artists need these interspaces to travel between art forms, processes, and materials to reinvigorate their practice and reimagine their identities. Kathy, the poet/novelist based in Australia, said, "That other medium gives you that kind of distance."[43]

Analogies to other art forms or processes inevitably led to discussions of identities, and I was completely unprepared for the ways that artists shapeshifted across disciplines and identities. A writer became a chef. A potter talked about being a farmer. A physicist became a DIY artist working with junked small appliances. A poet spoke of Antarctica and scientific research. These shifts in the interviews showed the capacity to draw past threadbare definitions of craft into new ways of being. The analogies were always volunteered, I never asked for them, but they became unavoidable digressions and foundational to how they talked about their work and identities. I got the sneaking sense that the poet might become a scientist or, if not become one, occupy scientific thinking. The writer, Kathy, drew an analogy that captures this proclivity: "If you are really a writer, you want to learn other things. Learning doesn't mean you go and imitate them. It's like going to the museum ... In other art forms, whether its architecture or it used to be the guilds, arts students go to museums and copy paintings ... you can learn things from different genres."[44]

Building comparisons across disciplinary and medium boundaries provides more than interview data, it illuminates two other ideas. First, it presents new articulations between disciplines and processes, and second, it offers a portrait of artisthood that is distinctly nonspecialized. Artists are nonexperts that become experts when conditions and context dictates, and in this manner, they are scientists or mathematicians asking why and how. A poet, Claire, brings this point out more fully, saying, "I actually think that mathematics and poetry are really closely related to each other, and they're practiced and require a certain aesthetic sense and a feel for the texture of language because of course mathematics is a language although we don't teach it that way, but that's what it is."[45] Moving away from disciplinary expertise allowed interviewees to test material consciousness (resin, ink, text, clay, leather, textile, music, wood, movement) alongside phenomenal and store consciousness. It was as if they were sketching analogies to test their process philosophies and the flexibility of a discipline. Characterization of craft drew from the haptic and the tactile when it appeared that the interviewee was becoming—to their mind—too abstract. Material consciousness served a primary role in defining craft in a particular art form; however, responses congealed around *characteristics* of a material more than a *technique*. Constructive principles are based in materiality and they extend into the conceptual when students work within strict limitations. In this way, limitations may serve the function of assisting students in the building process by imposing working constraints. This fact, a material's physical limitations, reflects the productive tension between method and material. Creativity can be a productive result of material constraints, but if those constraints are nonmaterial and arrive as institutional hindrances, then thinking is unduly constrained.

Marian, an art and architecture professor working in textiles and mixed media, articulated the challenges for students working in a new material:

> I want to integrate into the understanding, the tangibility: how it was built. How is the thing holding itself up and responding to gravity, and how is it suggesting

its tectonics, how is it suggesting how it's built in its formal characteristics and how it's put together. If that's something I want students to get to down the line, then one of the ways I start that is having them spend a lot of time working with the material and feeling its limitations because I really believe that the greatest creativity happens within the strictest of limitations.[46]

External limits are one thing, but Marian's description also suggests that "every material has its own internal structure." For artists working across materials and disciplines, internal structures are redefined when different materials come into contact. This cross-pollination, inevitably, holds the potential to change artists' approach to process and the way they define themselves and their material.

Nicholas and Charlotte describe leather by identifying its elemental nature and its origins with the cow and the tanner. The materiality Nicholas associated with clay, his first medium, implied that it didn't have the elasticity he desired. The nature of clay (after twenty-five years as a potter) felt uninteresting and tired. Nicholas used the farm he shares with Charlotte as a metaphor for art, saying, "Our farm is this giant slice of art that we talk about all the time. It's this big giant three-dimensional living, changing geometric thing."[47] Using the farm as a metaphor, Nicholas and Charlotte discussed the "observational nature" of art and the seasonal fluctuations in the farm's operation. For Nicholas, natural metamorphoses and seasonal changes described his way of seeing the functional *and* aesthetic as unified. Working with leather, he and Charlotte saw a union between the ways they wanted consumers to see their work and the way natural world enlivened them. Nicholas offered up the term "plant blindness" to describe consumers' inability to see the care they put into their work, a kind of craft blindness. Plant blindness, or the inability to identify, appreciate, or use a plant in nature, became analogous for Nicholas to customers' craft blindness to the quality of their leather purses, shoulder bags, or belts as distinct from mass-marketed junk. The analogy to blindness comes from an able-bodied worldview, but as a metaphor it does capture consumerist attitudes toward artifacts—what they cannot see. For Nicholas, consumers internalize and exhibit the inability to know the difference between the well-made and the poorly made thing. Craftspeople who navigate art processes with a reader, consumer, audience, or student in mind must work at educating them on materials.

Materials are not static as much as they are *the conditions* within which artists operate. For a self-taught artist and physics outreach educator, Erik, the stochastic arts tradition is alive. He was troubled by consumers' relationships to "junk or throwaway culture" and chose to build exhibits from discarded small appliances and other found items discarded as rubbish.[48] These artifacts and their repurposing as science exhibits were to work against the physics blindness that encompassed kids and adults. In his experience as a student he felt alienated from science courses and wanted to tinker, manipulate, experiment with found objects, not traditional laboratory equipment. Physics' separation from the physical world bothered him. Additionally, and because physics remained outside the worldview of more and more kids, Erik chose to focus on everyday items for his artwork as a way to disrupt and resist unexamined consumerism. Relationships between process and material become more than an outcome and in the process of the practitioner's labor "the good" emerges in the tradition of Aristotle's stochastic arts. Erik and Nicholas's pursuit in art is tied to the redemption of the consumer or the science student who may take the material world for granted or leave it unexamined or unexplored. Process, material, and audiences for art interconnect, and they reveal the virtue of process as more than the object produced. Objects, then, extend the vision of the artist and audience *together*.

Material choices are not purely about material outcomes, though they appear to be, and the internalized expression of an idea and the political implications of a material choice matter as much. Gary Alan Fine references this point in his ethnographic study, writing that "the choice of material is not merely a technical matter. Rather, it is or can be, political. Material choices are easily transformed into the moral and the evaluative."[49] Charlotte, the leather artist, described her transition from being a vegetarian to a leather artist, and she suggested that it took time and "killing lots of chickens" to understand her relationship to food, art, and ethics. She said,

> It was a psychological jump. There's this whole ethical thing tied up with it, which informs, I think, what I do. Like Nicholas was saying, he doesn't want to waste leather. I want to make something that honors this animal that was once alive and has an afterlife as a purse. So that definitely inspires me: the fact that you're working with what was once a living creature.[50]

The ethics and politics of the material weren't always a prominent discussion point in the interviews, nonetheless, those artists who addressed the topic of materiality or the origins of materials were interested in how those sources reflected their internal vision and the reception of artifacts. The choice of materials is a principled one and attached to the artist from conception, through process, and onto a reader, audience, consumer, or student. Based on the interviews, process is not an isolated or detached activity performed for its own sake.

The fact that discussions of material operate in conjunction with process should be no surprise. Artists spoke about material through the lens of internal processes and sometimes in reference to the productive tensions between artists and consumers. Consumers in the last two decades have become more driven by ethical considerations (material source, production methods, producer identities) in their purchases, but it remains questionable whether they are more attuned to sourcing, construction principles, and the artifacts they buy. Nicholas pointed to the fact that he could only remember one person meaningfully deliberating on the construction process of the leather handbags he and Charlotte make. Few farmer's market customers asked how they attained their leather. Despite the fact material considerations often circle artists back to ethical and moral construction principles, the thinking through process that delivers the purse to the shoulder is made through the handwork of the artist. But the tanner and the cow who sacrificed the hide are more obfuscated in this transaction.

Artists concerned themselves with origins as much as objects, and in the interviews, they desired to produce objects that honored the origin of a material through an ethical process. Reflections on process bring into focus the ways that artists want process to subvert material outcomes. Lena, a French photographer, designer, and painter, responded: "Art is a way of breathing, looking, seeing—it is not a product." Similarly, Erik, a found-object artist and scientific educator, believed that his collaborative process with students required them to pivot toward phenomenal consciousness; he said, "What we're getting less and less is the pure experience piece … the meaning of a personal engagement is important, to feel it in your hand … where we can articulate it or not, it should be valued." Process' virtue superseded the saleable product for many artists, and Chase, a weaver, argued passionately that the monetary value could never match the ten weeks or more he spent weaving an artifact. The selling prices for his wool, silk, alpaca, and worsted acrylic bags, area rugs, table runners, and linens could not reflect the time he had spent. The market value, therefore, was arbitrary to him; he said, "the thrill of making something, of using my brain, hands, feet, and back, and to make something … it's not quantifiable."[51] Relationships between material and process are continually revitalized through the artist's commitment to an internal and external cause. Even in cases where the bottom line remained in primary focus, they sought to remind themselves and consumers that the process and its precedents in material or history very much matter.

A furniture designer, Lawrence, manufactures luxury home goods exclusively in the United States because it allowed him to produce seating, lighting accessories, and other interior effects with the knowledge of their source. His education did not involve training in the ethics of design, and his coursework focused on art history rather than on technique at a private art school on the West Coast. Discussing the work of some of his peers, Lawrence said,

> Other kids in my program were making these pieces ... they didn't know design history and they didn't know the history of furniture design, so they weren't able to reference that stuff and they were referencing without knowing that they were referencing it, which is can be dangerous ... I think there's a danger in not understanding what came before.[52]

Ahistorical design struck Lawrence as "in danger" of being imitative or derivative. Like an ignorance to source material, ahistorical or acultural design obfuscates the maker from materials and processes that came before. This mystification that separates artist or audience from sources and processes may be a condition of late capitalism, where consumers are marketed craft with the assurance that it is craft. The reality is more complex for artists. Interviewees suggested, such as Nicholas, that he needed to overcome people's ignorance or inability to *see* relationships between the material and the processes of making. The natural world served as an analogy to this inability to see objects for what they were.

Erik, the physicist and found-object artist, argued that this inability was *learned* or *socialized* behavior, and not a congenital condition. He spoke about children's interaction with his science exhibits and how they approached them with wonder and openness. Accompanying adults, on the other hand, were more likely to insist upon explanations of physics phenomenon and remain hands-off when they encountered spaces for material exploration. Erik related these adult behaviors to a world that has been dulled to interactivity with found or discarded objects. The junk items Erik includes in his science exhibits form a resistance to the capitalist ideologies and "throwaway" culture. His philosophies as an educator *and* artist are built around discarded goods, and within these materials, he challenges kids and adults to reassess their understanding of science. The latest technology does not *extend* science in Erik's philosophy; it creates barriers that alienate people from material and mechanical know-how and the wonderment that accompanies scientific phenomenon. Young children do not need to experience the scientific method according to Erik, and his teaching philosophy modifies the scientific method in line with handwork and away from intimidating physics terminology. For Erik, Nicholas, Lawrence, and Chase, barriers exist between the audience and the artist. These impasses are opportunities for drawing focus to sources, histories, science, or the natural world. These processes can be invisible in a consumerist or educational model bent on commodification or standardization. By drawing awareness to processes otherwise obfuscated in the conception, design, and execution of their art form, artists in the study saw their work as larger than making artifacts for consumption. Art objects illuminate and offer viewers and audiences the exigence for reconsidering their relationship to the world.

Whether or not an audience or reader truly sees the object, artists navigate thresholds between material and formal considerations. Forms offer a vehicle for developing concepts and expressions. Blake, a poet and nonfiction writer, and Camilla, a musician and poet, discussed form like a material-conceptual vessel, as a "vehicle for thought." Thought drives the search for form in a way that's similar to how a painter might make a choice of canvas or attempt a technique with the brush. Sometimes a particular poetic form moved them to write, but more often they described navigating *ideations* through a genre or form. Camilla suggested that form drives thinking and thinking drives form; she said,

> And it's a particular kind of thinking for me ... or essay writing but when I'm doing a poem it's because I want to think in a particular way. Audre Lorde says "poetry gives name to the nameless" and that's the kind of work I think I'm doing or what I try to do. I can't. It's inarticulable. And so I find a way to triangulate or to kind of get at something, to communicate something that's not really possible to say and that's my artistic practice.[53]

In the search for the nameless, poetry serves well, and for Camilla, this means that literary genres have different capacities and potentials for expression. Blake complemented Camilla's discussion points by suggesting that the exploration of form activates ways of thinking that, eventually, move beyond their original intention, and become larger because of it. He said,

> For me, they're very different, very different practices. Often with a poem, I'm trying to surprise myself because I don't want to be fully in control of it. Or if I feel in control of it in the beginning, I want to get to a point where I break out and the poem is beyond me ... I think control is a dangerous thing, artistically speaking. The product can only be as good as an artist, whereas sometimes when the poem escapes us, it can actually be better than anything we're capable of producing ... So there's a way in which I try to reach that point with poems.[54]

Blake and Camilla's comments present form as a vehicle for ideas. Camilla, as a musician, also explained that content can shift based on the medium; she said,

> So my songs don't tend to be about the same thing my poems are about. And I end up thinking differently because it has different elements ... that's why we travel, sometimes being forced into new circumstances leads to better craft. Because craft has something to do with the brain. Thinking through something, then shaking your brain in a new way of thinking.[55]

New ways of thinking are born then of shifts in circumstances, in materials, in forms, and in the migration across thresholds in consciousness and toward a place "beyond me."

For Camilla and Blake, the movements across genres or mediums create new pathways in consciousness. From these new thresholds, material or formal constraints activate different ways of thinking and making. New possibilities for the artist emerge from intention but are sharpened by openness to and movement away from deliberate plans of action as an artist. Once intention creeps in, the door closes and the artist is left without an openness and flexibility that serves their ideas. Allowing more open expression in creative writing requires a more fundamental shift away from the artifactual, product-based model of instruction and program design to one modeled on processism and triangulation. In the interviews, artists constructed analogies to process, deliberated on the origins of materials and histories of their discipline, and finally and most importantly, they articulated the material, formal, and experiential dimensions as the work of consciousness. From the conversations, I saw artists triangulate between metaphors, materials, and other disciplines. Their explanations indicate that craft consciousness draws focus to the inner workings of practice *and* to the external conditions artists navigate in their attention to the material, philosophical, pedagogical, or historical. Among the infinite motivations artists may have for making, it is the *conceptual* and the *explorative* we may be missing in our teaching of writing.

III. Conceptual Processes, Spiritual Awakenings, and Institutional Influence

Conceptual exploration remains foundational to artists and is more critical than simple formal or material knowledge. In Chapter 2, material consciousness and phenomenal consciousness are interlinked with mind consciousness and the ability to access or act upon the potential energy of making. The action in art is *conceptual*, and in the processes described by many artists, form or material is secondary to the exploration of an idea. Ideation focuses processes toward a material. Artists lead with an idea and then find mediums to assemble the expression of the concept. It would seem odd to consider the conceptual and process based on superseding or preceding the material, but in most cases, artists followed Kim Grant and Gary Alan Fine's research conclusions: *art is all about process*. The artifact is not the thing—the performance or the process is the thing. If artifacts currently overshadow processes and conceptual thinking in creative writing programs, how might creative writing studies scholars design workshop and program models based on conceptual and processist ideologies? This question is taken forward in Chapter 4, but before moving to practical application, it's vital to discuss how artists reflect on process as a vehicle for ideas.

Conceptual exploration was tantamount to process in interviewees' responses, though it often led artists in different directions. Riana, a conceptual artist and photographer, emphasized this point: "The direction for me became the idea; there has to be an idea because for me it's the idea you need ... and you could use a photographic series ... In order to develop a good set of images, coming up with an idea or 'concept' helps to move the work forward."[56] For Riana, the photographic series was one way to build out an idea. The series did not determine the concept, and like Blake and Camilla, the form is a thinking device, a kind of technology, and a way to explore. Lena, the photographer and designer, related this thinking to an internal, spiritual journey: "But it's only an inner space, it's not like you're a gallerist—it's completely internal—it reflects and I produce well at the edge of strong emotion."[57] Lena described the edges as a negotiation between internal forces and external forces such as deadlines, and for her, mediums like photography reflected the motivations and spiritual impulses she followed. Photos could be journalistic or more expressive and it was a matter of determining her motivation and impulses before directing the work. Training in technical dimensions was useful in understanding lighting, for example, but the spiritual, experiential, and process dictated what she made. Process philosophies govern motives in a medium and allow artists to express something bigger than themselves. Spiritual forces arise from encounters, according to Lena, and she spoke about processes as a way to explore personal, spiritual dimensions: "To create that space—not to intrude on the creative expression—and to sort out the links spiritually that are misplaced or false." The links Lena described drew the emotional and spiritual into conversation with the expression, and she discussed process as a way to determine what was "misplaced or false" in the linkages between spiritual, material, and artistic cause. For Lena, the linkage between the inauthentic and the authentic expression comes down to understanding the internal dimensions of self and process.

Erik, the found object artist and educator, described the impediments in scientific education that robbed him (and his students) of the hands-on experience of the natural world. For him, the spiritual awe was stripped from science in order to make it more standardized and hierarchical. Scientific knowledge has been abstracted from the experience for him and his students; he said, "It sets expectations that someone needs to take something from that's predetermined … What we're getting less and less is the pure experience piece … the meaning of a personal engagement is important, to feel it in your hand like electricity … whether we can feel it or not, it should be valued."[58] The process of alienation described by Erik was echoed in his own experience as a student, and he became determined to nurture students first into "a wondering for … a stirring of curiosity for physical phenomenon and second into a sense of agency."[59] Riana, Lena, and Erik's observations suggest that process builds through agency and the need to undertake spiritual and conceptual exploration, and in this endeavor, they encounter the impediments and potentialities of a form or material. Artists explore the inner spiritual and imaginative dimensions in resistance to external institutional forces.

Erik resists traditional scientific education when it is packaged as lab templates and mathematical formulas. His resistance echoes the historical action of craft as a disruptive force, the contrarian's cause, and whether discussing Anni Albers or Ruth Asawa, it's difficult not to see craft consciousness as oppositional to institutional structures. AnaLouise Keating's concept of *thresholds* is instructive here though, and it accounts for the ways craft consciousness can serve as a form of resistance *and* as catalyst for the process of spiritual and conceptual exploration. Oppositional consciousness can configure the processes and identities of artists in an institutional context, but their process ebbs and flows between the institutional forces that dog their practice and interior forces that inspire them. For Chase, a weaver, much of our chat was devoted to a discussion of the forces pushing him toward a commercial or profit-making model. He said he made up prices for his weavings because they no longer equated with his labor hours, and folks who came to his shop wanted to dicker over prices in a manner that insulted his practice. Chase, Lena, and Erik comment on the antagonisms they face, and whether the challenges precipitate from inner or outer forces, living artists seek to diminish or circumnavigate impediments to process.

Capitalism encroaches upon craft artists, but the effects of this infringement are felt to different degrees and intensities. For a glass artist, Steve, it meant that the stained glass business was being under bid by international manufacturers. This shift in global manufacturing, coupled with the diminished demand for stained glass art in churches, meant that he had to close his shop after our interview. Demands on the artist can change process but their success was not measured in dollars, and oftentimes, the antagonisms of capitalistic forces are diminished when a consumer or audience values their work. Artists spoke with conviction about those who understood their labor and as more than a commodity. Chase, the weaver, told an anecdote about a man who came in and haggled over prices with him and treated his work as ornamentation. He laughed and kicked the man out of his studio. Afterward, he told the story of an eight-year-old girl who brought him a hand-drawn picture as a gift, and he let her pick out whatever rug she wanted on the wall, no cost. The sentiment was palpable among those with whom I spoke. They wanted their labor to be valued for its process and not simply as a manufactured outcome. Artifacts are embodiments of the internal and external processes used in construction. Given the energy devoted to the process of construction, artists did not align fluidly with transactional nature of capitalism. More often interviewees described process through the lens of interactions with customers or fellow artists. The exchanges that enlivened them did not have a monetized value, they came from the networks and communities that sustained them. For a Hollywood actor I spoke with, Dana, he described acting work on commercials for national broadcast, television roles as a supporting actor, and theatre performances. And yet, his description of acting was grounded in the ways that *community* was built among actors. Acting gave him opportunities to make a living, but more than this fact, he found that his BFA and theatre experiences afterward gave him a sustaining community he valued.

For the artist, finding one's agency is critical to navigating internal and external forces. Interviewees I spoke with described the ways that they set out on conceptual journeys to map ideas into forms through a chosen material. Impediments in process are naturalized not only in materials but also in conditions dictated by educational institutions and capitalist markets. Artists are naturalized into materials through experience, but they also grow in sophistication as they are socialized to the conditions of process. Process comes down to the forces within and the forces without, between internal desires and the shaping influence of institutions, professional fields, and the enterprise of teaching students. In the next section, I discuss how artists from nondominant traditions experience these energies in the development of their identity and practice.

IV. Artists Out-of-Category and Metamorphoses within Craft Consciousness

Artists of color or those who self-identified as artists from marginalized communities represented seven of the twenty-five artists I interviewed. From the group I spoke with, many talked about the ways that institutions and individuals impeded their efforts as artists. Joseph, a spoken-word poet and performance artist, said,

> It's a little orthodox because I got kicked out of the on-level English class I was in, and my principal gave me two choices: either I stay in the office or I go to the AP English class. And I thought I was smart enough. I went the rest of the year … we read Shakespeare sonnets. And writing, I kept doing it and doing it and doing it.[60]

For Joseph, oral delivery and performativity were central to his music and spoken word. If the audience isn't moved by his performance, there is nothing to build from and nowhere to go. Joseph moved outside educational institutions for training because school had been an environment where he had not always found a supportive, enriching environment. Support in educational contexts had come from one faculty member who was willing to facilitate his poetic development, and he took this seed of mentorship forward through a practice that he developed outside of the BFA/MFA structure of New York City.

Litzy, a violinist and photographer, provided a narrative from her BFA experience that reflected what I heard from Joseph. Her comments echoed the sentiments I heard from peers in my creative writing MFA more than a decade ago:

> I ended up going to music school. I thought that what I wanted to do. Music. I was always a technical player. The expressive parts I struggled with … Most music school are classically based or jazz, and I wasn't able to learn that, if that makes sense, which was part of the reason I left … The classical world is elitist, and I found in school I didn't like who I was, and I didn't like the way the people around me were acting. At least in my situation, it was very fake and a toxic environment. They would say, we're a family, we're a studio, but at the end of the day, it was like "you are my competition." I'm going to end up taking you out, or whatever, but it ended up being not a very good environment for me. It's not a supportive environment because it's a cutthroat environment when you leave.[61]

For Litzy, the toxicity and competition of the classical music program at her college became a context in which she could not persist.

Litzy suggested that illusion of a familial structure in competitive arts programs is primarily paternalistic and modeled on a social contract that was superficial and deeply flawed by strict individualism. Litzy found relief only when she left school:

> As I have gotten older, I started moving to other mediums and thinking about art in different ways. After I dropped out of music school, I got anxious because I couldn't put my creative energy anywhere. I did photography and experimented with paint. It has been cool moving around and experimenting with different forms of art and interacting with different artists in this town.[62]

Litzy and Joseph's narratives demonstrate the level to which marginalized artists can be estranged from educational institutions and art training programs. The nature of this rupture intensifies beyond primary and secondary education in their stories, and it indicates that competition and the compulsion toward professionalization (or standardization) are not received as a benefit to those from nondominant traditions. Litzy referenced the individualism of her BFA program and how it created the "fake" and "toxic" conditions that forced her to withdraw. Socialization in arts training programs can be fueled by individualism and an every-artist-for-themselves model. In the wake of this dominant ideology, collectivity and collaboration are oppositional and ancillary to the competitive and, therefore, more highly regarded MFA program. Creative writing MFA programs can be evaluated based on alumni publications rather than on the community of artists they build or based on the persistence of alumni who continue writing after graduation.

In Litzy's interview and or in the narratives of Joy Harjo and Sandra Cisneros, personal hostilities run in parallel to the competition amplified in the name of professionalization. Competition serves as a social pressure, but among the interviewees I spoke with, many felt that specialization was an even greater pressure. A dancer and a professor at a small liberal arts college, Diane, spoke in opposition to specialization and narrow interpretations of dance as a field in isolation; she said, "I'm multiracial, I have to be interdisciplinary. So I'm integrated. So the idea of integration in the arts is not that big for me. That's who I am. It's been multidisciplinary, interdisciplinary. Dance is all about integration."[63] Speaking about her undergraduate education, she said, "It wasn't until college when I was told that dance was art ... I got into abstractions in all the arts there." To feel integrated in art, Diane approached her teaching with an interdisciplinary method, and her elaborate description of practice as a multiracial artist was to suggest, along the lines of Anya Achtenberg, that specialization and linearity were counterproductive to her and those like her.

Statements from artists of color indicate the ways that communities in graduate programs either fostered opportunities to flourish or they force artists into training models that fit a narrowed conception of their identity or circumscribed their practice. In music, poetry, and painting, the parameters of dominant craft and aesthetics construct and maintain partitions between disciplines, and nowhere was this fact more prominent than in the interviewees with artists who don't fit categorical or identity boxes. Not all artists felt alienated and not all graduate programs create insurmountable socially oppressive conditions. An Iranian-born actor, Dana, described his MFA program at an interdisciplinary arts university on the East Coast as an opportunity to explore and stabilize his identity in acting. He said,

> I had an opportunity to reconcile my cultural background or faith background and my own sexual identity. These were all things that were very much still in flux and having acting and the arts ... that experience and that community. A tribe even larger than those that I knew through acting ... it wasn't just "I have friends" and rehearsal; it created a confidence that trickled into ... a different sense of myself.[64]

Both Diane and Dana's experiences contrast with those of Litzy and Joseph, and the difference, at least in this small group of interviewees I spoke with, was that Diane and Dana had supportive communities in undergraduate and graduate interdisciplinary arts programs. The interview group is too small to make larger claims about the ways that interdisciplinary arts programs may better foster openness and tolerance, but it was clear among interviewees that specialization was unnatural and it created conditions where artists out-of-category did not have room to explore process and who they are.

The findings among artists out-of-category were not the same for self-taught artists who represented nearly half (eleven) of the interviewees. Nonetheless, those who were self-taught or identified with a marginalized group reflected on interdisciplinarity and the need to approach process and materials from outside dominant making practices. For one professor and scholar, Madin, the desire to move into art was based in collaboration and the wish to connect with other artists.[65] As an outsider to art as an academic scholar, Madin arrived to art without formal training, and it meant he felt doubly outside, in a way. His desire to write poetry to accompany a photographic series meant he was willing to push at disciplinary and institutional boundaries. As stated earlier, the findings revealed that the majority of artists preferred to work in more than one medium *or* had left behind one medium for another. This fact, perhaps more than any other, was the most significant finding of my interview process. Some eighteen out of the twenty-five artists moved between art forms or had previously studied or practiced in an art form different than their current one. For my interview analysis, this meant any label I fixed was inevitably changed later in the conversation. Becoming an artist means moving through processes and concepts that are not bound to training in one genre or medium. The intersectional nature of craft is reflected in the consciousness of the artists I interviewed. Craft consciousness, if it is observable in the words we speak, comes through describing the triangulation between material, phenomenal, and access consciousness. Artists narrate their lives through materials, experiences, and actions, and in the anecdotes or metaphors, their lives are based in *metamorphoses* and *evolutions*.

A potter becomes a painter who becomes a leather artist who farms an apple orchard. Or a scientist becomes a poet who becomes a nonfiction writer. Transitions across material consciousness were not the exception but the rule, and I found identities were like the layers of consciousness described by Thich Nhat Hanh's *manas*. The self we cling to today will not be who we are tomorrow. Artists know this, and as they develop a store consciousness, new coats are worn over old coats. They say as much: "I don't know if you know this, but I started out as a _____." In transitioning between one identity and another or one medium and another, the objective was clear: keep on moving—not toward specialization—but toward a new version of themselves.

Artists spoke in terms of nature and the ecological more than they talked about specialization or formalism. Material and phenomenal experiences accumulate or are left behind for financial, spiritual, or ethical reasons. Among the identities that artists claimed in our conversations, I was surprised how nearly all identified as *observers of nature*. Initially, I ascribed this to the outdoor cafe where the interview was conducted, however, interviewees with whom I talked with indoors or in windowless dance studios also described with intensity their relationship to the natural world. Whether as a site of inspiration or interactivity, artists and scientists seemed cut from the same cloth. Claire, a poet, described the relationship: "I'm sure you've seen this too once you're really working as any sort of artist or any sort of scientist at the very highest level, you have much more in common with each other than you have differences with each other."[66] In Claire's mind the process of intense observation and experimentation connected the poet and scientist. In addition to connecting the intensity of scientific and artistic observation, other artists saw nature as a site for inspiration and emulation. Lawrence, a furniture designer, described his relationship to nature: "I draw inspiration from a ton of stuff, but I'm very nature based though. Like the tactile quality of things, the materiality of things is always nature based, and the color. My color theory comes from nature; I'll color match leaves with paint chips. I'm into the idea of the natural world."[67] Nature served as a source for inspiration, a subject to represent, and as a way of thinking through processes in their minds. I did not anticipate artists' focus on nature, and their points served to expand the ways that we may consider interactions in the natural world and with collaborating scientists. Erik, the found-object artist, stated, "I want to almost create the feeling you'd have in nature on the bus. A good day in nature—I'm observing—I'm present. No agenda there."[68]

Erik and Claire (poet) argued that science was *the* site in which their art form found definition. Principles in the ecosystemic and aesthetic were melded in my conversations with artists, and in Chapter 4 I explore new coalitions between the artistic and scientific and how they may be applied to the MFA in creative writing. I argue that creative writing education should adopt more ecosystemic strategies for interdisciplinary or transmedium exploration. If creative writing involved seeing artistic practice as material, phenomenal, and mental explorations based in collaborations with art forms outside writing, it may create new and more inclusive opportunities for young artists. An ecosystemic orientation in writing would involve collaboration, material exploration, and an understanding of apprentice and experienced writers as members of a collective.

Among the artists I interviewed, many did not remain in the genre, medium, method, or professional circumstances in which they began. I found that identity was more of a kaleidoscopic rendering, multicolored, serendipitous, and accidental. Artists "fell into" or discovered mediums in ways that reflected exploratory thinking and making practices that evolved with the artist. Leslie suggested that *exposure* was fundamental to her evolution as an artist: "I was exposed to so many different materials, but I always prided myself on doing drawing, painting, and printmaking. Then, I fell into printmaking."[69] Transitions between mediums were notable and more remarkable for the ways that they changed the manner in which artists observed the world, conceptualized their own identities, and adapted new practices in their work. Claire, a poet, suggested this evolution as a journey across identities:

> I think I was going to be a poet firefighter when I was six. Then of course I was going to be a poet and an oceanographer and then a poet and a lawyer, and a

poet and diplomat, and then a poet and a professional poker player. Then when I started school, I actually had a double major in English and Theatre and I was going to be a poet and actress because that's practical.[70]

Claire gave a humorous and facetious rendering of her evolution as an artist, a journey that flouts linearity and prescriptions. Disciplinary boundaries are tantamount to the boundaries cordoning off identities and bodies in MFA programs.

A dancer and choreographer, Diane, described in detail how her interdisciplinary, multiracial identity as a dancer was enmeshed in collaborations; she discussed her work with musicians, abstract painters, poets, and choreographers. Another dancer, Jasmine, reflected on her evolution as an artist disinterested in the presentational elements of the solo show. She wanted to break proscenium and engage the audience in a participatory journey in a way that captured her experience dancing in Guinea. African and Caribbean dance, as Jasmine pointed out, involves participation and emotional responses that challenge Western notions of the passive, observing audience.[71] Jasmine and Diane both saw the stage as a site for embodying practice or "putting dance on other people" as choreographers. Their engagement with students and audiences was presented as a collaborative and participatory dialogue that advanced toward a more inclusive and interdisciplinary understanding of performance.

As with authorship in the Western tradition, performance appears guided toward the soloist performing rather than toward a more direct engagement with the audience. Collaboration in dance between performer and audience is pivotal in West African dance, for example, but as I spoke with musicians rather than dancers, I also found a holistic approach to performance. Delia and Andrew, a couple collaborating as a violinist and songwriter in a local band, discussed their last recording session as a band and how they were advised by the record producer to see their part in each song as working in conjunction with one another.[72] The band philosophy may be oppositional to the soloist's mentality, an attitude that dominates writing or visual mediums, such as writing or painting. The pure soloist was not a prominent figure among those whom I interviewed, and painters and poets alike collaborated and sought out other mediums from which to draw inspiration. No *one* discipline held the market on collaboration, and whether it was dancers, designers, ceramicists, painters, poets, or actors, each detailed their work with others during their journey and evolution as artists. The findings challenge the popular perception that the MFA in creative writing is about developing individual talent for the literary marketplace. To be clear, writing workshops appear collaborative, but they serve an odd dish of protocol, artifice, and social pressure that is more collaborative-*like*. Cultivating individualism through the guise of the smart, apathetic reader, the workshop falls away from collaboration and defaults to a persona somewhere between slush-pile editor and caring friend. In Chapter 4, I will discuss Felicia Rose Chavez's anti-racist workshop model and its potential for redesigning traditional workshop.

For the moment, though, it's worth entertaining the counterargument that students in creative writing must remain focused on material understanding in specific genre categories because there is little *time* to do anything else during the MFA. Read, read, read. Write, write, write. MFAers read in literature classes and workshop their "stuff" or writing-in-progress in cohorts of peers for a period of two to three years. Such a short time window might be just enough time to write, but I wondered in conducting interviews how the MFA in writing came to be narrowly focused on formalism when the studio arts had already established broader, more integrative, interactive models. Of course, I cannot suggest that studio arts MFAs are without the hierarchies of class, gender, race, sexuality, or ability, but artists spoke candidly about the ways that interdisciplinary models freed them to explore. The findings were clear for creative writing, and stated simply, strict genre boundaries based in formalism and dominant craft discourse have deleterious effects on who can call themselves a creative writer, and it delimits the pedagogical, collaborative, and development of craft consciousness. To preserve dominant craft discourse in its current form and to expand these models of MFA programs in creative writing is to radically limit the potential for an inclusive, anti-racist creative writing education. Talking with a poet-firefighting-oceanographer-diplomat-poker player convinced me that specialization in a genre is an antiquated and exclusive model that can and should be reframed through craft consciousness and through a more integrative, interactive arts or cross-genre approach in creative writing. Writers out-of-category, and those for whom the current program and workshop design has failed, must insist on an alternative model because, along with being based in neocolonialist, patriarchal, capitalist, and white supremacist ideologies, current models do not reflect the nature of arts practice for contemporary artists. Those artists that live and breathe their practice, no matter the discipline, find that collaboration, interactivity, and community serve to support their original visions as artists. Starting with individualist, specialized model of instruction, ironically, does not support the true nature of the labor. Artists search out collaboration and inspiration outside of themselves and as they become someone different again and again and again.

Research One universities in the United States have defined creative writing through specialization. In these larger research-focused institutions, specialization plays a foundational role in defining professional identities for the marketplace, and as a result poets must be poets and fiction writers must be fiction writers for the purpose of tenure and promotion. But what I found to be true on the ground and in the minds of artists in this classification simply doesn't bear this out. Poets must be poets only for the institutional purposes, and perhaps this is why creative writers often published in a second or third genre before heading onto the job market. Among the smaller group of artists I interviewed from Research One universities (three total, one painter, two writers, one of whom was from Australia), specialization was nonessential to their practice. They moved across genres, transitioned between mediums, and showed a propensity for collaboration. There were no negative repercussions for changing genres or mediums. Although the sample size is too small to build out broader conclusions along these lines, it is clear that MFA programs in creative writing do not match the work faculty do as professional artists. The institutionalization discussed in the first section of Chapter 2 serves to remind us of craft's corruption within institutions. How does the institutional apparatus of the MFA program silo creative writers in an infrastructure of socialized disciplinary conditions, genre categories, tenure and promotion criteria, and other infrastructure that's potentially damaging to practice? Reconstructing these institutional and disciplinary structures is no small task, but it requires, first and foremost, a recognition of the nature of artists' process.

Discussion: Craft Consciousness and Artistic Ontologies, Ecosystems, Political Systemics

My findings demonstrate that creative writing MFA programs should transition toward craft consciousness as a process philosophy and conceptual space that better aligns with artistic thinking and the internal nature of practice. By naming an ecosystemic approach, I am referring to the sum and total of interactions in consciousness and the material or conceptual actions undertaken in artistic process. To naturalize writers into practice, rather than a genre, we must see the mind as analagous to nature. The processes of the artistic mind are ecosystemic and should not be dictated by formalism and its emphasis on material objects.

The interviews make clear that craft reflects the interior dimensions of process as it allows artists to migrate across mediums through an evolving artistic practice that is interactive, collaborative, and iterative. Craft consciousness builds through theory *and* praxis, through theoretical renderings that define consciousness (Chapter 2) and through conversations with living artists (Chapter 3). These findings will never be fully complete and must be replenished as craft reconfigures itself through future definitions and in response to the specific sociocultural conditions artists work in. The present findings do confirm, however, that creative writing has missed the process-turn in art and that MFA programs are outmoded and oppositional to the ways artists think. Like artists in the studio arts, MFA programs in creative writing are situated in local cultures based in a diverse set of geographical, departmental, institutional, and cultural contexts. Given these circumstances, what is needed is a varied approach to workshop, program design, and collaboration. Although it was not the objective of this study, scholars must investigate creative writing programs in the United States in order to determine how they compare to international programs. Future qualitative studies could prove that innovations exist beneath the surface of dominant craft. Dominant craft sets up writers to imagine identity as a fixed ideological-artistic-institutional position when it is, in practical terms, a process of becoming.

Craft operates across consciousnesses in ways that reflect differently at different times in an artist's life. The migrations discussed in the findings section are bound to more than identity or discipline, and they move within an artist's changing sense of process and explorations from project to project. Training creative writers under the banner of genre does not serve the long game, and it is my argument that craft consciousness incorporates *process philosophies* and insights from formal, generic, material, or cultural contexts outside of writing. For creative writing to become a more inclusive field predicated on practitioner knowledge (i.e., Mayers's *craft criticism*), we need to see new prototypes emerge in workshop and in MFA/PhD program design.

Designing creative writing workshop and programs through craft consciousness allows students to more easily access collaborative partnerships, form meaningful peer and faculty relationships, and draw forward process philosophies that embolden students to take risks. Rather than cowing writers into line with literary tradition and workshop protocol, the defining features of the MFA should be flexibility, reciprocity, and inclusivity. Jenni Sorkin references the legacy of the Arts and Crafts Movement and the vast and diverse network of craftspeople it represents. To move beyond *craftlike* or those activities that reference craft without "doing craft," creative writing must embrace the radical feminist intervention that craft represents. Subverting institutional, patriarchal, colonialist, and capitalistic evocations of craft would mean eliminating the distortions and exclusions the term currently supports in MFA programs.[73] Among the critics and apologists of creative writing alike, there is a tendency to see craft as the stiffened rationale for institutionalization or as a distinguishing marker of specialization in a genre. These connotations are far from innocuous; they directly affect artists as the interview findings suggest, and these external impediments serve up the term as an intrusion like marketing fodder rather than as a radical intervention. The intervention should place processism before (or in complement to) materialism. Processes, interactions, and explorations educate the writer as an artist. The writer navigates a plurality of consciousnesses and process philosophies through the internal and external forces that surround their labor, and these consciousnesses form a nexus in craft and they determine— more than an MFA degree—*what it is to be an artist.*

Gary Alan Fine can be forgiven for bemoaning the loss of training in technique in the MFA in studio arts because his sentiments are echoed in the materialist nostalgia of John Ruskin's sentiments of the dawn of the Arts and Crafts Movement. In the hands of William Morris and those influenced by his nineteenth-century philosophies, craft held the radical potential to be anti-industrial, anti-capitalistic, and even anti-colonialist. Future iterations would domesticate or categorically dismiss the term as the labor of women and other marginalized artists. The craft artists I interviewed sometimes accepted characterizations that differentiated them from fine artists, nonetheless, they resisted technical reductions or imagined ways to circumnavigate the idea through sharp metaphors or analogies. Fundamentally, external criteria and social expectations drive the term toward domination and exclusions that are harmful. The injury to the writer detaches them from the object *and* the writer from other artists. Artist interviews, oral histories, and craft criticism recover what is taken from marginalized artists. These resources intersect through process and will work against neat and easy prescriptions of the identity and culture of an artist. Utilizing craft criticism and intersectional aesthetic traditions beyond dominant craft in the classroom will alleviate some of the pressure exerted on marginalized artists. Practically speaking, definitions based in formalism, materialism, or technical discourse operate to reduce the breadth of methods for making for writers. The findings signal a shift toward process that's overdue, and it remains to be seen how craft consciousness can be applied to writing program design, teaching contexts, and artists' collaborations.

Conclusion

No qualitative study design is perfect. But I found through the interviews my study of the veracity of what I suspected, namely that craft consciousness is observable through the verbalizations artists give to their thinking. The multidimensionality of craft consciousness is not easy to embody or teach. It invites creative writers to integrate process and composing philosophies from outside of their discipline and in a way that is akin to an internal ecosystem. Ecosystems exhibit dynamic changes and processes that happen across (and because of) *interactions*. Craft consciousness represents those available processes and deep store consciousness that the artist can put into action. To develop this internal awareness, the potential energy of the developing artist must be supported through teaching that is not yet prominent in graduate programs in creative writing. These new mechanisms can be activated through existing structures—the workshop and the program—but they can also be discovered through collaborations that broaden creative writing into art and science.

In Chapter 4, I draw forward pedagogical and programmatic applications for craft consciousness. In this effort I will rely on the pedagogical scholarship from Janelle Adsit's *Inclusive Creative Writing* and Felicia Rose Chavez's book *The Anti-Racist Writing Workshop: How to Decolonize the Creative Writing Classroom*. Both Chavez and Adsit seek to shift the pedagogical dimensions of workshop and educational practices in creative writing toward a more decolonized, anti-racist, and inclusive model. Chavez speaks to the challenge before creative writing studies scholars, namely, dismantling structure built for exclusion; she writes,

> Admitting that neutrality does not exist—that we currently fuel politicized, race-based writing workshops—is the first and most important step toward change. To bring down the monument of white-centered ideology, we've got to dismantle not only the pedagogical infrastructure of white bias, but also the white supremacist ego of domination and control behind the decision-making.[74]

The neutrality of craft is a myth. Painted over or elided in this myth are the ways of making that are cultural and socially embedded and that do not prescribe to current workshop models based in material outcomes. Using Felicia Rose Chavez, Janelle Adsit, and Matthew Salesses's research as support for my argument, I will present pedagogical imperatives based in craft consciousness and its stride toward equity. Additionally, I will begin to draw conversations on workshop into broader questions of graduate program design using Keller

Easterling's book *Medium Design*. Easterling's argument aligns with processism and the dynamic change and *interactivity* necessary to train creative writers. From the concept of medium design, and using an urbanist's spatial vision, Easterling argues that we distinguish between the disposition of objects and their interaction with space, humans, and their natural surroundings. Medium design expresses itself in complement to craft consciousness insofar as it suggests that objects' orientation, arrangement, and connection to space and the artist matter more than its thingness. As it applies to creative writing, medium design and craft consciousness prioritize what Gilbert Ryle calls "know how" rather than "know that."[75] Through expanding the field from its roots in literature, craft consciousness highlights the interactions and activities that artists undertake in their labor. It presupposes that mediums and forms morph through their multiple uses and as they are situated in different contexts. How we build creative writing programs in the future will depend upon how they function for those participants and faculty that populate them. To this point, creative writing has neglected the diverse and dynamic cosmologies of artists who study and mentor in graduate programs. The spirit of Chapter 4 defines craft consciousness as a term of renewal from which new collaborative potentials are born. For creative writers, collaboration with scientists and other artists, may define the field for decades. From the research of the final chapter, I hope to draw writers toward practicalities and imaginative futures in line with craft consciousness.

4

Craft Consciousness Futures

If you'll remember, this book began inside a bus without any guidelines. It just so happens that tonight, myself and the Physics Bus founder, Erik, will be giving a Zoom presentation to the patrons of a local library. We don't know who will be in the audience, but I do know Erik will be disappointed because the high-flying spectacle he orchestrates will be properly domesticated by an online interface. No propane fireballs and no electric shocks to jolt the kids. No parents wondering about the liability insurance. What I have to rally Erik around is the conversation we're having on craft and DIY science, which he already sees as less valuable than the hands-on work with kids. Their wonderment is a fuel, kinetic energy put in motion to an internal cause rather than external criteria. Lessons lessened. He still runs the Free Science Workshop during the pandemic, and yesterday he showed me a replica of Paul McCartney's electric guitar that a neighborhood kid made with cereal boxes, wire, and paper clips. The kid who made it has perfect pitch and can play any tune he hears by ear. After school, he walks over the Free Science Workshop to tweak this monstrosity of ingenuity and to receive subtle, almost invisible guidance from Erik. These are the lessons of craft. The quiet turn inward is the model we need, what Ralph Waldo Emerson would call our revelatory inner compass, "Trust thyself, every heart beats to that iron string."

Craft consciousness needs practice, needs modeling, needs the need of the artist or scientist to go further. I will convince Erik by the night's end that in the absence of in-person, hands-on experimentation and material exploration, we will have a conversation that helps the audience to recalibrate what we know to be science, and maybe even craft. In what we hope is the waning of the Covid pandemic, the online conversation cannot supplant what could have been. What we can build in the absence of play is the energy for future experimentation. For creative writing, craft consciousness can be revolutionary and radically liberate the ways we teach, design, and collaborate in graduate programs. The purpose of this chapter is to move theory into praxis and to see where it may build new models or paradigms for future workshops and MFA programs. Before setting forth, let's start by reviewing how craft operates in the field and how it may be modified through craft consciousness. First, historical analysis and pedagogical examinations of craft locate the term in technique and oftentimes omit more complex understandings of the term outside of materiality. Materialism animates the dominant ideologies of literary formalism, and it works in lockstep with the institutional and educational codification of craft under the banner of technique or knowledge of literature. Legacies in process philosophies do the essential work of providing an alternative cosmology in process metaphysics and artistic practice. Following from this first point, dominant aesthetic traditions treat craft as oppositional to art, especially fine art, and the rehabilitation of the term becomes possible through bridging intersectional aesthetic traditions and the craft criticism by marginalized or out-of-category artists. Graduate programs in creative writing are programs in the arts, and our histories remain inextricable from studio and craft arts. Contemporary MFA graduate programs in the studio arts are process based, and this reality has yet to reach creative writing because of disciplinary and institutional boundaries erected in the name of specialization and professionalization. Traditions in craft are never removed from the labor of women and those often not otherwise recognized as Artists in the capital sense. The marginalization and overt discrimination of women artists under the moniker of craft may require new or alternative terms like design, though, craft studies scholars have recovered and expanded our conception of the term through drawing it toward performance, embodiment, and the phenomenal consciousness internalized by the artist. Artists are not solitary, as we are often led to believe, and craft consciousness connects them to registers of consciousness inside themselves *and* among the collective of artists. The network of collaborators that support the writer are legion and beyond the scope of literature alone. To define craft consciousness we need to describe an internal awareness to the external criteria that artists traverse in their evolving practice and identities. Drawn from neither a single source nor one specialization, artists explore their identities, and they need a critical heuristic in process to capture what it means to become someone new again and again.

Process philosophies are set in contrast to the Western static categories that separate *techné* (craft) from *episteme* (knowledge) in the Platonic tradition; processism in the philosophical tradition takes as its central notion that *change is perpetual* and what Alfred North Whitehead refers to as the *dynamics of life* are foundational to reality. My argument stands with the evidence gathered from practicing artists that their being is not a static entity, and even late in their careers, they are still becoming artists and exploring new processes and mediums. MFA programs in creative writing and their program architects may argue that there is not *the time* to allow for the exploratory thinking and process philosophies that develop over a lifetime; and as a consequence, funding considerations allocated by genre and rankings remain the vehicle through which we define workshops, programs, funding, and tenure lines. The specialized university program creates the illusions of specialists, and a kind of specialist that remains beholden to teaching students in the categories of their hire. Poets begat poets in a sense, and from this model, we have carved out an institutional legacy in which writers emerge as genre-focused specialists seeking tenure positions in that genre. This circuit is closed, artificial, and even with the most inclusive of intentions, we tend toward the static and are governed by philosophies that tire and focus resources and labor toward a writer-in-kind, more than a thinker. Creative writing education becomes inclusive through craft consciousness, a collective mode of thinking that values collaboration over exclusivity, processes over products, and cultivates an ontological path for apprentice writers who may challenge or experiment with principles in form, genre, process, and aesthetics. In this last chapter, I sketch out ways in which we might imagine *ontological principles in becoming* that map onto those teaching practices, arts processes, and identities that remain dynamic and pliable in writerly development.

Displacing the static teaching begins by investigating further the ways that artists embody craft consciousness as a *thinking practice* and how this modality has the potential to lead toward more inclusive ways of making. Without being predicated on the static nature of the individual as a commodity to be groomed, educators may pivot toward pedagogical innovations that are disruptive to institutional mechanisms bent on the specialized individual. It is worth entertaining another counterargument before proceeding, namely, that we should not be in the business of messing with the interior workings of the artist. One might say that we need not tread into the psychobabble of the head because such teaching may unwittingly alienate or damage the writer's education.

These counterarguments presume we are not damaging apprenticing artists through current workshop practices and pedagogies, and I suggest that we are involved in a fundamentally ideological exercise when we create a course reading list and are silencing writers through workshop methods and program designs that privilege those advantaged already. Bringing the writer to a reexamination of their deepest held beliefs about literature and literary production is foundational to MFA program work in the classroom, and it remains only a step further to invite students toward process philosophies that hold the potential for them to reconsider and reexamine how they produce work. In the second section of this chapter, I examine the ways that craft consciousness practices might inform the teaching of workshop and spaces in the craft seminar or hybrid forms courses. As teachers we have the opportunity to change pedagogical philosophies to align with inclusive practices and processes that invite other art forms and collaborations in. Building on philosophies in craft consciousness, rather than dominant craft discourse, means abandoning the textbooks of craft and inviting living artists (nonwriters) to discuss composition or improvisation. Such teaching is disruptive to the specialist seeking to concentrate in a genre, but it is fundamental to craft's historical action as a form of resistance, transgression, and it positions us to fight against industrialization, capitalism, and even environmental injustice. Craft consciousness is a pedagogical method that envisions the writer as a perpetual generalist who adapts, improvises, and finds making principles where they can and how they desire. Seen in the light of the pedagogical and ontological, the final section of the chapter speculates about institutional frameworks where interdisciplinary, postdisciplinary, and transdisciplinary knowledge can be shared from within and outside the academy. More than vocabulary that radiates with academic splendor, these concepts are meaningful in detaching dominant craft discourse from the mechanisms of oppression. Drawing on examples from institutional settings, the final section synthesizes the ways that material conditions in creative writing can find articulation with other art forms and disciplines, especially the sciences. Through these points of realignment, craft consciousness activates thinking, teaching, and spaces we occupy in schools and through artistic practice. New creative writing programs can be established outside the United States to use craft consciousness to inform workshops, new courses, and the interdisciplinary relationship between creative writing and other practitioners. Perhaps creative writing's movement beyond literary studies becomes an engagement in practitioner disciplines outside the university and among those whose art is non-academic and whose insights offer us engagement with new communities.

This book has tussled and labored with the old oppositions that mire craft in standardization, commodification, and institutionalization, and this last chapter serves to propose changes that lead to new futures for the field. In this effort, I will begin with teaching and lean on the work of Janelle Adsit, Felicia Rose Chavez, and Matthew Salesses who, among other insights, have drawn sharper focus to the ways that workshop, programs, and craft can become inclusive and anti-racist. Their scholarship demonstrates practical ways forward and it names the unnamed, the operating assumptions of the literary canon, dominant aesthetics, and the separation of artists of color from their own process through white supremacy. My effort in this chapter is to redouble their research and to find ways to integrate the liberatory ethos of craft consciousness into the workshop. To draw craft consciousness into the pedagogical motives against racism, sexism, ableism, homophobia, and other forms of discrimination, the old way of understanding craft has to be discarded and recast in the name of greater freedom for all writers. How that happens—how we reclaim craft in the name of something better—requires a collective of future creative writing studies scholars and artists to return to the term with new eyes. As Chavez writes, workshop operates on a lot of "assumed knowledge" and it is through interrogating the values that we share that creative writing can reassess "the good" of its educational mission.[1]

Building from Chavez and Adsit's research, the second section of this chapter engages more fully with the elements of program design by using theorist Keller Easterling's concept of *medium design*. A kindred concept to craft consciousness and processism more broadly, medium design articulates one of the pivotal facets of craft consciousness: the interplay between objects and organisms. Medium design, like craft consciousness, draws artists away from materialist assumptions, and toward the ways that people, objects, and their activities correlate to dynamic processes and use. Applied to creative writing program design, craft consciousness and medium design require artists to build new kinds of MFA programs that are nonspecialized and bound to process and to experimentation across thresholds in consciousness. Designing undergraduate and graduate programs requires a specific understanding of the local culture, student populations, and institutional orientation of an MFA program. My objective is to sketch out considerations that allow for the activities and practices in craft consciousness to be supported within MFA programming. The final section of the chapter serves to affect the motives of collaboration between artists and scientists. The future of creative writing lies in displacing Western notions of the individual artist and facilitating opportunities for collaboration and partnerships with the scientific community. The Anthropocene and the current environmental disaster require an urgency of a magnitude not known before in human history. Artists bring more than awareness to environmental justice causes—they represent translators of form, storytellers, and shifters of consciousness that may shake the world from its self-destruction. Collaboration across disciplines and the fields of science and art may be one of the last ways we can hope to reach a crisis point where collective, international efforts will be taken to save us. Craft consciousness draws us toward the ambitious objectives above, to new workshop models, program designs, and collaborative futures.

Pedagogical Principles in Craft Consciousness

I. Collective Knowledge and Community Building

What do you bring with you to workshop as a writer? What Felicia Rose Chavez calls "cultural and creative heritage" remains undiscussed and invisible in current workshop models at the graduate level.[2] Our "assumed knowledge" of literature, craft, and workshop locates itself in materialist legacies of formalism and is built to disqualify many from the literary elite. This reality makes workshop pedagogy a didactic, formulaic continuation of exclusions in art. Felicia Rose Chavez, in her book *The Anti-Racist Workshop: How to Decolonize the Creative Writing Classroom* (2021), outlines the fundamental assumptions that underlie current workshop practices silencing the BIPOC writer. Although a graduate cohort may come from different states, countries, and upbringings, writing workshop is laser-focused on two elements: the submission and the author. Our assumptions about what we mean we talk about literature or craft appear undifferentiated from one student to the next. By necessity it would seem, and to remain artificially objective, workshop students are told to concentrate on the material of the text itself. Students arrive to workshop and to an understanding of literature and craft by default and by legacies not written by them or for them. From the beginning of coursework, MFA programs build toward author *differentiation* and against developing an inclusive cohort. Graduate cohorts are socialized and oftentimes come to love and support each other through workshopping and off-campus events that surround and encompass their activities. In *Talking Art*, Gary Alan Fine discusses this socialization process and its connection to admiration, sexual desire, intellectual stimulation, friendship, and professional support (editing, brainstorming, discussion). If claiming authorship forms the center of the MFA, it does so to elevate the individual over the collective in the name of professionalization. Collectivity is seen as "good" for socializing and "bad" when writers must consider their peers as competition. A literary tradition that alienates disabled, non-hetero, indigenous, classed, and gendered writers is further intensified by the social conditions that dislocate MFA peers from each other.

As a fiction writer in MFA workshops, I was struck by my cohort's radically different sense of what literature even was. For some writers it meant bestselling fantasy and for others it meant lyrical flash fiction. I found it strange we never wrote collaboratively (though I shouldn't have been), and it was only through speaking in workshop that we rendered our affiliations and ambitions to the world. We were satellites that began orbiting different professors in a similar time–space galaxy that shared common aesthetic ground. I never accessed the network of referrals and mentorship because I associated it with the punitive. I had been kicked out of college once, worked in a green bean cannery in the summertime where we knew if we got injured, we'd be fired. The MFA program was a mystifying enterprise where I was labeled as a farm kid from Wisconsin who wrote like blue-collar folk. I felt honored, in a way, to be different than the class of writers around me, and being white and male gave me the same privileges I felt in the cannery where I was offered promotion from the cleanup crew, not based on seniority but based on my whiteness. Still, when I came to the workshop, I felt that my peers' version of literature was curated to fit their identities and class traditions, not mine. I wanted to write stories with a wild sense of control and to yield to their insights because I was the understudy, the kid who grew up eating venison or the fish we caught. These stories could have been welcomed into the hearts of my peers, but often they led me back to where they wanted to me to go, to a refinement and to engagement with craft that mimicked their version of literature. Be more Hemingway, be more Steinbeck. It translated for me as—write like the version of literature we know. Be *that*, not you.

Alienation through workshopping is not an ideological-pedagogical anamoly. And for those who are differentiated in workshop because of their race, gender, sexuality, and upbringing, the assimilation to the norms of literature and dominant craft appears as an irrefutable necessity. I was a puppy in workshop. I would contort to everything everyone said in feedback, and I wanted desperately to please and be pleasing with what I wrote. What I was left with was Frankenfiction, self-parody, being a hick and hayseed for my readership, so I might approximate their love for Ray Carver. The readership of workshop pivots toward the middle brow because it has yet to acknowledge the cultural and creative heritages MFA students use to define literature for themselves. Felicia Rose Chavez discusses how she and students of color have to shield themselves from biased assumptions and cultural and creative heritage of the white supremacist literary arts tradition. If a cohort doesn't intervene through their discussions, dominant literary tradition bends the writer under its heft.

How can a cohort negotiate the living organism of contemporary literature as practitioners without pressing the writer into a dominant tradition that is alienating?

I received my MFA program acceptance based on my background as a lower-middle-class white male writer, and it stood to reason that those professors that identified with my position were drawn to my work and approved of it. Other program faculty were aggressively dismissive of my submission on the grounds that they were in poor taste ("classed") or not consistent with the dictates of realism ("surreal or mystical"). I remember distinctly a long workshop discussion on a story I wrote from the perspective of a dog, not his point of view, but simply a thinly veiled story about a barn dog named Mr. Bill that came with the deed to our farmhouse. The workshop leader hated it with an announced loathing he verbalized, and I received emails from my peers afterward as condolence. A sweet gesture, not given to everyone. I learned that dogs may never be characters, and I moved on in my puppy dog way taking workshop feedback as commands. Reflecting now as a teacher, the opportunity lost was for a discussion of how we define literature and what literature can be about. Can literature draw itself to characters not often seen in literature (barn dogs) or to those human and nonhumans at the margins? I wanted to make visible the story of those unseen because I saw *that* as the function of literature. What we missed was a conversation among the collective about what constitutes literature. That conversation does not happen when the writer is silenced and made an accessory to the drive to *tear a story apart*. Felicia Rose Chavez provides an analysis of this silencing and its implications for writers of color. Workshop upholds dominant white, Western aesthetics through conscious and subconscious gestures and procedures. She writes,

> Whether consciously or subconsciously, we shun artists into self-imposed silence in order to prevent them from succeeding on their own terms, insisting instead that they judge their work according to our personal values and assumptions. For artists of color, workshop can function as a rite of erasure, tyrannizing self-expression into silence in order to reinstate and reproduce (white) creativity, (white) imagination, and (white) autonomy. Seen in this light, criticism becomes more about the individual egos of workshop participants than about the art being workshopped.[3]

It's easy to dismiss personal anecdotes of workshop, which vary from program to program and student to student, still, white supremacy and domination is upheld by both the procedures of workshop and the ideologies of Western individualism. To develop a voice, an individual pursuit, creates in the cohort a striving for differentiation that gets gummed up in a defense of dominant aesthetics. Exclusions are made based on tastes and through chats that arrange cohorts into racial, gendered, and classed hierarchies that mirror the inequities of our culture. The desire to uphold aesthetic and literary traditions is a legacy of white supremacy, gendered subjugation, and the domination of the marginalized through an educational apparatus. Craft consciousness can intervene, and it presents the collective, the network, and the community as non-oppositional to the writer. Doesn't each writer's understanding and production of work depend on the formations in consciousness they navigate? What greater benefit to the cohort is there than to hear how each defines literature and their writing process?

A creative writing cohort that builds toward a collective serves the individual *and* the group of peers simultaneously. Inclusive pedagogical practices have been examined by creative writing and craft studies scholars, and future research across fields should strengthen intersectional aesthetic coalitions, processist principles, and teaching spaces where *collectivity* displaces a laser focus on the *individual*. Workshop could provide a space that includes non-hierarchical teaching and exploratory modes of making. In *The Anti-Racist Workshop*, Chavez practices this community building through nurturing trust and collective agency; she writes, "To foster a supportive arts community, participants must exercise joint ownership of the writing workshop. This goes beyond sharing physical space. Real community is collective rather than individualistic, active rather than passive, centered on trust rather than transaction." Trust building is not easier once students enter an MFA program where competition and professionalization hang over the socialization process. Felicia Rose Chavez, Janelle Adsit, and Matthew Salesses provide a incisive and elaborate set of teaching practices that lead toward an inclusive, communal space for workshopping. In particular, I would draw attention to chapter four in Chavez's book, chapter three in Adsit's book, and Salesses's chapter on "Alternative Workshops." From their thorough set of pedagogical practices and models, I argue that collaborative writing, or cowriting, should take a central role in early MFA workshops. Why? If students build together, as the examples from artist interviews demonstrate, they are likely to be challenged in their way of thinking about literature. How does craft consciousness reconfigure itself in light of the mind of another writer? Why am I invested in a particular aesthetic approach? Where do traditions in canonical literature mirror or differentiate themselves from marginalized aesthetic traditions? To produce contemporary literature means understanding the past within the present and determining how our assumptions mingle and modify with the mind of a collaborator. The socialization process in MFA programs moves quickly, repetitively, and obsessively into differentiating one writer from another. What if a new process delivered a way to build inclusion into the workshop method, craft discussions, and program design?

Stepping toward collaborative arts production appears transgressive, if not heretical in workshop models because aesthetic domain is ceded to the egoist, not to the collective. Workshops are a form of intentional community that skew toward dysfunction and toxicity when they foster competition with a capitalist shrewdness.

As a formative community for the writer, MFA programs should move toward "occasions of experience" in Whitehead's concept where peers are encouraged to migrate toward collaboration and processes that expand their understanding of literature *and* art. Foundationally, a cohort is built on experiences that are traversed through workshops and seminars that oftentimes polarize textual interpretation and textual production. Process and artistic practice are left outside the workshop door, which feels very un-workshop. Chavez points to this phenomenon, and in her workshop, she focuses writers on process, practice-based activities that return creative writers to the embodied activity, that is, writing. She asks students to handwrite, to freewrite, to return to the corporeal of the making process. Chavez models how craft consciousness can be expressed in workshop. It is a space of discovery that hinges on the building of a community, first, foremost, and forever. Within this nurturing community, writers are free to define craft in terms they understand, and eventually, these definitions change based on conversations with each other. She writes,

> It is not merely a small gesture; inviting students to collectively define craft concepts—concepts that will guide their reading of one another's texts, inform their workshop critique, and direct their self-evaluations—is, in practice, an unprecedented act of acceptance: they belong, for real. Engage them as individuals, exercise their critical thinking skills, and collaborate on communal knowledge construction. In doing so, we ensure that every workshop is reflective of its participants, as opposed to our personal perspectives.[4]

Constructing understandings of craft through conversations together, the MFA cohort develops a critical vocabulary that can be shared and expanded through exploring process from outside of writing. The term "craft consciousness" applies to the higher order work of building knowledge as a network, and it flies in the face of the competitive, individualistic drive at the heart of current models. Competition is currently seen as the stimulant to productivity rather than an impediment to writers.

One wonders how cohorts might change the exclusionary principles animating workshops and programs if they pivoted toward collective action, collaboration, and an investigation of intersectional aesthetic traditions. Collectivity is summarily eliminated from the institutional apparatus of the MFA program. *There isn't the time, only time to write.* Time is used as a rationale for expediency, and it suggests that MFA students are invested in an MBA-like model of self-entrepreneurship. This his sentiment amplifies a legacy of pedagogy that is invested not in the whole but more in determining the value of competing artistic visions. Artists-in-training need not be cordoned off from their peers, and it's obstructive for writers to imagine their work apart from collaboration. Adopting craft consciousness and a processist philosophy to workshop allows students to interrogate basic question of literary and aesthetic traditions and its supporting vocabulary in dominant craft. No cohort becomes inclusive through dominant craft discourse, and craft consciousness generates an alternative social, pedagogical, and collaborative workshop and program ethos. As suggested by countless writers of color, the MFA is a site where design, traditions, and histories of literature signify BIPOC writers and their practice as outside of taste and their presence is seen only in elective concessions, rather than as a foundation. Workshop is not where submissions are reviewed and feedback given—it is a site where bodies are negotiating a presence or absence—and the collective *makes* (or eliminates) space for each artist. Process philosophies provide the opportunity to negotiate across formations in consciousness and to integrate new invention practices (Vitanza, Hawk), disrupt oppositional consciousness (craft vs. art), and determine traditions that are germane to the community. In Chapter 2, we discussed the formations in consciousness as material consciousness (material knowledge), phenomenal consciousness (experience), sense consciousness (of the body and senses), and store consciousness (the deep-seated sense of self). To this point, material consciousness dominates the sway of creative writing workshops and programs, and this legacy devotes itself to the individual while it gives lip service to community building. Craft consciousness reimagines the program and workshop in the tradition of women and marginalized artists who have been undervalued and elided in the drive for training that is devoted to the solitary white male author in the Western aesthetic tradition. How does craft consciousness serve the whole while it allows the individual writer the agency to explore the thresholds of consciousness? Bringing their experience, their sense of being in the world, their knowledge of art, the writer communes with their peers in an open, collaborative space. Writers develop agency through explorations that allow them to play and pry through those traditions in art that are determined by them and for them. This section, with the focus on collaboration and collective knowledge building, lies at the nexus of craft consciousness and the historical legacies of women and writers out of category. From Chapter 2, we know these legacies form a lens for making contemporary literature, and it will be the work of this chapter to further map this framework onto workshop methods, program design, and collaborations with artists and scientists.

II. The Nature of Workshop: Multiplicities and Contradictions in Space

More than any other feature, it is *power* that defines the writing workshop environment, and it is power that faculty and peers may or may not wield when they discuss a writer's submission. Traditionally, the workshop leader structures critique in the Socratic fashion whereby the faculty member becomes the implicit determinant of aesthetic value. Silenced, sequestered from the discussion, the author retreats to become the proxy benefactor of the discussion. Felicia Rose Chavez points to the problems in this traditional workshop procedure and how it serves to disenfranchise writers of color through social and aesthetic domination. She writes,

> Normal workshop caters to (white) creativity, (white) imagination, and (white) autonomy on the page, safeguarding "pure art" from the thorny nuisance of politics … Incorrect workshop leaders teach their students of color to read and write by cleaving their consciousness in two, prioritizing the normal, white perspective above their own, abnormal, perspective.[5]

The traditional workshop is a space of pro forma and not given to play or exploratory pedagogies or politics. Chavez points to the ways this method shepherds writers toward a middle ground of the apolitical and to the production of literature that appeases the white imaginarium. How can this power imbalance be reimagined? In an essay for *New Writing: The International Journal of Theory and Practice of Creative Writing*, I discuss an alternative to the Socratic method. In a *neosophistic workshop*, the facilitator invites participants to examine contradictions, points of tension, or aesthetic recommendations in their feedback to a writer on a submission.[6] In a neosophistic model, a model developed in the tradition of Plato's rivals the sophists, the workshop professor does not implicitly or explicitly become the determinant of aesthetic taste. Claire, a poet I interviewed, described an alternative model that parallels the neosophistic model and argues for the principle of multiplicity.[7] She never makes a determination of whether a workshop submission is "good or bad"; and instead, she asks students to render multiple readings and multiple directions for a poem. The effect of an approach that draws multiplicity and contradictions to the fore allows the workshopee to act upon the revisions that serve the poem rather than readers. When aesthetics are overly determined by the leader and readings are domesticated in order to map onto the workshop leader's aesthetic, the submission ossifies and becomes rigid to rewriting. For workshops, a neosophistic or a reading approach that emphasizes multiplicity renders feedback in a mode that is more process based. Claire tells students she is happy to tell them after class whether she thinks a poem is bad or good, but she realizes the space is freighted with her identity as the implicit arbiter of aesthetics. Her restraint is far more constructive than we realize at first glance.

Workshop feedback has a way of excluding potentialities in rewriting, and it serves to narrow contributions to those verbal performances that align aesthetic values to match those of the workshop leader, a point discussed extensively in Anna Leahy's edited collection *Power and Identity in the Creative Writing Classroom* (2005).[8] No matter their qualifications or author status, workshop leaders appear destined to make the final aesthetic or constructive judgment of a submission. And why shouldn't they? What is author status if not an intellectual-artistic rank above student apprentice? The problem with this rationale remains with the workshopee and their need to develop a consciousness of craft. The judgment, as the poet Claire argues in her interview, positions the workshop leader as the arbiter of taste rather than the facilitator interested in the expansive possibilities of the submission in the writer's hands. Where the revised submission can go is premised not on fixing it or appeasing the faculty leader but in introducing new potentialities. Submissions function as test cases that need not be evaluated for publishability or act as a placeholder for one's status in the social hierarchy. Workshops formatted in the Socratic tradition are positioned to do the work of establishing aesthetic and social hierarchies. They don't provide a capacious avenue in reimagining a submission's next iteration, and they may condition the artist to align the next submission with demands of the cohort or workshop leader. The social order may begin to dictate the terms of craft more than an internal sense of what the story or poem wants to be. More potentially destructive is the way that feedback in the Socratic tradition delimits the constructive or process principles at work in the submission. As readers, the workshop cohort tends toward consensus, and we have taken this value as an occasion to negotiate meaning in a submission draft as opposed to volunteering more energy in its *future value*. The future of a submission is predicated on revitalizing and expanding the author's efforts in exploring the piece: its formal components, its content, scenes, causation, and the processes negotiated in a second or third pass through. We eliminate the author from conversations about a submission in order to eliminate their *intention* from corrupting our reading. Allowing the author back into the conversation feels conciliatory and an afterthought in many workshops. Participants often hold tightly to close reading strategies while they arrange themselves in the social order, and these activities marginalize practitioner knowledge and curtail the development of craft consciousness. How else might they be tasked? If peers were given a writer's submission in order to rewrite and rethink them as pieces of their own imagination, material consciousness could be explored in a way that shifts the power of workshop into the writer's hands.

Before discussing the details of an *improvisatory workshop*, it's worth pausing to ask a simple question: What workshop models may form in the vacuum created by the displacement of the traditional Socratic workshop method? As noted in the previous section, one way to move the pedagogical compass away from the fetishizing of the individual is to have workshop function as a space of exploration. In the second half of this section, I identify workshop models that reflect craft consciousness. Models for workshop are more variable than they first appear, but the permissions to explore new methods for workshopping make tradition the default. In constructing new models, the fine and performing arts are logical sites for searching out new ways of teaching writers. Developing artists are trained across disciplinary structures and practitioner knowledge is shared in the spaces of critiques, studios, and design contexts. From the previous chapter, I discussed the ways that fine and performing arts programs operate with process and material-conceptual exploration at the center of their mission. Process-based workshops are the norm in composition studies, so why is there such a fidelity to traditional workshop and its obsession with material outcomes, when spaces for making and providing feedback take on a variety of forms across the arts?

For creative writing, the *improvisatory workshop* mentioned above is a good place to start as it involves cowriting and collaboration that can translate for undergraduate and graduate students. An improvisatory workshop tasks the peers with rewriting and rethinking a submission in workshop. After a student submits their work, peers begin the process of revising the work according to their understanding of the material, phenomenal, sense, and other formations in consciousness. Should they remain true to the submission's spirit or can they generate something that departs from the original? Peer feedback is *not* action—though the traditional workshop would have us believe it is—and workshop participants who take the action to rewrite a submission devote to the action of the mind more than the mouth. What appears as a sacrilege to the notion of individual authorship actually stretches peers to consider their aesthetic choices in light of authorial intention or in their *perception* of authorial intention.

Workshop participants, in this arrangement, can be prepared by reading sections of Janelle Adsit and Renée Byrd's *Writing Intersectional Identities: Keywords in Creative Writing* (2019), which outlines the challenges in *representation* and assuming identities, subjects, characters, forms, and aesthetic traditions that may not be their own. The process of rewriting someone else's work affords them the opportunity to access experiences and senses in the world that deviate from their own. Thinking as a writer means occupying an empathetic, reflexive position of a character, in the case of fiction, or channeling the rhythm of a monologue or interrogating a line break. Each of these choices is explained in the workshop that follows. In this context, and after rewrites are completed, the originating writer leads the workshop and a conversation on what the students produced. In an inversion of the power structure, the writer does not endure the speculations or flippant responses that appear endemic to traditional workshop. Peers must discuss the choices they made and why they made them. How did they avoid appropriation or essentializing a character with a disability? Where do they lack knowledge of literary traditions outside those they identify with? By transposing authority to the writer, the improvisational workshop sparks a discussion of how craft decisions get made through the lens of cultural studies and intersecting aesthetic traditions. How does occupying a character of a different gender challenge their understanding? Where do they locate the challenges in representation cited by Adsit and Byrd, and how do they anticipate moving past them to develop a more nuanced and complex understanding of material and phenomenal consciousness?

In the ideal scenario, these questions create a productive crisis in the consciousness of the writer. But this crisis is indispensable and it brings to light the double consciousness that writers from nondominant traditions face under the thumb of dogmatic, exclusionary literary or aesthetic traditions. Students take risks in this model, they learn, they get flustered writing through stretching their own phenomenal consciousness. Material explorations restore agency to the writer who, after dispersing their original submission, provides context to peers about the submission and then listens to the conversation about the submission and its complementing rewrite. The workshop leader acts as facilitator by guiding the workshop back to points of disagreement or discomfort. Improvisatory workshops, like the neosophistic model, serve the critical function of restoring agency to the writer through unsilencing them and encouraging the faculty member to support the development of craft consciousness through exploratory, collaborative play. Without devoting time to minutiae or highly speculative verbal feedback in the traditional workshop, peers take their suggestions to the writer in the form of conversation *and* an attempted rewrite. By triangulating between material, phenomenal, and access consciousness, the writer develops a mind for the work of revision with content that did not originate in their own mind. The benefit of this approach shifts the power of the workshop within the cohort who would otherwise stand in judgment of a submission. In place of a verdict or an aesthetic evaluation, peers are summoned to action with text. They have to *assay* using the original submission, and in this action, the writer hears from peers as collaborators in craft; this persona change from editor to peer makes the space more functionally "a workshop." Through the process-based model of the improvisatory workshop, peers can adapt the piece of writing beyond the textual to non-discursive artifacts. What if a peer created a poem in response to a flash fiction piece or a poem became a video essay? Processes are the cornerstone of workshops, and it becomes *mutually* enriching when writer and peer move beyond the perfunctory exercise of reading and responding.

To my point, when *play* becomes pedagogically grounded in improvisational workshops, it generates alternatives and adaptations that were never possible before. In the words of David O'Grady, a researcher at UCLA's Game Lab, "games are born out of adaptation, they live in the adaptations of those who play them, and they perish when they no longer prove adaptable … Play, in short, is a subversive act."[9] As O'Grady suggests, workshop has become a game that appears no longer adaptable. Tired and mechanical. Play in workshop subverts the materialist and formalist dogma that determines the value of the writer and the writer's submission. Valuation of a submission on the grounds of past literary or aesthetic traditions is no longer sufficient; it eliminates process, excludes the writer it's supposed to benefit, and forces the cohort into a game of justling for social hierarchy. Craft consciousness plays with the permissions of workshop, and it challenges the traditional model by suggesting that the focus is on internal awareness of the writer and the community that surrounds them. The good of creative writing is not finding out whether your stuff is any *good*—because who knows for sure—rather, it lies in helping the writer examine the formations in craft consciousness and how they can enact them through practice.

Workshops based on play disrupt a focus on the individual author, and it sets the parameters for an inclusive cohort that operates on potentials and interactions rather than on judgments. Additionally, program faculty may consider ways for the MFA cohort to develop methods in workshop that are determined by the participants, what I call an *open workshop method*, much like an open syllabus. In this model, workshop participants in a given context select the method of workshopping that best serves them. For the faculty member, this model can be adapted to principles of craft consciousness and draw from workshops models based in the arts. Felicia Rose Chavez develops the *anti-racist workshop* in the mold of process philosophies and craft consciousness. With experience in studio arts culture herself, Chavez has adapted the Liz Lerman model from dance choreography to her own anti-racist writing workshop. For Chavez, the Lerman model is anti-racist because it allows the writer to take ownership and agency regarding their submission. She writes,

> Lerman delineates three specific workshop roles: facilitator (or workshop leader), artist, and responders. The artist moderates the workshop discussion, but it is the facilitator who guides the process along, intervening step-by-step to help the artist and responders more clearly articulate their ideas. This goes beyond checking students when they deviate from the process; it's our responsibility as workshop leaders to confront and challenge students' racist, sexist, classist, and homophobic behavior clearly, directly, and in the moment. Yet it's equally emboldening for the artist to shut that shit down. How many times do we as people of color want to say something, but we can't, or we don't, or we won't, out of fear?[10]

Chavez's adaptation of the Lerman method demonstrates how workshop methods can create a more inclusive environment, a workshop space that need not originate in the traditions of English Studies. Writing workshops can serve like studio spaces in the arts where production takes place in physical space and through a socialization into craft consciousness. Workshops framed by craft consciousness move toward collective practice, collaboration, and processes by pushing artists toward new disciplines and literary forms. A workshop conceptualized in this manner deviates toward improvisatory, collective, and inter- or transdisciplinary motives governed by artists working together to bring agency to the writer. Creative writing workshops utilizing a craft consciousness model become inclusive because they are considerate of processes, identities, and traditional wisdom not conventionally positioned to do the labor of art making in dominant craft discourses and traditional workshops. Who produces and how they produce it becomes central and it pushes the cohort of artists away from a funneling toward the exclusions or taste-making that defines genre, form, and the discipline. Local cultures in MFA programs should have the freedom to consider models of workshop that can be constructed and adapted to their needs on the ground. The inheritance of workshop is based in traditions that have impeded and constrained the ways writers are socialized into artistic practice. Alternatively, and in light of craft consciousness, we are beholden to redefine workshop as a site for making where writers construct the parameters of process for them and their cohort. Developing on the neosophistic, improvisatory, open, and anti-racist workshop models, creative writers will develop (and have developed) models that function to redistribute power and bring process to the forefront of workshop procedure. Matthew Salesses rifts on workshop design through his "Alternative Workshop" chapter, and the exercise is an ideal demonstration in what is needed. He advances fourteen workshops in half as many pages, rifting on the traditional workshop with an artist's flair for adaptation.[11] Craft consciousness invites these new workshop models to form around process and inclusive pedagogy, and from these values, new disciplinary coalitions are explored. For the artist, these coalitions can be adapted to the reality of life, a condition in which they are free to transition between materials and disciplines and develop hybrid or emerging forms of expression. The next section transitions toward discussing how MFA program design can reflect craft consciousness and create opportunities for writers to traverse boundaries in form and discipline. How workshops determine method will impact what gets produced by writers, and it is more critical than ever to push the field toward exploring emerging and hybrid forms of writing and non-discursive art traditions.

MFA Program Design + Hybrid and Emerging Forms

How we design the experience of creative writing programs has been determined by a commitment to literary studies and to populating English courses with majors. Undergraduate programs serve the student desire for more creative writing workshops, and I argue that they should continue to fulfill this need while providing a more inclusive and diverse set of pedagogical approaches. Graduate programs are another matter, and they serve a different function in training artists. The design of MFA programs influences the experience of the writer as much as workshop, and in this section, I examine the ways that design philosophies from Keller Easterling may help us to integrate process philosophies and craft consciousness into creative writing. In *Medium Design: Knowing How to Work on the World* (2021), Easterling frames the challenges facing the world and their implications for design. From political division, climate change, and pandemics, Easterling describes the emaciated conditions of our public discourse, which is stuck in oppositional binaries or circulating in constant loops of argument and counterargument. Like AnaLouise Keating's discussion of oppositional consciousness, Easterling proposes an alternative to intractable squabbling, and her approach to design takes interactivity, contradiction, and potentialities as the natural state of things.

Easterling critiques the obsessions of capitalism in materiality, in thingness, in outcomes, and in assessment. These principles have created gross social inequities and interfere with the work of remaking the world in a humane fashion. To her point, Easterling shies away from giving *medium design*, her critical term, a concrete definition, and instead, she describes the conditions from which it emerges, writing, "Rather than prescribing solutions, like buildings, master plans, or algorithms, medium design works with *protocols of interplay*—not things, but parameters for how things interact with each other. For everyone accustomed to looking for solutions, these forms of interplay may be perplexing."[12] By examining the "protocols for interplay," the designer, artist, educator, parent, politician, scientist, activist—anyone—can conceive of "the good" through the process of interaction among humans and nonhuman entities. Processes of interactivity determine design within a medium—not the assembly and distribution of things. Commodities in design are made every day, and from dishwashers to skyscrapers, designers often follow capital toward a design outcome. The artifact. Easterling points to the failures of material consciousness within our political, economic, military, and climate crises. These perpetual states of calamity indicate that humanity is stuck in binaries and loops of discourse that trouble us and push us ever closer to nonexistence. Medium design, like craft consciousness, does not represent a panacea, but it moves us toward processism as it sheds values in materialism. We are inculcated with the value of outcomes, and creative writing is no exception; it educates MFA writers with professional, material outcomes at the center. We *must* publish. These values march writer after writer through MFA programs, but it misses the interplay and potentials that define what it means to be an artist. To recover the mission of creative writing, as I suggested in Chapter 1, means finding a way to engage with the interactive dimensions that bounce the artist through the world. Easterling writes to this point: "Interplay can rewrite an organization, set up interdependencies, or initiate chain reactions. It is the design of platforms for inflecting populations of objects or setting up relative potentials within them. It is less like designing objects and more like adjusting the faders and toggles of organization."[13] Creative writing needs rewriting. Its MFA/PhD programs now span continents, and yet, the interplay, interdependencies, and potentials remain untapped or dormant. To adjust the toggles and faders of creative writing, new relationships must be formed at the program level and through work to explore the dynamic potentials of new partnerships. Interdependencies need not be by-products of MFA programs, and collaborative interactions can become the foundation from which the mission and organization of creative writing is rewritten. The interviews from Chapter 3 demonstrate that artists seek out interactions from beyond their specialized training.

These collaborations with other artists and this need to search for new materials or forms for expression represent the paradigm shift Easterling advocates for in medium design. Craft consciousness inflects on program design in creative writing through a similar mechanism—and as it insists on a more inclusive, intersectional approach to workshop and literary and aesthetic traditions—it also situates interactive processes in consciousness as the foundation for the field. Processes in consciousness are developed (and supported) through explorations and interactions between the artist and the world. The cosmologies of radical craft, with their historical and future potentials to resist capitalistic or institutional overtures, present the potential for new organizational structures. Drawing writers toward an examination of processes, potentials, and interactions outside of the textual is the first step. Writers need literature, but literary studies need not be our only collaborator. In the section that follows I look at specific examples of how the interactions across generic, material, and disciplinary boundaries are reimagined in multi-genre and integrated arts programs.

Interactions across genre boundaries are signaled by shifts in terminology. Multi-genre or cross-genre designations are familiar terms in creative writing, and they name the ability in the design of the program for writers to work between or across literary genres. Oftentimes, MFA programs affiliated with arts colleges and universities, such as CalArts or Pratt, permit writerly migrations. These journeys are not the norm, but they subvert the fidelities to genre in the name of the in-betweens. Programs of a multi-genre or cross-genre nature invite students to the opportunity to bend through genre to locate themselves in prose poetry, lyric essay, or autofiction, for example. Traditions in these between-genre categories have literary traditions and they allow writers to work out-of-category. Nonetheless, according to the AWP Guide to Writing Programs, just thirty programs internationally advertise "cross genre" and only twelve programs list "multi genre" as an MFA concentration.[14] Of course, this doesn't mean that individual programs don't allow students to do cross genre or multi-genre work. It *does* mean, however, that programs are not organized or designed to support the work. If writers and artists compose across genres and disciplines, how can MFA programs reflect the *interactions* and *potentials* that connect textual with non-textual art?

At Ithaca College in Central New York, a new graduate program in "Image-Text" explores the relationship between photo, image, and literature. The program works across disciplinary categories in photography, writing, and design, and students complete practicum courses that extend beyond the discipline they were admitted in (photographer or essayist). Seminar courses utilize an "interdisciplinary framework" and rely on practitioner knowledge and an exploration of arts practice.[15] Students complete critiques, field placements, and theses that demonstrate an affinity between fields and across disciplinary categories. The MFA in Image-Text prepares students to make contributions "to literary and media arts fields, including print and online publication and exhibition, and encompassing experimental fiction, documentary and journalistic practices."[16] Fusing journalism, creative writing, photography, painting, media and digital arts, the Image-Text MFA defines creative writing through its interactions with non-discursive, image-based arts fields. The frailty of this program and others like it are defined by their in-betweenness; in fact, Ithaca College has recently recommended cutting the program for budgetary reasons.

As Easterling might suggest, the Image-Text MFA program does not translate to objects that material culture would like to see as exemplary. What the program does emphasize represents a future thinking that is needed. Literary genres exist between visual and textual frameworks in the digital world, and MFA programs that adapt to this reality are positioned to discuss the question of the moment—how does literature occupy the space between text and image and/or other mediums? A commitment to cross genre or multi-genre approaches in creative writing represents a first step, and it initiates an inquiry into process and interactions that are not just interdisciplinary but post- or transdisciplinary. Strict disciplinarity and specialization, as I have argued, interferes with the explorative and interactive pursuits germane to artistic practice.

The design of the Master of Studies in Creative Writing at the University of Oxford represents a step in the right direction. Coursework in the first year vacillates between fiction, poetry, and drama, and the program draws a careful line between critical analysis and creative production. In the second year, students begin to work on specializations, but the dramatic writing includes radio, television, stage writing, sits alongside fiction, nonfiction, and poetry. Each writer explores the spectrum of genres before choosing one. The migration of writers toward a specialization should be spurred on by a commitment to exposure and exploration of mediums and their processes. In this way, an MFA student need not declare a genre before matriculating and specialization would be backdropped rather than front-loaded in the MFA program. Medium design principles, applied to creative writing programming, suggest that specialization is unnecessary and counterproductive to developing a deeper and broader understanding of process. Applied to a specific medium, craft consciousness should be inclusive of the ways other art forms compose and other artists conceive of their conceptual work. To remain at remove from the intersections across mediums leaves the writer to study literature at the exclusion of other non-textual mediums.

Programs at Pratt Institute, like those at the University of Oxford, Ithaca College, or The School of the Art Institute in Chicago, offer expansive opportunities for writers to explore processes in other art forms. Pratt Institute MFA describes the transdisciplinary movement students undertake, and their website reads,

> Students work in a variety of mediums, lineages and forms, including fiction, poetry, performance, non-fiction, translation, cultural criticism, investigative journalism, documentary, digital media, image/text, and visual practices. We encourage collaboration and the exploration of hybrid approaches to writing a set of interactive processes that can potentially generate new and transformative social spaces.[17]

Interactive processes are essential to the development and socialization of writers. Currently, cross genre, multi-genre, or transdisciplinary writing programs are no more than a unique subspecies of MFA programs that are overwhelmingly dominated by specialization. How can we propagate new MFA program designs more intentionally and in a way that reflects craft consciousness rather than dominant craft discourse?

If we jettison literary studies within MFA program design in exchange for practitioner knowledge in other art forms, don't we risk positioning writing as *production* only and not as a site for interpretation? The process philosophy that grounds craft consciousness must be inclusive of literature, though it fundamentally pivots the teleological cause of creative writing toward processes, interactions, and potentials outside writing. Currently, we write more than we read by most estimates and this frequency, as Deborah Brandt reminds us, changes the social habits of professional writers. We now skew toward production over interpretation in our lives as thinkers.[18] Text is being produced at a rate that is unprecedented in human history, and it remains to be seen how this productive phase will transform our intellectual and artistic lives. I argue that process-based MFAs are designed to provide us with a way *back to reading*, and it brings writers to understanding of literature within the broader interactions and composition practices in other non-textual mediums. Easterling references philosopher Gilbert Ryle's distinction between "knowing what" and "knowing how."[19] The latter form of the knowledge is for practitioners. By moving the *knowing how* to the center of program design and pedagogical implementation, writers are exposed to an ecosystem of processes, materials, and mediums that interact and overlap. Working through forms, genres, and processes captures dynamic change that is endemic to artistic identity and thinking.

Hybrid or interdisciplinary art forms cannot and should not replace traditional literary forms. They can change, however, our perspective on how they interact with readers. As an illustration, I teach an undergraduate bidisciplinary course, "The Video Essay," with a media studies professor and documentarian, Dr. Leah Shafer. In the course, students read and write experimental creative nonfiction essays and produce expressive as well as analytical video essays. The video essay is an emerging form in media studies, and it has legacies in the essay tradition of Montaigne and those essayists who experiment with form such as Rebecca Solnit, Ander Monson, Carol Maso, or Dinty Moore. Essay films, such as Chris Marker, Maya Deren, and Hollis Frampton's work, provide meaningful, productive sites for understanding the process of video essay production. Students are challenged to think about the ways that the video essay does not present *one* definition. And we examine the kaleidoscopic definitions that emerge from the literary tradition, film studies, and the avant-garde. Students experiment with processes through still image manipulation, execute erasure poems, partner-up for in-class performances, learn new sound and visual effects, and create a collaborative video essay in pairs. The course shows them that video production can be more than a supercut or a YouTube vanity project of self-promotion and that the essay tradition protracts into video artifacts that meld essay and film traditions together.

Reinscribing new and old media with life might be one of the teleological "ends" of the field in the next decade based on the creative writing studies scholarship of Trent Hergenrader and Adam Koehler. And it is at our peril that we do not adapt a critical understanding of processes in order to respond to a world that is print and digital.[20] Understanding creative writing through the lens of craft consciousness means building legacies in process, interaction, and potentials that should inflect on how we design MFA programs. How we implement new program designs in creative writing will change how we understand what it means to be an artist in the twenty-first century, a time, Easterling reminds us, that is fraught with crises of a global scale. Seen in light of our world's precipitous destruction, the ability of craft to disrupt destructive processes becomes crucial to understanding our world and our potential extinction. Integrated arts programs and the future collaborations with scientists and other stewards of the natural world will determine the true contribution creative writing can make to the collective good.

Creative Writing Futures in Integrated Arts and Scientific Collaboration

Keller Easterling argues as a processist that we must apply our efforts to the *interplay*, not to the object. We are at sea in a surfeit of things, mostly disposable, that encourage us to ignore *processes* of production. As Erik, the creator of the Physics Bus, demonstrated in the introduction of this book, we become caught up in throwing things out, in disposing of the materials and ignoring their value, their second lives, and the processes that things teach us. Loop upon loop of consumption make us think that the thing is what we're after. And creative writing has not been immune to this materialist entreat. More literary publications means more readers and potentially more glory for the individual MFA Program, but does more really give us more? The future of creative writing must be framed in process, and as we reconsider pedagogy and MFA program design in this vein we must examine our interplay with the arts *and* sciences. Much of this book has focused on integrating histories, theories, and scholarship from craft studies and art into creative writing. This last section initiates another potential collaboration with the sciences. Opening toward collaborations with scientists, environmentalists, activists, educators, and artists impacts the ways we teach writing and how our writing interacts with the world of readers. The Physics Bus project draws together art and science in order to make visible the dynamic processes and physics phenomenon that go unrecognized as we move in the world.

How does craft consciousness protract into the sciences and to issues of urgency? One of the more practical answers to this question lies in modeling creative writing programs on integrated arts programs. The *Alliance for Arts in Research Universities* keeps a complete list of Integrated Arts, Humanities, STEMM Programs in Research Universities, Community Colleges, and Liberal Arts College.[21] The list demonstrates the capacity of institutions in higher education to create bidisciplinary coalitions in a manner that expresses the interplay between fields. Notably, writing, and creative writing more specifically, plays a less prominent role in these collaborations, and the list demonstrates that institutional structures may be flexed away from specialization. Integrated arts models do have a legacy as subspecies in writing programs, such as Cal Arts Integrated Studies Program, Sweetland Center for Writing at the University of Michigan, and among more specialized programs like those at the University of Florida (Creative Science Communication). Some institutions integrate collaborations into the curricular structure, as with Emory University, the University of Michigan, La Guardia Community College, while others utilize specialized centers to do the work, such as the Oberman Center for Advanced Studies at the University of Iowa. As it applies to creative writing, we must reexamine the interplay in local contexts between the individual MFA Programs and the science programs of an institution. Environmental Studies programs can serve as a model for this approach, and the examples at the University of Montana or the Envisioning Ecology Program at Virginia Tech draw together writers, farmers, environmentalists, activists, and student writers.

Interdisciplinary programs can be dominated by what would seem logical institutional pairings, between engineers and scientists, or designers and medical humanists, though, the draw of programs toward collaboration also fits with the ethos of craft consciousness. Creative writers collaborate with scientists, as Claire, the poet, mentioned in her trips to Antarctica with a research team. It is worth imagining how craft consciousness enlists writers to think about the interplay between writing and science. Environmental humanities programs or environmental studies programs offer models for MFA program design where the interplay between urbanists, writers, artists, activists, and hard and social scientists is held as the preeminent model. How creative writing adapts to the anthropogenic moment requires writers to imagine their collaborations from beyond the confines of English Studies and writing.

As an example, at Hobart and William Smith Colleges, the TRIAS Writer Program offers a traditional writer's residency for the academic year. The TRIAS writer spends their two semesters curating a reading series, teaching one writers' workshop, and working toward their current writing project. The 2019 resident, fiction writer Jeff VanderMeer, struck up a conversation at a dinner party with a biology professor, Dr. Meghan Brown. The two began talking casually about salamanders. It turned out VanderMeer was writing a spy thriller that would eventually be "set in a near future of neighborhood drone patrols and a more advanced climate catastrophe than our own."[22] Brown contributed an "an ecology of species" to the novel and VanderMeer integrated her work into the built world of the novel. Of this collaboration, Brown wrote an email describing the collaboration: "Designing biologically-plausible species was a delightful tangent from my typical scholarship but with the shared goal of learning and teaching about species interactions."[23] The collaboration between Brown and VanderMeer extended their writing and thinking beyond the specialized quadrants of biology and fiction writing. On their current book tour, Brown and VanderMeer have engaged scientific journalists, climate activists, and readers of literary fiction. Their example serves to demonstrate how scientists and writers entangle through process and through mutually beneficial practices. For creative writers, the path to collaboration and exemplars in the sciences and arts begins with looking. Felicia Rose Chavez, in the *Anti-Racist Workshop*, discusses how venturing into critiques in the arts changed her perspective on how to support the agency of writers of color in writing workshops. Chavez models the ways pedagogical models may cross-pollinate, and Brown and VanderMeer show how collaboration and interactions across disciplines generate new species of collaboration.

From examples of interplay across science and creative writing, we can ask the question Easterling pushes forward in medium design—how can relational perspectives open up craft and creative writing to new collaborations and ideas? Like interplay, the idea of the *relational* and the *intersectional* should determine how we practice and study creative writing. Intersectional aesthetics, as discussed in Chapter 2, must not appropriate aesthetic traditions from one group or another, instead, it is the relational and intersectional nature that displaces the monolith of dominant craft. Dominant craft, in its stagnancy and adamancy, ignores the relational, action-based models for making. In medium design, as with craft consciousness, our physical and conceptual worlds are seen at the intersections and as the realities of what comes before and after the object's life in the world.

Relational aesthetics as defined by Nicholas Bourriand require us to reconsider art making; he writes, "the role of artworks is no longer to form imaginary and utopian realities, but to actually be ways of living and models of action within the existing real, whatever scale chosen by the artist."[24] The relational aesthetics discussed by Bourriand and the extra-disciplinary activities of writers discussed by Udelson, like medium design or craft consciousness, suggest that interactions form the locus of art. Easterling and Bourriand position intersectionality and relationality as fulcrums for understanding art, science, and culture. For creative writing, collaborations with scientists and artists change how we understand the mission of creative writing. How can we design these collaborations or interactions into MFA programs? And, how does craft consciousness inflect upon these collaborations without participating in the same looping antagonisms? By drawing toward science and other art forms, relational circumstances dictate that writers move out of isolation and toward the social relationships that define them and their work. Moving toward relational art, as Bourriand suggests, remakes the artist as a *catalyst* rather than as a monolith. To catalyze curiosities, the Physics Bus operates in conjunction with the Free Science Workshop, a community space where kids can come after school to tinker. The model for community-based science education is predicated on the relationship of the center to the students. Set within the community, not outside of it, the Free Science Workshop draws its value from the community members that interact and coexist in the space. As writers rethinking the parameters of creative writing's mission, it's our relationship with the world and its citizenry that should determine our educational mission.

Conclusion

Keller Easterling reminds readers that medium design does not "solve" the problems of the world, and as with craft consciousness, it is important to see that a new term does not necessarily lead to new ways of seeing or becoming. To create an alternative to dominant craft, writers have to *see* differently. The new movement within creative writing has to be premised on alternative workshop methods, new program designs, and the reclamation of craft from its illusion of neutrality. In his book, *Craft in the Real World: Rethinking Fiction Writing and Workshopping* (2021), Matthew Salesses uses a practical approach for displacing dominant craft by proposing a host of alternative workshop models, analyzing traditions in Asian literature, and defining craft through an approach that is culturally situated and empowering. He writes,

To really engage with craft is to engage with how we know each other. Craft is inseparable from identity. Craft does not exist outside of society, outside of culture, outside of power. In the world we live in, and write in, craft must reckon with the implications of our expectations for what stories should be—with, as [Audre] Lorde says, what our ideas really mean.

As Salesses writes, "craft is a set of expectations," which set the path from which we begin to understand ourselves and each other.[25] Opening up craft toward interiority changes how we see creative writing and the artist. Training writers to see, to feel, and to create requires us to evaluate and act upon relationships, interactions, and potentialities. Process remains at the foundation of *becoming an artist*. It cannot be the product. In this book, I have sought to engage with the prescriptive dimensions of dominant craft, but the truth of the matter is that craft consciousness requires actions to change how we teach, collaborate, and design MFA programs. Without these actions the term is just a term, easily discarded or repurposed for something else. My argument rests upon collective action and the momentum created by creative writing studies scholars and artists alike who are doing the work to pursue a diverse and inclusive approach to teaching. How writers move in the world has been a curiosity to me for a long time, and the interviews of this book draw upon the stories of living artists because they do the work of art, and as writers, we must follow practitioner knowledge because that's who we are. As practitioners, institutions and the marketplace will continue to influence and impede practice, but it need not determine who we are and how we teach. Craft histories and the work of craft studies scholars reflect the humanizing gesture needed in our field. Through recovering craft from the discourse of domination, writers are free to define the traditions that matter to them and the writers they teach. To radicalize craft, writers need only remember the causes from which the term has been summoned before, and like conjurers of the past, often women and marginalized artists, craft consciousness is a way of thinking that lives inside us. It is not manufactured or marketed, it lives inside ways of knowing and making that are inherited and found. My mother, a seamstress, worked under the table for the only fancy furniture store in our small town in Wisconsin. When the owner gave her expensive fabric, sometimes she would cabbage a swatch here or another there to construct something small for us. Summer shorts. Or picnic napkins. These remnants are who artists are, and sometimes, they cut a bit of cloth off the fabric roll to assemble something new. My hope for this book is that readers will see it as a remnant, which, if you ask a seamstress, a chef, or a woodworker, is a very cherished thing. What's left behind becomes an occasion or opportunity for a future good. I can think of no better way to think of craft consciousness than to imagine it as a headspace where what we know and what we don't know about art making is commingled and wholly rewired.

Appendix

Chart of Artist Interviewees

Pseudonym	Medium(s)	Training	Country of Origin
Leslie	Graphic Design, Printmaking	BFA, MFA	United States
Madin	Writing (Poetry and Scholarship)	PhD	United States
Camilla	Music, Writing (Poetry)	PhD, MFA	United States
Blake	Writing (Poetry, Nonfiction)	PhD, MFA	United States
Litzy	Music, Photography, Painting	BFA (withdrew)	United States
Steven	Glass	Apprentice/Self-Taught	United States
Lena	Interior Design, Photography, Painting	Self-Taught	France
Katie	Writing (Poetry, Nonfiction)	MA, PhD	United States
Dana	Acting, Theatre Arts	BFA	United States
Amadou	Music	Self-Taught	Senegal
Chase	Weaving	Self-Taught	United States
Riana	Conceptual Art, Photography	MFA	United States
Catherine	Sculpture, Painting	Self-Taught/Apprentice	Italy
Diane	Dance	BFA, M.Ed., EdD	United States
Doug	Poet	Lecturer	UK

(continued)

Continued

Pseudonym	Medium(s)	Training	Country of Origin
Erik	Mixed Media, Found Objects	Self-Taught	United States
Andrew	Music (Songwriter)	Self-Taught	United States
Delia	Music (Classical)	BFA	United States
Sebastiano	Sculpture, Painting, Fashion	Apprentice/Self-Taught	Italy
Charlotte	Leatherwork	Apprentice/Self-Taught	United States
Jasmine	Dance, Choreographer	MFA	United States
Kathy	Writing (Novel, Young Adult)	PhD	Australia
Marian	Mixed Media, Letter Press, Textiles	PhD, MA (2)	United States
Nicholas	Pottery, Leatherwork	Apprentice/Self-Taught	United States
Joseph	Performance Art, Spoken Word	Self-Taught	United States
Marigold	Painting	BFA, MFA	United States
Lawrence	Furniture Design	MFA	United States

Notes

Introduction

1 Janelle Adsit, *Toward an Inclusive Creative Writing: Threshold Concepts to Guide the Literary Writing Curriculum* (London: Bloomsbury, 2017).
2 "University of Oregon: Creative Writing," https://crwr.uoregon.edu/diversity/.
3 Sonya Larson, "Degrees of Diversity: Talking Race and the MFA," *Poets and Writers*, September/October 2015. http://www.pw.org/content/degrees_of_diversity.
4 Matthew Salesses, *Craft in the Real World: Rethinking Fiction Writing and Workshopping* (New York: Catapult, 2020), xv.
5 Salesses, *Craft in the Real World*, 34.
6 "Harvard Transdisciplinary Research in Energetics and Cancer" T.H. Chan School of Public Health. https://www.hsph.harvard.edu/trec/about-us/definitions/
7 Alfred North Whitehead, *Process and Reality* (Cambridge: Cambridge University Press, 1929). In Chapter 4, the distinction between *being* and *becoming* is discussed closely and in relation to the term *craft consciousness*. In contrast to the cosmologies of Heidegger and Descartes, Whitehead develops a metaphysical theory in the early twentieth century that presents "occasions of experiences" as constitutive of reality; reality is neither fixed nor static; Jon Udelson, "Bad Grades, Making Bank, and Hating Piano: The Divergent Trajectories of Two Creative Writers' Semiotic Becomings," *Journal of Creative Writing Studies* 6 (1) (2021), 1–3.
8 In an essay for the *Creative Writing Studies Journal* (2021), scholar Jon Udelson "argues for a theoretical and empirical approach to studying creative writers' semiotic becomings" in order "to validate creative writers extra-literate and extra-disciplinary experiences." Importantly, his argument has direct application to creative writing pedagogy and the benefits of looking *outside* of training in writing to understand how we teach and what extradisciplinary practices writers engage in as they form an identity as writers. In Chapter 3, I directly discuss Udelson's qualitative research, though notably, and for my purposes here, the concept of "becoming" is located in the theoretical and cultural context of processism and processual traditions in art making rather than in semiotic or literacy studies' use of the term.
9 Sonja Foss, *Rhetorical Criticism*, 5th ed. (Long Grove, IL: Waveland Press, 2017), 147.

10 Kevin Dunn, *Global Punk: Resistance and Rebellion in Everyday Life* (London: Bloomsbury, 2016).
11 Glenn Adamson, *The Craft Reader* (London: Bloomsbury [formerly Berg Publishing], 2010).
12 National Aids Memorial. https://aidsmemorial.org/theaidsquilt-learnmore/.
13 Glenn Adamson, "Goodbye Craft," in *Nation Building: Craft and Contemporary American Culture* edited by Nicholas R. Bell (London: Bloomsbury, 2015); Howard Risatti, *Theory of Craft: Function and Aesthetic Expression* (Chapel Hill: University of North Carolina Press, 2013); Sandra Alfondy, *NeoCraft: Modernity and the Crafts* (Halifax: Press of the Nova Scotia College of Art and Design, 2008); T'ai Smith, *Bauhaus Weaving Theory: From Feminine Craft to Mode of Design* (Minneapolis: University of Minnesota Press, 2014); Jenni Sorkin, *Live Form: Women, Ceramics, and Community* (Chicago: University of Chicago Press, 2016); Sandra Corse, *Craft Objects, Aesthetic Contexts: Kant, Heidegger, and Adorno on Craft* (Lanham, MD: University Press of America, 2008); Richard Sennett, *The Craftsmen* (New Haven, CT: Yale University Press, 2009); Matthew Crawford, *Shop Class as Soulcraft: An Inquiry into the Value of Work* (New York: Penguin, 2010); Alexander Langlands, *Cræft: An Inquiry into the Origins and True Meaning of Traditional Crafts* (New York: W.W. Norton, 2018).
14 Tim Mayers, *(Re)Writing Craft: Composition, Creative Writing, and the Future of English Studies* (Pittsburgh: University of Pittsburgh Press, 2005).
15 Adsit, *Toward an Inclusive Creative Writing*; Wendy Bishop, *Released into Language: Options of Teaching Creative Writing* (Portsmouth, NH: Heinemann, 1998); Kate Haake, *What Our Speech Disrupts: Creative Writing and Feminism* (Urbana, IL: NCTE, 200); Anna Leahy, *Power and Identity in the Creative Writing Classroom: The Authority Project* (London: New Writing Viewpoints, 2005).
16 Crawford, *Shop Class as Soulcraft*; Langlands, *Cræft*; Sennett, *The Craftsmen*; T. J. Jackson Lears, *No Place for Grace: Anti-Modernism and the Transformation of American Culture 1880–1920* (Chicago: University of Chicago Press, 1994); Glenn Adamson, *Thinking through Craft* (London: Bloomsbury, 2015).
17 D. G. Myers, *The Elephants Teach: Creative Writing since 1880* (Chicago: University of Chicago Press, 1996); Mark McGurl, *The Program Era: Postwar Fiction and the Rise of Creative Writing* (Cambridge, MA: Harvard University Press, 2009); Eric Bennett, *Workshop of Empires* (Iowa City: University of Iowa Press, 2015); Mayers, *(Re)Writing Craft*, Dawson, *Creative Writing and the New Humanities*.
18 Howard Singerman, *Art Subjects: Making Artists in the American University* (Berkeley: University of California Press, 1999).
19 Helen Molesworth, *Leap before You Look: Black Mountain College 1933–57* (New Haven, CT: Yale University Press, 2015); Sorkin, *Live Form*; Smith, *Bauhaus Weaving Theory*; Corse, *Craft Objects, Aesthetic Contexts*.

20 David Pye, *The Nature and Art of Workmanship* (London: Herbert Press/ Bloomsbury, 2008).
21 European Southern Observatory "Science with the VTLI," http://www.eso.org/sci/ facilities/paranal/telescopes/vlti/science.html.

Chapter 1
"*What Is the Good?*" The Seeds of Virtue in Craft Histories and Creative Writing

1 Ruth Asawa and Albert Lanier Interview, *Smithsonian Archives of American Art*, June 21–July 5, 2002. Web.
2 Aldo Leopold, *A Sand County Almanac* (Oxford: Oxford University Press, originally 1949, 1989).
3 For a fuller discussion of rhizomic theory as it relates to knowledge, see Gilles Deleuze and Félix Guattari, *A Thousand Plateaus* (Minneapolis: University of Minnesota Press, 1980). In contrast to a vertical and hierarchical representation of knowledge (discussed as *arborescent*), Deleuze and Guattari argue for a *rhizomic* structuring of knowledge that allows for multiple readings and a "mutualism" or shared participation across differing fields or genres. The metaphor presents a lens for understanding how craft consciousness benefits from intermedium understandings of artistic practice.
4 Besides Wendy Bishop, there are considerable and significant figures who initiated a discussion of creative writing as a subject of study. Notably, and at the early stages of creative writing studies, creative writers were active contributors (see *Creative Writing in America*, edited by Joseph Moxley). Among the early scholars, Pat Bizzaro, Stephanie Vanderslice, Kate Haake, and Tim Mayers, there were contributions across a host of pedagogical, theoretical, and historical studies of the field.
5 Tim Mayers, *(Re)Writing Craft: Composition, Creative Writing, and the Future of English Studies* (Pittsburgh: University of Pittsburgh Press, 2005).
6 Italo Calvino, *Six Memos for the Next Millenium* (New York: Vintage), 124.
7 Stephanie Vanderslice and Rebecca Manery, *Can Creative Writing Really Be Taught?: Resisting Lore in Creative Writing Pedagogy* (London: Bloomsbury, 2017).
8 Bruce Horner, *Terms of Work for Composition: A Materialist Critique* (Albany, NY: SUNY Press, 2000), 176–7.
9 Anna Leahy, Lia Halloran, and Claudine Jaenichen, "Text(ure), Modelling, Collage: Creative Writing and the Visual Arts," *New Writing: The International Journal of Practice and Theory of Creative Writing* 11 (1) (2013), 1–17.
10 A longer discussion of the philosophical and theoretical differences between being (Heidegger) and becoming (Whitehead) is taken up in Chapter 2.

11 Aristotle, *Nicomachean Ethics*, trans. Terence Irwin (Indianapolis, IN: Hackett, 1985), 1.
12 Ibid., 152.
13 "About Writers' Workshop: History," https://writersworkshop.uiowa.edu/about/about-workshop/history (April 2, 2018). Web.
14 Jeffrey Walker, *The Genuine Teachers of This Art: Rhetorical Education in Antiquity* (Columbia: University of South Carolina Press, 2012). Note the epilogue and its discussion of *technê* and contemporary creative writing.
15 Plato, *Charmides*; *Ion*; *The Republic*; *Sophist*; *Theaetetus*, trans. Benjamin Jowett, http://classics.mit.edu. Web.
16 Plato, *Ion*. trans. Benjamin Jowett. Web.
17 "Episteme and Techne," *Stanford Encyclopedia of Philosophy*. Web.
18 Matthew Crawford, *Shop Class as Soulcraft: An Inquiry into the Value of Work* (New York: Penguin, 2010).
19 David Pye, *The Nature and Art of Workmanship* (London: Herbert Press, 2008).
20 Aristotle, *Poetics*. trans. Gerald F. Else (Ann Arbor: University of Michigan Press, 1967).
21 Longinus, "From *On the Sublime*," *Poetry Foundation* (January 3, 2018). Web.
22 John Ruskin, *The Seven Lamps of Architecture* (Mineola, NY: Dover, 1989).
23 Glenn Adamson, "Goodbye Craft," in *Nation Building: Craft and Contemporary American Culture*, edited by Nicholas Bell (London: Bloomsbury, 2015), 32.
24 Glenn Adamson, *The Craft Reader* (London: Berg, 2010).
25 T. J. Jackson Lears, *No Place for Grace: Anti-Modernism and the Transformation of American Culture 1880–1920* (Chicago: University of Chicago Press, 1994), 57.
26 Ibid., 32.
27 Alexander Langlands, *Cræft: An Inquiry into the Origins and True Meaning of Traditional Crafts* (New York: Norton, 2018), 10.
28 Ibid., 11.
29 Crawford, *Shop Class as Soulcraft*, 5.
30 Ibid., 7.
31 Ibid.
32 Richard Sennett, *The Craftsman* (New Haven, CT: Yale University Press, 2009), 6; *The Culture of the New Capitalism* (New Haven, CT: Yale University Press, 2007); Hannah Arendt, *The Human Condition* (Chicago: University of Chicago Press, 1959).
33 Ibid., 7.
34 Bean Gilsdorf, Interview with Glenn Adamson, *American Road Signs* (May 30, 2011). Web.

35 Richard Sennett, *The Craftsmen* (New Haven, CT: Yale University Press, 2008). Acknowledgments section.
36 Ibid., 120.
37 Margaret Atwood, *Bluebeard's Egg* (New York: Houghton Mifflin Harcourt, 2012), 276.
38 Wendell Berry, *The Gift of Good Land: Further Essays Cultural and Agricultural* (Berkeley, CA: Counterpoint Press, 2018). Web.
39 Kaamu Daáood and The Army of Healers, "Liberator Spirit" from *Leimert Park* (Album), Mama Records, 1997.
40 D. G. Myers, *Elephants Teach: Creative Writing since 1880* (Chicago: University of Chicago Press, 1996), 146; Mark McGurl, *The Program Era: Postwar Fiction and the Rise of Creative Writing* (Cambridge, MA: Harvard University Press, 2009), 15.
41 Myers, *Elephants Teach*.
42 Stephen Wilbers, *The Iowa Writers' Workshop* (Iowa City: University of Iowa Press, 1980).
43 D. W. Fenza, "Creative Writing and Its Discontents," *Association of Writers and Writing Programs* (March 1, 2000). Web.
44 Howard Singerman, *Art Subjects: Making Artists in the American University* (Berkeley: University of California Press, 1999), 6.
45 "History of Yale School of Drama," https://drama.yale.edu/history (March 2, 2018). Web; "Columbia University School of the Arts: A History," https://arts.columbia.edu/history. Web.
46 John C. Gerber, *Pictorial History of the University of Iowa* (Iowa City: University of Iowa Press, 2005), 112.
47 Myers, *Elephants Teach*.
48 Paul Dawson, *Creative Writing and the New Humanities* (London: Routledge, 2005).
49 Ibid., 64.
50 Eric Bennett, *Workshop of Empires* (Iowa City: University of Iowa Press, 2015).
51 Ibid., 27.
52 McGurl, *The Program Era*. Although Bennett credits Mark McGurl with sparking the impetus for his book, it should be noted that Wendy Bishop's research in creative writing studies serves as the pioneering scholarship in the field. See bibliographic information in *Composing Ourselves as Writer-Teacher-Writers: Starting with Wendy Bishop*, edited by Patrick Bizzaro, Alys Culhane, and Devan Cook (New York: Hampton Press, 2011).
53 Ibid., 46, 72.
54 Ibid., 409.
55 Ibid., 81.
56 Ibid., 15.
57 Ibid., 36.

58 Dawson, *Creative Writing and the New Humanities*, 126.
59 Ibid., 209.
60 Ibid., 211.
61 Matthew Salesses, *Craft in the Real World: Rethinking Fiction Writing and Workshopping* (New York: Catapult, 2020), 100.
62 Ibid., 101–2.
63 Ibid., 117.
64 Mayers, *(Re)Writing Craft*.
65 Ibid., xiv.
66 Ibid., 13–14.
67 James Elkin, *Why Art Can't Be Taught* (Urbana: University of Illinois Press, 2001); Ian Hartshorne and Donal Moloney, *Teaching Painting: How Can Painting Be Taught in Art Schools?* (London: Black Dog, 2017); Vanderslice and Manery, *Can Creative Writing Really Be Taught?*.
68 Janelle Adsit, *Toward an Inclusive Creative Writing: Threshold Concepts to Guide the Literary Writing Curriculum* (London: Bloomsbury, 2017).
69 Bill Beckley, "Image Boink Text: The Erotic Relationship of Language and Art," in *Social Medium: Artist Writing 2000–2015*, edited by Jennifer Liese (New York: Paper Documents, 2016), 15.
70 Adsit, *Toward an Inclusive Creative Writing*, 58–9.
71 *de-canon: A Visibility Project*, https://www.de-canon.com/blog/2017/5/5/writers-of-color-discussing-craft-an-invisible-archive (May 5, 2017). Web.
72 See *Bauhaus 1919–1928*, edited by Herbert Bayer, Walter Gropius, Ise Gropius, https://www.moma.org/documents/moma_catalogue_2735_300190238.pdf, 18. Web.
73 T'ai Smith, *Bauhaus Weaving Theory: From Feminine Craft to Mode of Design* (Minneapolis: University of Minnesota Press, 2014), 8.
74 Ibid., 9.
75 Helen Molesworth, *Leap before You Look: Black Mountain College 1933–57* (New Haven, CT: Yale University Press, 2015).
76 See Anna Rhodes, "'Theatre Piece #1 Revisited: A Happening' A Celebration of the Original 1952 Happening," *College of Fine and Applied Arts at Appalachian State University* (March 1, 2018). Web.
77 Myers, *Elephants Teach*, 77.
78 Adsit, *Toward an Inclusive Creative Writing*, 58.
79 Jacques Derrida and Avital Ronell, "The Law of Genre," *Critical Inquiry* 7 (1) (1980): 55–81.
80 Andrea K. Scott, "Ruth Asawa Reshapes Art History," *New Yorker* (September 29, 2017). Web.

Chapter 2
Six Thought Experiments in Craft Consciousness

1. Sonja Foss, *Rhetorical Criticism: Exploration and Practice*, 5th ed. (Long Grove, IL: Waveland Press, 2018).
2. See "Index of Adagios," Chapter 4 in D. G. Myers, *The Elephants Teach: Creative Writing since 1880* (Chicago: University of Chicago Press, 1996), 77.
3. "Process Philosophy," *Stanford Encyclopedia of Philosophy*, October 26, 2017. Retrieved from https://plato.stanford.edu/entries/process-philosophy/.
4. Ibid.
5. Howard Robinson, "Materialism in the Philosophy of Mind," 1998, doi:1 0.4324/9780415249126-N032-1. Routledge Encyclopedia of Philosophy, Taylor and Francis, https://www.rep.routledge.com/articles/thematic/materialism-in-the-philosophy-of-mind/v-1.
6. Terry Eagleton, "Introduction: What Is Literature?" University of Dartmouth. https://www.dartmouth.edu/~engl5vr/Eagle1.html.
7. Ibid.
8. Susan Sontag, "The Aesthetic of Silence." *A Susan Sontag Reader* (New York: FSG, 1982).
9. Mary Ann Cain, "Problematizing Formalism: A Double-Cross of Genre Boundaries," *College Composition and Communication* 51 (1) (September 1999): 89–95.
10. David O. Dowling, *A Delicate Aggression: Savagery and Survival in the Iowa Writers' Workshop* (New Haven, CT: Yale University Press, 2019).
11. Sandra Cisnernos, *A House of My Own: Stories from My Life* (New York: Knopf, 2015), 127.
12. Joy Harjo Interview, University of Iowa Center for Advancement Chat, Old Caps Series, November 11, 2020. https://dailyiowan.com/2020/11/11/united-states-poet-laureate-joy-harjo-speaks-on-poetry-time-at-iowa/.
13. Janice Lauer and Kelly Pender, *Invention in Rhetoric and Composition* (Anderson, SC: Parlor Press, 2003), 121.
14. Kelly Pender, *Techne: From Neoclassicism to Postmodernism: Understanding Writing as a Useful, Teachable Art* (Anderson, SC: Parlor Press, 2011).
15. Martha A. Gonzales, *Voices from the Ancestors: Xicanx and Latinx Spiritual Expressions and Healing Practices* (Tucson: University of Arizona Press, 2019).
16. Ibid., 31.
17. Byron Hawk, *A Counter-History of Composition: Toward Methodologies of Complexity* (Pittsburgh: University of Pittsburgh Press, 2007), 16.
18. Ibid, 169.
19. Ibid.

20 Tim Mayers, *(Re)Writing Craft: Composition, Creative Writing, and the Future of English Studies* (Pittsburgh: University of Pittsburgh Press, 2005), 47.
21 Ibid., 71.
22 Ibid.
23 Ibid., 72.
24 Ibid.
25 Gil Scott Heron, "I'm New Here," from album *I'm New Here* (XL Recordings, February 8, 2010).
26 Gil Scott Heron, from album *I'm New Here*, 2010.
27 Sontag, "The Aesthetic of Silence."
28 Sontag, Susan, *As Consciousness Is Harnessed to Flesh: Journals and Notebooks, 1964–1980* (New York, FSG, 2012).
29 Gloria Anzaldúa, *this bridge we call home: radical visions for transformation*, edited with AnaLouise Keating (New York: Routledge, 1981), 540.
30 Lara Medina and Martha A. Gonzales, *Voices from the Ancestors: Xicanx and Latinx Spiritual Expressions and Healing Practices* (Tucson: University of Arizona Press, 2019), 3.
31 Gloria Anzaldúa, *Light in the Dark/Luz en la Oscuro: Rewriting Identity, Spirituality, Reality* (Durham, NC: Duke University Press, 2015).
32 Ibid.
33 Esther Díaz Martín, *Voices from the Ancestors: Xicanx and Latinx Spiritual Expressions and Healing Practices* (Tucson: University of Arizona Press, 2019).
34 "Making the Interior Visible," An Interview of Dawoud Bey by Louis Bury, *BOMB Magazine*, April 5, 2019. https://bombmagazine.org/articles/making-interiority-visible-dawoud-bey-interviewed/.
35 From Chapter 2, "Marginalized Aesthetics," Janelle Adsit, *Toward an Inclusive Creative Writing: Threshold Concepts to Guide the Literary Writing Curriculum* (London: Bloomsbury, 2017), 49.
36 Anya Achtenberg, "Notes in Journey from a Writer of the Mix," in *How Dare! We Write: A Multicultural Creative Writing Discourse*, edited by Sherry Quan Lee (Ann Arbor, MI: Modern History Press, 2017), 101.
37 Ibid., 101–2.
38 Lorraine O'Grady, "Some Thoughts on Diaspora and Hybridity: An Unpublished Slide Lecture (1994)," *BOMB Magazine* 153 (Fall 2020): 70–4.
39 Jennifer Liese (ed.), *Social Medium: Artists' Writing, 2000–2015* (New York: Paper Documents, 2016).
40 Nathan Vincent, *Queer Threads: Crafting Identity and Community*, edited by John Chaich and Todd Oldham (New York: Ammo Books, 2017), 125.
41 Pierre Fouché, *Queer Threads: Crafting Identity and Community*, edited by John Chaich and Todd Oldham (New York: Ammo Books, 2017), 128.

42 Harmony Hammond, *Queer Threads Crafting Identity and Community*, edited by John Chaich and Todd Oldham (New York: Ammo Books, 2017), 129.
43 Adsit, *Toward an Inclusive Creative Writing*, 58.
44 Ibid., 60.
45 Ibid., 66.
46 Tobin Siebers, *Disability Aesthetics* (Ann Arbor: University of Michigan Press, 2010), 15.
47 Ibid., 3.
48 Victor Vitanza, "Abandoned to Writing: Notes toward Several Provocations," *Enculturation* 5 (1) (2003). Retrieved from http://www.enculturation.net/5_1/vitanza.html.
49 Ibid.
50 Gil Scott Heron, from album *I'm New Here*, 2010.
51 AnaLouise Keating, *Transformation Now!: Toward a Post Oppositional Politics of Change* (Champaign: University of Illinois Press, 2014).
52 Howard Risatti, *A Theory of Craft: Function and Aesthetic Expression* (Chapel Hill: University of North Carolina Press, 2013), 13; R. G. Collingswood, *The Principles of Art* (London: Oxford University Press, 1938).
53 Ibid., 12.
54 Sandra Corse, *Craft Objects, Aesthetic Contexts: Kant, Heidegger, and Adorno on Craft* (Plymouth: University of America Press, 2008).
55 Ibid., 64–5.
56 Christine Smallwood. "Through Clenched Teeth: The Cold, Frenzied Genius of Kleist," *Harper's Magazine*, April 2020. Retrieved from https://harpers.org/archive/2020/04/through-clenched-teeth-michael-kohlhaas-heinrich-von-kleist/.
57 Kate Haake, *What Our Speech Disrupts: Feminism and Creative Writing Studies* (Urbana, IL: NCTE, 2000), 12.
58 Dowlings, *A Delicate Aggression*.
59 Keating *Transformation Now*, Location 170.
60 Daphne M. Grace, *Beyond Bodies: Gender, Literature, and the Enigma of Consciousness* (Leiden, Netherlands: Brill, 2014), 48; Susan Blackmore, *Consciousness, A Very Short Introduction* (London: Oxford University Press, 2005), 3.
61 Ned Block, "On Confusion about a Function of Consciousness," *Behavioral and Brain Sciences* 18 (1995): 227.
62 Thich Nhat Hanh, "The Four Layers of Consciousness," September 14, 2017. Retrieved from https://upliftconnect.com/thich-nhat-hanh-the-four-layers-of-consciousness/.
63 Janelle Adsit, *Toward an Inclusive Creative Writing: Threshold Concepts to Guide the Literary Writing Curriculum* (London: Bloomsbury, 2017), 3. & *VIDA Report: Women in Literary Arts* (2017 Count Overview) Retrieved from https://www.vidaweb.org/.

64 Toni Morrison, *Source of Self-Regard: Selected Speeches, Essays, and Meditations* (New York: Knopf, 2019); Charles Johnson, *The Way of the Writer: Reflections on the Art and Craft of Storytelling* (New York: Scribner, 2016); Sherry Quan Lee (ed.), *How Dare! We Write: A Multicultural Creative Writing Discourse* (Ann Arbor, MI: Modern History Press, 2017).

65 Matthew Salesses, *Craft in the Real World: Rethinking Fiction Writing and Workshopping* (New York: Catapult, 2020), 14.

66 William Kentridge, "The Creative Process of a Master Artist," *TEDx Johannesburg*, November 15, 2016. Retrieved from https://www.youtube.com/watch?v=SmaXqktW3A8.

67 Jessica Lopez Lyman, "Imposter Poet: Recovering from Graduate School," in *How Dare We! Write: A Multicultural Creative Writing Discourse* (Ann Arbor, MI: Modern History Press, 2017).

68 David Mura, "The Student of Color in the Typical MFA Program," *Gulf Coast*, April 21, 2015. Retrieved from http://gulfcoastmag.org/online/blog/the-student-of-color-in-the-typical-mfa-program/.

69 Dr. Joseph Young, University of Wisconsin-LaCrosse, Class Lecture on Richard Wright's "The Man Who Lived Underground."

70 Thomas Nagel, "What Is It Like to Be a Bat?" *Philosophical Review* 83 (4) (October 1974): 435–50.

71 Thich Nhat Hanh, "The Four Layers of Consciousness," September 14, 2017. Retrieved from https://www.lionsroar.com/the-four-layers-of-consciousness/.

72 Xánath Caraza, "Writing Is as Necessary as Air to Me," in *Voices from the Ancestors: Xicanx and Latinx Spiritual Expressions and Healing Practices* (Tucson: University of Arizona Press, 2019), 98.

73 Block, "On Confusion about a Function of Consciousness," 227–47.

74 Dan Tippens, "Ned Block on Phenomenal Consciousness, Part I (Interview)," May 18, 2015. Retrieved from https://scientiasalon.wordpress.com/2015/05/18/ned-block-on-phenomenal-consciousness-part-i/.

75 Hanh, "Four Layers of Consciousness."

76 Ibid.

77 Ibid.

78 Anzaldúa, *Light in the Dark*.

79 Hanh, "Four Layers of Consciousness."

80 T'ai Smith, *Bauhaus Weaving Theory: From Feminine Craft to Mode of Design* (Minneapolis: University of Minnesota Press, 2014), 13.

81 Ibid., xxxiv.

82 Ibid.

83 Gunta Stölzl, "Weaving at the Bauhaus," *Bauhaus Journal*, "Offset" 7 (1926). Retrieved from https://www.guntastolzl.org/Literature/St%C3%B6lzl-on-Bauhaus-Weaving/Gunta-St%C3%B6lzl-Weaving-at/.
84 Smith, *Bauhaus Weaving Theory*, 6.
85 Ibid., 141–2.
86 Ibid., 143.
87 Jenni Sorkin, *Live Form: Women, Ceramics, and Community* (Chicago: University of Chicago Press, 2016), 13.
88 Mayers, *(Re)Writing Craft*, 72.
89 Ibid., 55.
90 Randolph Lewis, *Navajo Talking Picture: Cinema on Native Ground* (Lincoln: University of Nebraska Press, 2012).
91 Bianca Viñas, "The Motion of a Poetic Landscape: An Interview with Sherwin Bitsui." Retrieved from https://hungermtn.org/motion-poetic-landscape-interview-sherwin-bitsui/.
92 David Garneau, "Can I Get a Witness?" in *Sovereign Words: Indigenous Art, Curation and Criticism*.
93 Trinh T. Minh-ha, *When the Moon Waxes Red: Representation, Gender and Cultural Politics* (London: Routledge, 2014), 13.
94 University of Iowa, "A License to Write: The Iowa Writers' Workshop Experience," February 8, 2010. Retrieved from https://www.youtube.com/watch?v=prSIokFqBdU.
95 Jenni Sorkin, "Craftlike: The Illusion of Authenticity," in *Nation Building: Craft and Contemporary American Culture*, edited by Nicholas Bell (London: Bloomsbury, 2016), 80.
96 Ibid., 85.
97 Ben Ristow, "A Line of Print, A Stroke of Paint: A Visual Rhetorical Analysis of Creative Writing Programs," in *Can Creative Writing Really Be Taught?* edited by Stephanie Vanderslice and Rebecca Manery (London: Bloomsbury, 2017).
98 *VIDA: Women in Literary Arts*, 2014–17 archive. Retrieved from https://www.vidaweb.org/the-2017-vida-count/.
99 Sorkin, "Craftlike," 85.
100 Ibid., 85.
101 Petre Vlad Glaveanu with editors Lene Tanggaard and Charlotte Wegener, *Creativity: A New Vocabulary* (London: Palgrave, 2016).
102 Oli Mould, *Against Creativity* (Brooklyn, NY: Verso Press, 2018), 82.
103 Siebers, *Disability Aesthetics*, 20.

Chapter 3
Radically (Un)Becoming: Qualitative Perspectives on Crafting an Artistic Practice

1. Alexander Langlands, *Cræft: An Inquiry into the Origins and True Meaning of Traditional Crafts* (New York: Norton, 2018).
2. Glenn Adamson, *Thinking through Craft* (London: Bloomsbury, 2007); T'ai Smith, *Bauhaus Weaving Theory: From Feminine Craft to Mode of Design* (Minneapolis: University of Minnesota Press, 2014); Matthew Crawford, *Shop Class as Soulcraft: An Inquiry into the Value of Work* (New York: Penguin, 2010).
3. Kate Haake, *What Our Speech Disrupts: Feminism and Creative Writing Studies* (Urbana, IL: NCTE, 2000), 12.
4. "About Us." Yale School of Drama. Retrieved from https://www.drama.yale.edu/about-us/.
5. Margaret H'Doubler, *Dance: A Creative Art Experience* (Madison: University of Wisconsin Press, 1940).
6. Walter R. Miles, "A Biographical Memoir of Carl Emil Seashore, 1866–1949." *National Academy of Science*, p. 298.
7. Jenni Sorkin, *Live Form: Women, Ceramics, and Community* (Chicago: University of Chicago Press, 2016).
8. Gary Alan Fine, *Talking Art: The Culture of Practice and the Practice of Culture in MFA Education* (Chicago: University of Chicago Press, 2018), 41.
9. Ibid., 40.
10. Ibid.
11. Kim Grant, *All about Process: The Theory and Discourse of Modern Artistic Labor* (University Park: Pennsylvania State University Press, 2017), 110–11.
12. Ibid., 169.
13. Ibid., 12.
14. Ibid., 186.
15. Ibid., 40.
16. Ibid., 41.
17. Ibid.
18. Gregory Light, "From the Personal to the Public: Conceptions of Creative Writing in Higher Education," *Higher Education* 43 (2) (March 2002): 260.
19. Ibid., 274.
20. Kyung Min Kim, "A Humanized View of Second Language Learning through Creative Writing: A Korean Graduate Student in the United States," *Creative Writing Studies Journal* 3 (1) (2018): 2.

21 Yan Zhao, *Second Language Creative Writers: Identities and Writing Processes* (Bristol, UK: Multilingual Matters, 2015), 2.
22 Jon Udelson, "Bad Grades, Making Bank, and Hating Piano: The Divergent Trajectories of Two Creative Writers' Semiotic Becomings," *Journal of Creative Writing Studies* 6 (1) (2021).
23 Ibid., 2. Udelson directly references Paul Prior's essay "How Do Moments Add Up to Lives: Trajectories of Semiotic Becoming vs. Tales of School Learning in Four Modes" from *Making Future Matters* (2018).
24 Ibid., 2.
25 Ibid., 3.
26 Ibid., 2.
27 Vicki Halper and Diane Douglas, *Choosing Craft: The Artist's Viewpoints* (Chapel Hill: University of North Carolina Press, 2009).
28 Milton Van Dyke, *An Album of Fluid Motion* (Stanford, CA: Parabolic Press, 1982).
29 Adamson, Glenn (ed.), *The Craft Reader* (London: Berg Press, 2009).
30 Matt Ratto and Megan Boler (eds.), *DIY Citizenship: Critical Making and Social Media* (Cambridge, MA: MIT Press, 2014).
31 Marian Interview, Art and Architecture, Textiles, and Mixed Media, Small Liberal Arts College.
32 Kathy Interview, Poet and Novelist, Teaches at Large Public University in Australia.
33 Lena Interview, Photographer, Painter, Designer, Self-Taught.
34 Riana Interview, Conceptual Artist, Textiles, Photography, MFA.
35 Nicholas and Charlotte Interview, Potter and Leather Artists, Self-Taught.
36 Ibid.
37 Sebastiano and Catherine Interview, Sculpture, Painting, Mixed Mediums, Self-Taught.
38 Ibid.
39 Ibid.
40 Delia and Andrew Interview, Violinist and Songwriter and Guitarist, Ivy League University and Self-Taught.
41 Leslie Interview, Graphic Designer and Printmaker, Small Liberal Arts College, Northeast United States.
42 Chase Interview, Weaver and Printmaker, New York, Self-Taught.
43 Kathy Interview, Poet and Novelist, Public National University, Australia.
44 Ibid.
45 Claire Interview, Poet, Research One University, Western United States.
46 Marian Interview, Art and Architecture, Small Liberal Arts College, Northeast United States.
47 Nicholas and Charlotte Interview, Potter and Leather Artists, Self-Taught, Northeast United States.

48 Eric Interview, Physics Educator and Found-Object Artist, Self-Taught, Northeast United States.
49 Fine, *Talking Art*, 52.
50 Nicholas and Charlotte Interview, Potter and Leather Artists, Self-Taught.
51 Chase Interview, Weaver and Print Maker, Self-Taught, Central New York.
52 Lawrence Interview, Furniture Designer, West Coast Arts School Training.
53 Blake and Camilla Interview, Poets, Nonfiction Writer, and Musician, PhDs, MFAs, Small Liberal Arts College.
54 Ibid.
55 Ibid.
56 Riana Interview, Conceptual Artist and Photographer, BFA, MA, MFA.
57 Lena Interview, Photographer, Painter, Designer, Self-Taught.
58 Eric Interview, Found-Object Artist and Science Educator.
59 Ibid.
60 Joseph Interview, Spoken Word and Music, Self-Taught.
61 Litzy Interview, Musician and Photographer, Self-Taught.
62 Ibid.
63 Diane Interview, Dance and Choreography, Teaches at Small Liberal Arts Colleges.
64 Dana Interview, Iranian-American Actor, BFA, Based in Los Angeles.
65 Madin Interview, Writing (Poet and Scholar), Professor, Small Liberal Arts College.
66 Claire Interview, Poet and Nonfiction Writer, Teaches at Research One University, Western United States.
67 Lawrence Interview, Furniture Designer, Private West Coast Arts School Training, Western United States.
68 Eric, Found-Object Artists and Scientific Educator, Self-Taught.
69 Leslie Interview, Graphic Designer and Sketchist, Teaches at Small Liberal Arts College.
70 Claire Interview, Poet and Nonfiction Writer, Research One University, Western United States.
71 Jasmine Interview, Dancer and Choreographer, Small Liberal Arts College, Northeast United States.
72 Delia and Andrew Interview, Violinist and Songwriter/Guitarist, Ivy League University and Self-Taught.
73 Sorkin, *Live Form*.
74 Felicia Rose Chavez, *The Anti-Racist Workshop: How to Decolonize the Creative Writing Workshop* (Chicago: Haymarket Books, 2021), 55.
75 Keller Easterling, *Medium Design: Knowing How to Work on the World* (Brooklyn, NY: Verso Books, 2020), 28.

Chapter 4
Craft Consciousness Futures

1. Felicia Rose Chavez, *The Anti-Racist Workshop: How to Decolonize the Creative Writing Workshop* (Chicago: Haymarket Books, 2021).
2. Ibid., 227.
3. Ibid., 154.
4. Ibid., 136–7.
5. Ibid., 111, 113.
6. Ben Ristow, "Performances in Contradiction: Facilitating a Neosophistic Creative Writing Workshop," *New Writing: The International Journal for the Practice and Theory of Creative Writing* 11 (1) (2013): 92–9.
7. Claire Interview, Poet, Research One University, Western United States.
8. Anna Leahy, *Power and Identity in the Creative Writing Classroom* (Bristol: Multilingual Matters, 2005).
9. David O'Grady. "Playfully Subversive: The Many Roles of Adaptation in Making Games at UCLA's Game Lab. Retrieved from http://www.tft.ucla.edu/mediascape/Fall2014_PlayfullySubversive.html.
10. Chavez, *The Anti-Racist Workshop*, 157.
11. Matthew Salesses, *Craft in the Real World: Rethinking Fiction Writing and Workshopping* (Boca Raton, FL: Catapult Press, 2021), 149.
12. Keller Easterling, *Medium Design: Knowing How to Work on the World* (Brooklyn: Verso, 2020).
13. Ibid., 11.
14. AWP Guide to Writing Programs. Retrieved from http://awp.org/guide.
15. "MFA Image-Text," Ithaca College. Retrieved from https://catalog.ithaca.edu/graduate/communications/image-text-mfa/.
16. Ibid., "MFA Image-Text," Ithaca College.
17. "Graduate Writing Program," Pratt Institute. Retrieved from https://www.pratt.edu/academics/liberal-arts-and-sciences/the-department-of-writing/graduate-writing/.
18. Deborah Brandt, *The Rise of Writing: Redefining Mass Literacy* (Cambridge: Cambridge University Press, 2014).
19. Easterling, *Medium Design*, 67.
20. Trent Hergenrader, *Collaborative World Building for Writers and Gamers* (London: Bloomsbury, 2018); Adam Koehler, *Composition, Creative Writing Studies, Digital Humanities* (London: Bloomsbury, 2017).
21. *Alliance for the Arts in Research Universities*. Retrieved from https://www.a2ru.org/projects/list-of-integrative-arts-humanities-and-stemm-programs-in-research-universities-community-colleges-and-liberal-arts-colleges/.

22 Noah Berlatsky, "Review: Climate Collapse Comes for the Spy Thriller in Jeff VanderMeer's Sly Genre Game," *Los Angeles Times*, March 30, 2021. Retrieved from https://www.latimes.com/entertainment-arts/books/story/2021-03-30/review-climate-collapse-comes-for-the-spy-thriller-in-jeff-vandermeers-sly-genre-game.
23 Meghan Brown, email, March 31, 2021, "Novelist + Biologist + Journalist."
24 Nicholas Bourriand, *Relational Aesthetics* (Colson: Le Presse du Reele, 1998).
25 Salesses, *Craft in the Real World*, 32.

Index

ableism 109
Achtenberg, Anya (*see also* out-of-category) 67, 152
acting 149, 152
Adamson, Glenn 6–7, 25, 30, 131
　Thinking Through Craft 29
Adsit, Janelle 41, 43, 47, 71, 85, 160, 166, 177
　marginalized aesthetics 67
　threshold concepts 41
aesthetics
　citizenry 122
　disability (or diffabled) 72, 108
　indigenous 102
　intersectional 43, 72, 101, 115, 188
　marginalized (*see also* Adsit, Janelle) 81, 110
　relational 188
　survivor (or survival) 70
　Western 38, 43, 100
AIDS Memorial Quilt 6
Albers, Anni 46, 96
Albers, Josef 46
Alfondy, Sandra 94
Alliance for Arts in Research Universities 187
Anzaldúa, Gloria 9, 65, 94–5
　conocimiento 65, 69, 102
　nepantla 94
Arendt, Hannah 29
Aristotle 8
　Nicomachean Ethics 19
　On Rhetoric 22
　Poetics 22–3
Art Institute of Chicago 184
artisan 26, 137
artist (or artistic)
　collaborations 132
　colonies and communities 53, 149
　identity formation 152
　labor 149
　market and market value 143

metaphors 133, 138–9
migrations 18, 133, 158
multiracial 151–2, 155
as teachers 129
art making
　commercial pressures 148
　ecologies of making 153
　global manufacturing 149
　interplay 181
　metaphor and analogies 139
Arts and Crafts Movement 6, 25–6
Asawa, Ruth 13, 49
Association of Writers' and Writing Programs (AWP) 3, 15, 34
Atwood, Margaret 30
authorship 168, 175

Baldwin, James 89–90
Bauhaus 20, 32, 35, 45, 47
becoming 2, 5, 18–19, 44, 48, 52, 76, 111, 125, 152, 158, 165, 190
being (*see also* Heidegger) 37, 45, 63
Bennett, Eric 32, 35–6
Berger, Otti 97
Berry, Wendell 31
Bey, Dawoud 66
BFA program 150–1
Bishop, Wendy 16, 115
Bitsui, Sherwin 100
Blackmore, Susan 82
Black Mountain College 20, 32, 35, 45–6
　happenings 47
Blanchot, Maurice 76
Block, Ned 82, 91
BOMB Magazine, oral history 86, 127
boundaries
　disciplinary 140, 182
　genre 182
　material 182
　medium 140
Bourriand, Nicholas 188–9
Brander, Matthew 35

Brandt, Deborah 185
Brown, Meghan 188
Buddhism 83, 89
  manas 83, 92, 94, 153
  meditation 95
Byrd, Renée 177

Cain, Mary Ann 56
CalArts 182, 187
capitalism 28–9, 102, 104, 107, 144, 148–9
  bourgeois 25–6, 32
  disembodied labor 28–9
Caraza, Xánath 90
catharsis 23
ceramics 98–9, 122
Chavez, Felicia Rose 10, 156, 160, 166–8, 170–1, 174, 179, 188
Chicago, Judy 122
Cisneros, Sandra 57
collaborations
  intersectional 189
  relational 189
College Art Association (CAA) 34
Collingswood, R. G. 78, 121
colonialism 100–1
Coltrane, John 31
Columbia University 34
composition studies 61
conceptual art 119
consciousness (*see also* craft consciousness)
  access 83, 91, 178
  class 102
  collective 101, 106
  critical 102
  cultural 87–8
  formations 82–3, 86, 90, 92–3, 108, 111, 131–2
  hard problem 83
  material 30, 83, 85–7, 111, 119, 140, 178, 181
  mind (or root) 91
  non-oppositional 77
  oppositional 74–7, 93, 98, 110, 124
  phenomenal 83, 85–6, 88–9, 111, 140, 143, 178
  sense 89, 111
  store 83, 91–2, 140, 153

thresholds (and threshold theory) 74, 76, 81–2, 98, 132
consciousness studies 53, 82
consumerism and market pressure 142–3, 148
cooptation 102
Corse, Sandra 75, 79
cowriting 172
craft 138
  alienation from 87
  apolitical or acultural 88
  appropriation 105
  authenticity (or authentication) 26, 28, 47, 104–6
  blindness 141
  codification 24, 41
  collectivity 32, 44, 103, 172
  colorblind ethos 87–8
  commodification 137
  cosmologies 182
  criticism (*see* craft criticism)
  democracy 35
  disruption 31, 51
  explorative (opening up) 59
  external criteria 131
  feminization 45, 97, 159
  functionality (or functionalism) 93, 99
  haptic 99
  heuristic 41–2, 47, 131
  identity 58
  inclusivity 32, 42
  institutionalization 41, 58, 109–10
  intermedium 95–7
  internal and spiritual forces 147
  intervention 44, 159
  know-how 137, 161
  marginalization 32
  migrations 41
  morality 25
  network of practitioners 106
  nostalgia 26, 119
  objects 136
  performative 95
  performativity 150
  practitioners 38
  prescriptive method 60
  preservation 27, 29
  pure craft 86
  radicalization 190

real world (Salesses) 33
rhetorical awareness 38, 47
socialization 121
soul-building 24, 28
standardization 55, 59
technique 33, 35, 48, 79, 121
virtue (or virtuous practice) 18–20, 24, 48
weaponized 87
craft arts 78
craft consciousness 64, 70, 96, 103, 106, 108, 113, 138, 148, 157–8, 160, 164–6
collectivity 171
definition 3, 5, 48, 51, 54, 92–3, 130, 134, 190
MFA program design 173, 182
pedagogy 167
writing workshop models 180
craft criticism (*see also* Mayers) 33, 39, 41, 62, 68–9
craft studies
embodiment 94, 136
feminism 94
craft theory 79
craft-like (*see also* Jenni Sorkin) 104–5
craftsmanship 45
craftspeople (or craftsmanship) 97, 103, 135–7, 141
Crawford, Matthew 22, 28
creative nonfiction 145
creative writing
convergences 126
ecosystemic 154
expulsion from the academy 40
genre specialization 157
identify formation 123, 125
mission 20, 47
multilingualism 124
pedagogy 166
professionalization 20
qualitative research 123
socialization 126
studies 16
textbooks or handbooks 84
creativity 34–7, 40, 103, 106–7, 112
systemic 36, 48
crocheting 93–4
Cunningham, Merce 47

Daáod, Kamau (and the Army of Healers) 31
dance 72, 116, 151, 155, 179
Dawson, Paul 33, 35, 37
de-canon archive 43, 86, 127
democracy 36
design 96, 143, 144, 161
ahistorical 144
ethics 144
furniture 144
inspiration from nature 154
interactivity 181–2
Dewey, John 34, 47, 53
diasporic artist 68
Diaz, Junot 42–3
DIY (Do-It-Yourself) 18
dominant craft discourse 3, 20, 38, 42–3, 48–9, 52, 54, 57–8, 61, 65, 88, 105
dominant literary tradition 169
Douglas, Diane 127
Dowling, David 57, 80
Dunn, Kevin 6

Easterling, Keller 10, 160–1, 167, 181–3, 185–6, 189
education
arts 151
experiential 19
interdisciplinary models
paternalism 151
scientific (physics) 144, 148
Elkins, James 40
embodiment 78, 94, 99, 122
Emerson, Ralph Waldo 163
Engle, Paul 34
episteme 8, 21
ergon (function) 21, 23
ethnography 117

farming 27, 31
feminism 51, 115, 159
Fenza, D. W. 33, 36
Fernandez-Williams, Sherrie 87
fetishization (art) 100
Fine, Gary Alan 115, 118, 126, 129, 142, 168
Foerster, Norman 33
formalism (literary) 47, 51, 56, 99, 109–10
formations (*see* consciousness)

Foss, Sonja 6, 51
Foucault, Michel 97
found object art 142–3, 148, 154
Fourché, Pierre 69
Frayling, Sir Christopher 113
Free Science Workshop 163, 189
Freire, Paulo 65, 102
Frost, Robert 112

gardening 30, 49, 112
Garneau, David 101
genre specialization 156
  cross genre 183
  image-text 183
  multi-genre 183
glass making 149
Glăveanu, Vlad Petre 107
Gonzales, Martha A. 59
Grant, Kim 115, 117
graphic design 138
Gropius, Walter 45, 96

H'Doubler, Margaret 116
Haake, Kate 79, 114–15
Halper, Vicki 127
Hammond, Harmony 70
Harjo, Joy 57
Hartshorne, Ian 40
Harvard University, T.H. Chan School of Public Health 4
Hawk, Byron 60–1
Haynes, David 3–4
Heidegger, Martin 48, 63
Hergenrader, Trent 186
heuristic 73
Horner, Bruce 17
Hubbard, Elbert 26

indigenous art 100
industrialization 25
interdisciplinarity 139, 151–2, 166
intersectionality 97, 101
Iowa Writers' Workshop 15, 33, 57, 104, 117
Ithaca College 183
Itten, Johannes 96

Johnson, Charles 85
Justice, Daniel 100

Kant, Immanuel 78
Keating, AnaLouise 75–6, 81, 110–11
Kentridge, William 86
Kim, Kyung Min 124, 126
knowledge
  practitioner 17
Koch-Otter, Benita 97
Koehler, Adam 186

Langlands, Alexander 27, 113
Larson, Sonya 3
Lauer, Janice 58
Leahy, Anna 175
Lears, T. J. Jackson 26, 37
leatherwork 135–6, 141–2
Lerman, Liz 179
Liese, Jennifer 68
Light, Gregory 123, 126
literacy narrative 124
literariness 71, 77
literary form 145–6
Longinus 23–4
  sublime 24
lore 17
Lukács, György 65, 102
Lyman, Jessica Lopez 87

Manery, Rebecca 17, 40
material, materiality, or materialism 30, 51–2, 56, 83, 109, 117, 164
  choice 142
  ethical considerations 143
  exploration 133
  internal structures 141
  repurposing 142
  sourcing 142
Martín, Esther Díaz 66
Marx, Karl 120
master-apprentice model 22
mathematics 140
Mayers, Tim 7, 33, 38–9, 62, 99
McGurl, Mark 33, 36
Mearns, Hugh 34
Medina, Lara 59
medium design 10, 96, 167, 181, 184
MFA Program
  collectivity 173
  commodification 122
  creative writing 41, 47, 103–5, 158, 164

disciplinary boundaries 155
education 118, 154
histories 115–16
Image-Text (Ithaca College) 183
institutionalization 157
multi-genre or cross genre 183
music 34
socialization 157, 172
specialization 157
structure and design 88, 122, 132, 158, 165, 167, 173
studio arts 34, 116, 118, 121, 122, 182
toxicity 151
transdisciplinary 184
metaphysics
process 51, 74, 99
substantive 51
Min Ha, Trinh 102
mix media arts 136, 140
modernity (and anti-modern) 26
Molesworth, Helen 46
Moloney, Donal 40
Morris, William 6, 26–7, 107, 120
Morrison, Toni 85
Mould, Oli 103, 107–8
Mountford, Roxanne 114
Mura, David 88
music (and musicians) 137, 145, 150, 155
Myers, D. G. 32–4, 53

Nagel, Thomas 88–9
Native art 100
New Classicism 58, 60
New Criticism 35, 56
New Humanism 35–6, 38
New Romanticism 58
New Writing (journal) 174
Nhat Hanh, Thich 82, 89–90, 94–5, 114, 153
North, Stephen 17
novel writing 139

O'Grady, David 178
O'Grady, Lorraine 68
Oliver, Mary 40
ontology 63, 88, 101, 165
Oppenheimer, Frank 1
out-of-category (artist or writer) 67–8, 70, 152, 156

painting 143
patriarchy 101–2
Pender, Kelly 9, 58
Peterson, Susan 98
photography 135, 143, 147, 150
Physics Bus 1–2, 127, 142, 163, 186, 189
Plato 8
Ion 21
poetry 99, 139–40, 145, 152, 154, 175
pottery 135, 141
Pratt Institute 182, 184
print making 138, 154
Prior, Paul 125
process turn (in art) 120
feminism 121
processism (or process philosophy) 2, 29, 31, 48–9, 51–3, 80, 114, 121, 131, 146–7, 149, 158, 161, 164
Program Era 36–7
progressive education 34
proscenium 72
Pye, David 31, 113
workmanship of certainty 23

qualia 82
qualitative research 123
collaborative interviewing 129
interview format 128, 130
study design and rationale 127–9
Quan Lee, Sherry 85

rhetoric 21
Rice, John Andrew 46
Richards, M. C. 98
Risatti, Howard 75, 78
Ruskin, John 25, 27, 120
Ryle, Gilbert 161, 185

Salesses, Matthew 4, 7, 33, 38–9, 43, 47, 85, 126, 166, 180, 189–90
Schapiro, Miriam 122
Schegel, Friedrich 76
Scheneeman, Carolee 122
science and art 187
collaborations 153, 161, 167, 189
observations 153–4
Scott-Heron, Gil 64, 74, 76
sculpture 49
Seashore, Carl 117

self (*see also* self-expression)
    instability (or unstable) 92, 102
    no self or new self 95
    past or future self 95
    boundaries of self 95
self-expression 119
self-taught artists 128, 152
Sennett, Richard 28–9, 132
Shafer, Leah 185
shapeshift 68
Siebers, Tobin 108
Singerman, Howard 34
Smallwood, Christine 79
Smith, T'ai 7, 45, 94–6
sociology 118
sociopoetics 33, 38
Sontag, Susan 64
Sorkin, Jenni 7, 94–5, 98, 104–6
    craft-like 104–5
    live form 98
spoken word and performance art 150
Stickley, Gustav 26
stochastic arts 21–3, 141–2
Stözl, Gunta 97
Studio arts 118–19
Studio Craft Movement 104
system theory 37

technê 8, 18, 21–2, 55, 58, 60
    atechne 64, 75
    post-techne 60–1
technology 144
telos 19, 23
thought experiment 51, 109
thresholds (*see* consciousness)
transdisciplinarity 4
transdisciplinary 166
TRIAS Writer Residency Program 188

UCLA (University of California-Los Angeles) 178
Udelson, Jon 125–6
University of Iowa 34, 117
University of Michigan (Sweetland Writing Center) 187
University of Montana 187
University of Oxford 184

Van Dyke, Milton 131
VanderMeer, Jeff 188

Vanderslice, Stephanie 17, 40
VIDA 85, 105
video essay (or essay film) 185
Vincent, Nathan 69
Virginia Tech 187
Vitanza, Victor 64, 75
voice 79
VONA 43

Walker, Jeffrey 21
Walsh, John Francis 84
weaving and4 textile arts 66, 97–8, 134, 138, 140, 148
    Anni Albers 96
    Bauhaus 96
    bordar (from Esther Martín Díaz) 66
Wenderoth, Joe 99
Whitehead, Alfred North 2, 48, 52, 114, 164, 172
Wilbers, Stephen 33–4
Wildenhain, Margueritte 98–9
Wright, Richard 88
writing workshop
    alienation 169
    alternative (*see also* Salesses) 180
    anti-racist (*see also* Chavez) 10, 156, 160, 170, 179
    collaborative 156
    community building 171
    conceptual exploration 120, 146
    embodiment 172
    improvisatory 176–7
    as laboratory 117
    Lerman method 179
    multiplicity 175
    neosophistic 174
    open method 179
    power 174
    process 120
    silencing 170
    socialization 120
    Socratic 175
    taste making 175
    whiteness 174

Yale University 34, 116
Young, Joseph 88

Zhao, Yan 124, 126